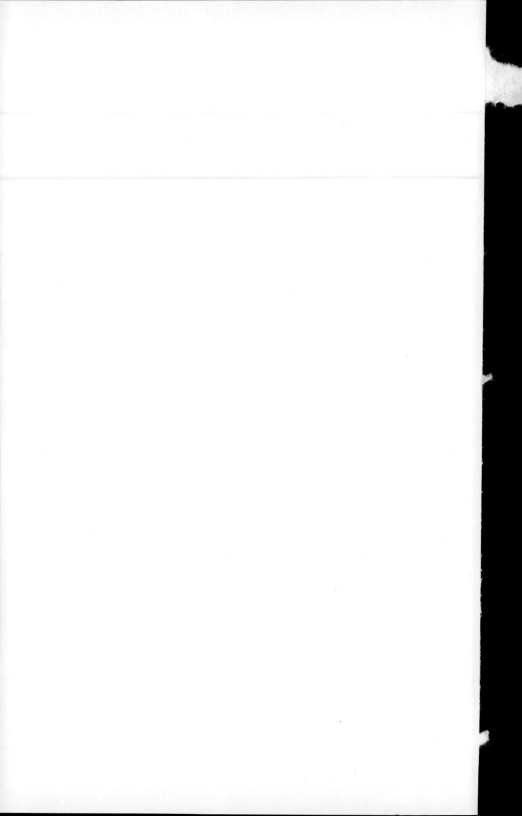

Thomas Davis and Ireland

Thomas Davis and Ireland

A BIOGRAPHICAL STUDY

Helen F. Mulvey

The Catholic University of America Press
Washington, D.C.

The paper used in this publication meets the minimum
requirements of American National Standards for
Information Science—Permanence of Paper for
Printed Library materials, A N S I Z39.48-1984.

∞

Library of Congress Cataloging-in-Publication Data

Mulvey, Helen, 1913–

    Thomas Davis and Ireland: a biographical study /
Helen Mulvey.

      p. cm.

    Includes bibliographical references and index.

    I S B N 0-8132-1303-7 (alk. paper)

    1. Davis, Thomas Osborne, 1814–1845. 2. Ireland—
History—19th century—Biography. 3. Authors, Irish—
19th century—Biography. 4. Nationalists—Ireland—
Biography. 5. Journalists—Ireland—Biography.
6. Young Ireland movement. I. Title.

DA950.23.D2 M85 2002

821'.8—DC21

  [B]

                                  2001053882

In memory of My Mother and Father

And My Sister M.A.M.R.

Contents

Preface and Acknowledgments   ix

Introduction   1

1. Early Life, 1814–1842   21

2. Backgrounds and Parallels   72

3. Journalism: Personal and
   Public Life, October 1842–1843   101

4. Public and Private Life, 1843–1845   142

5. The Last Summer: Annie Hutton   193

6. Davis and the Writing of History   205

7. Further Reflections and Epilogue   228

Appendix   243

Bibliography   255

Index   273

Preface and Acknowledgments

The study of Thomas Davis which follows comes out of a long interest in Irishmen who called themselves nationalists. What were they besides? Davis's first biographer was his Young Ireland friend Gavan Duffy, who published in 1890 his famous *Memoirs of an Irish Patriot*. The Davis who emerges from Duffy's pages is a character so saintly that it has invited disbelief. But many others besides Duffy, as we shall show, testified to the rare qualities of Thomas Davis. Davis from my own research stands up very well, and the viewpoint of the Duffy biography is not to be disregarded. I have, however, tried to present a more complicated and complete portrait, with attention to motivations, ideas, interests, friendships, and inconsistencies. Davis's life was short—he died at thirty-one—but what he left behind in his writings and in the memories of his friends suggests that had he lived longer many different careers might have been open to him, as a lawyer, an historian, a journalist, an historical novelist. I have not written a whole history of Young Ireland, nor a complete "Life and Times" of Davis, but I have given attention to the research of these last decades which has told us so much about the years 1830–1845. The concentration and emphasis is on Davis himself, what he thought and said, and did, and the vision he had for his country.

In the preparation of this work I have had the gracious assistance of the staffs of the Dublin libraries where I have done most of my research. For permission to quote from documents in their possession I thank the Royal Irish Academy; the Council of

Trustees of the National Library of Ireland; the Board of Trinity College, Dublin; the Dublin Corporation, Dublin Libraries (Gilbert collection). Thanks are also due to the National Gallery of Ireland for the photograph of Christopher Moore's bust of Annie Hutton; and also to the Dublin City Council for the photograph of John Hogan's statue of Thomas Davis, now in Dublin City Hall. I extend special thanks to Diane Monte of the Connecticut College secretarial staff for her work on the final typescript and her interest in the work as a whole. To the librarians at Connecticut College I am indebted for help with interlibrary loans.

Over several research summers in Dublin, I have enjoyed and learned from the conversations and opinions of several fellow scholars. Most especially I want to mention Professor Maurice O'Connell, not only for his great knowledge, but for the kindness and hospitality I always received from him and his late wife, Betty. Also I am grateful for the interest Dr. Jacqueline Hill of Maynooth College has taken in my work. Again, I have learned much from her about the period of the 1840s. I also want to thank for many kindnesses Professor Vincent Comerford, Richard Hawkins, Carla King, and Christopher Woods. Also thanks to Fergus O'Ferrall for sharing with me his essay on Thomas Davis and the Irish language. Also my appreciation to my niece Rosalind Rustigian for her support and encouragement during the writing of this work.

To the American Philosophical Society I am grateful for an earlier grant in support of my Irish studies. I also thank the Connecticut College Faculty Study and Research Fund for grants for summer research in Dublin.

Introduction

Historiography: Friends, Patriots, Scholars

Thomas Osborne Davis, the subject of the study which follows, is little known in the United States. In Ireland, however, his life is forever remembered for his work as a founder of and writer for the *Nation* newspaper, which appeared on October 15, 1842. Davis's two colleagues in this fresh journalistic enterprise were Charles Gavan Duffy and John Blake Dillon. Duffy was editor; Dillon was only an occasional contributor, but close to his two friends in all their plans and decisions. But it was Davis and Duffy who really made the *Nation,* sometimes writing nearly whole issues themselves. The young men, all under thirty, were members of Daniel O'Connell's Repeal Association, and in their newspaper gave every support to O'Connell's campaign to repeal the Act of Union which in 1801 had abolished the old Irish parliament and brought the two countries together into a legislative union. The aim of the young men was twofold: to work for the restoration of an Irish parliament, and to bring all Irishmen of whatever creed or class or origin into a confederacy to make Ireland the nation it had never yet been. They did not give themselves any special name, but were called "Young Ireland" by a journalist. And so the name, with many accretions, false and true, has come down to us.

Around Duffy, Davis, and Dillon there clustered very soon a

group of youthful contemporaries, Trinity College alumni, Catholic and Protestant, many of them lawyers and occasional contributors to the paper. There were John Pigot and John O'Hagan, close friends who were soon to go to London to complete their legal studies; there was Thomas MacNevin, witty, and unpredictable; there was Denis Florence McCarthy, the poet, later to become a distinguished student of Spanish literature. Michael Joseph Barry and Denny Lane worked for Repeal and Young Ireland ideals in Cork, and in Lane's case, wrote letters of encouragement and advice, and now and then came to Dublin. Michael Doheny, the later Fenian, was also in the circle but less close to it. Several men whose names are known in America as Irish Forty Eighters—Thomas Darcy McGee, John Mitchel, Thomas Francis Meagher, and Richard O'Gorman—were not in the original Young Ireland group but were to enter it in 1845 or shortly thereafter. Looking back, a lifetime later, on his early career as the *Nation*'s editor, Duffy left no doubt that Davis was the true leader, who had studied and reflected deeply on subjects of which his companions knew but little. It was a leadership that was never resented, coming as it did from a man whose kindness, grace of manner, and gifts for friendship matched his intellectual qualities, whose essays and verse, edited and published shortly after his death, were to preserve for Irishmen over the later century the memory and ideas of Young Ireland.

The sudden death of Thomas Davis in September 1845, a month before his thirty-first birthday, was for the Young Irelanders, according to their later writings, a disaster. For Duffy it was a catastrophic blow, and it is probably fair to say as severe as any he sustained in his long life. He went on with the *Nation,* gathering fresh recruits for its work, but never again was the exultant mood of the earliest years of the newspaper to return. The year of Davis's death saw the onset of the famine, and the terrible four years which followed speeded the Irish diaspora to the United States, to Canada, and to the Antipodes. Already, an older Irish world which had come out of the eighteenth century had been giving way to new trends and forces now accelerated by the famine; after 1850 political events were moving toward the "Irish question" of the middle and later nineteenth century. Duffy, finally acquitted of charges arising from his involvement in the revolutionary events of 1848, returned to his editorship of the *Nation* in 1849. Throwing his influence into the tenant rights movement, a cause which he thought might bring the diverging North and South of Ireland closer in feeling, he was elected to Parliament in 1852 from New Ross. Despairing, eventually, of any immediate hope of legislative independence for Ireland or indeed of any serious Irish reform, Duffy decided in 1855 to emigrate to Australia. Settling in the province of Victoria, he began a legal career but was soon involved in the political life of the recently founded colony. Serving both as prime minister and later as speaker of the Victoria House of Assembly, he was knighted in 1873 for his distinguished services as a British colonial statesman. Like McGee in Canada, another former Young Irelander, who was to be associated with Canadian confederation, Duffy shared and reflected on the extension of responsible parliamentary government to British overseas colonies, making inevitable comparisons with Ireland and its government.

Returning to Europe in 1879, Duffy, while arranging to live in the south of France, determined to devote his retirement to completing the history of Young Ireland, a piece of work already underway. Some of his friends thought he might resume his career in the House of Commons, contributing his long colonial experience to the problems of Irish politics, now under the domination of Charles Stewart Parnell. Duffy was not persuaded. Corresponding with his long cherished friend John O'Hagan, who would soon become a judge on the Irish Land Court, set up after the passage of the Land Act of 1881, Duffy rejected any idea of an Irish political career. If he did not complete his long planned work on Young Ireland, no one else would, and the ideas and intentions of that movement would be forever misunderstood. "The high principles of action which Davis preached are not only not practiced, but apparently not remembered," he wrote loftily to John O'Hagan.[1]

In the autumn of 1880, the first of Duffy's historical works, *Young Ireland*, was published in London. *Four Years of Irish History*, telling the story of the Young Irelanders from 1845 to 1849, came out in 1883. In 1890, the famous biography *Thomas Davis: The Memoirs of an Irish Patriot* appeared. It remains today the basic study of Davis's life. *A Bird's Eye View of Irish History*, included first in *Young Ireland*, was given a separate publication in 1882. In 1898, Duffy's two-volume autobiography, *My Life in Two Hemispheres*, revealed more of his own personality, but was silent on many matters of which one would like to know more. It is valuable, however, for his early life in Ulster, and for his middle years in Australia. Duffy's books were widely read and noticed by reviewers in England, Ireland, the United States, and Australia. Nor did Davis have to wait for the 1890 biography: he was a central character in the first Young Ireland volume. Complimentary copies of all Duffy's books sent to statesmen, to old friends and acquaintances, and to literary figures brought to him in return praise, questions, and criticism. The huge volume of letters which Duffy received can now be read among his papers in the National Library of Ireland.[2] They are fascinating for all they reveal of opinion and feeling on the Irish question, bringing together the perspectives of the 1840s and the realities of the 1880s. From the historian W. E. H. Lecky, from William Gladstone, from Samuel Smiles, from Matthew Arnold, from Cardinal Newman, from

1. C. G. Duffy, *My Life in Two Hemispheres*, 2 vols. (London: Fisher Unwin, 1898), II, 377–78. Cited hereafter as Duffy, *My Life*.
2. Gavan Duffy Papers, Box 8005, National Library of Ireland. "Young Ireland," Duffy wrote in the preface to the final edition of his *Young Ireland* (London, 1896), "has been the subject of a correspondence, which if published, would make a volume of the same size, and perhaps of equal interest."

Young Irelanders now grown old, from Davis's brother and nephew, from Smith O'Brien's son, from O'Neill Daunt, O'Connell's old lieutenant, from George Otto Trevelyan, from Lord Ripon in India, and from many others, the correspondence poured in.

Duffy's works are contributions of the greatest value to the history of early nineteenth century Irish political life, and no later work on the Young Ireland movement can be written without a careful study of his books. But he is biased, more particularly exalting Davis and all he stood for at the expense of O'Connell. Duffy's portrait of O'Connell was indeed so harsh that a fair amount of recent scholarship has gone into attacking his version of O'Connell's actions and motives.[3] To this Davis/O'Connell question we shall return in the body of this present work. Some of the original materials used by Duffy have disappeared, and their quotation by him still remains our only source for significant parts of the Young Ireland story. But to criticize Duffy is not to denigrate the valuable histories he did leave behind in surely one of the more active retirements on record.

Duffy had two clear purposes in his historical work: the first, to vindicate his Young Ireland companions, and to show their "truthfulness, simplicity, and real moderation;" the second was to appeal to the conscience of the "best class of Englishmen" to invite them to understand Irish history and learn "why Irishmen, not deficient in public spirit . . . were eager to break away from the Union and from all connection with England."[4] "I can scarcely hope," Duffy wrote to Gladstone on sending him a presentation copy of *Four Years of Irish History*, "that you will find leisure to

---

3. See, for example, Maurice O'Connell, "O'Connell, Young Ireland and Violence," in his *Daniel O'Connell: the Man and His Politics* (Dublin: Irish Academic Press, 1990), 61–88. Also Donal McCartney, "The Changing Image of O'Connell," in *Daniel O'Connell, Portrait of a Radical*, ed. K. B. Nowlan and Maurice O'Connell (Belfast: Appletree Press, 1984), 19–31.

4. Preface to the first edition of *Young Ireland* (London: Cassell, 1880).

read the book, completing the history of the Young Irelanders of a generation ago. But if you should look into it at any time you will see why men of honor and ability thought it easier to die than to endorse the system of government which existed at that period. . . . You have made signal and beneficent changes since then; but the chief difficulty remains. . . ."[5] As he came to the close of his long apologia for himself and the friends of his youth, Duffy had very much on his mind the bungled and disastrous Irish rising of 1848 and all the ills that followed. "We can now perceive," he wrote of the Young Irelanders in the closing pages of *Four Years*, "that their first work was their wisest and best, and that Irish nationality would have fared better had there never been a French Revolution in 1848. All that had been accomplished up to that time was swallowed up by famine, emigration, and unsuccessful insurrection."[6] Duffy himself, a moderate in politics, had been momentarily carried away by French events in 1848, and what he thought they might mean for Ireland. Now, in his histories of Young Ireland he was suggesting that the work of achieving some kind of Irish independence involved matters far beyond politics. Nationalist though he was, Duffy had observed the rise of democracy in Europe, in Australia, in America, and his words suggest his mature awareness that political agitators alone do not finally prepare people for responsibility and power. Education, a healthy public opinion, civic spirit, just social and economic conditions, a national literature, all these the first Young Irelanders had seen should accompany any political dissolution of the Irish old régime. Davis had seen this with especial clarity, even though he agitated for Repeal, supporting O'Connell, and believing work for Repeal and reform should proceed on parallel tracks. One wonders about Duffy, and about what he would not and could never

5. Duffy to Gladstone, January 29, 1883. Gladstone Papers, Add. MSS 44479, British Library.
6. *Four Years of Irish History* (London: Cassell, 1883), 778.

say. Did he, possibly, sometimes, in his old age, think that the Repeal movement of the 1840s, at least in the political form it took, was premature? Whatever his reflections, he never ceased to defend his course and that of his young colleagues in the 1840s. They did what they thought right at the time. Their motives and reputations were his sacred cause. And at their best they had left an enduring legacy.

In a biography of Duffy published in 1966, Léon ó Broin suggests that Davis became a figure of national dimension for Ireland only in the 1890s, principally because of Duffy's picture of him in his Young Ireland volumes.[7] To be sure, Duffy's biography made vivid and real for the generation of the 1890s the character, the aims, and the varied abilities of Thomas Davis. To say this, however, is not to say that he had been forgotten in the years after his death in 1845. In 1846, Duffy brought out a collection of Davis's literary and historical essays which has been the basis of all later collections, and which went through many editions.[8] Also in 1846 there was a small volume of Davis's poetry edited by Thomas Wallis, a friend widely believed at the time to have been an important influence on Davis's nationalist thinking.[9] In 1868, in a New York edition of the Wallis volume, John Mitchel, whose differences with Duffy would not normally make him a reliable witness, saw Davis as the sun around which Young Ireland revolved. In 1847, Thomas Francis Meagher, the romantic hero of the younger Young Irelanders, edited Davis's *Protestant Letters,* which had appeared originally in the *Nation.* Writing during the famine years, Meagher struck the note of lament: "Had he been

7. Léon ó Broin, *Charles Gavan Duffy: Patriot and Statesman* (Dublin: James Duffy, 1967), 148.

8. Thomas Davis, *Literary and Historical Essays,* ed. Charles Gavan Duffy (Dublin: James Duffy, 1846). (Library of Ireland)

9. *The Poems of Thomas Davis: Now First Collected,* ed. Thomas Wallis (Dublin: James Duffy, 1846). (The book is part of the Library of Ireland, the name given to a series of books written by the Young Irelanders.)

preserved till now his voice would be heard, amid the desolation of his day, inspiring love and hope and strength amongst us."[10] A more famous and crucial remembrance came from John O'Leary, the Fenian and later a friend of William Butler Yeats. Writing in 1896 in his *Recollections,* O'Leary recalled the year 1846, when recovering from an illness he came across the poems and essays of Thomas Davis. He wrote:

I felt in quite a new sense that I was an Irishman, and that for weal or woe my fate must be linked with that of my country. I do not think that either then or since I ever had much of that spurious Irishism of Moore's songs which associates Ireland with virtue and England with guilt. But Irish in a higher and better sense I think I may claim to have at least struggled to be, and in so far as I have fought the good fight to Thomas Davis more than to any other . . . is the credit due.[11]

We must now look in more detail at what Duffy actually wrote about Davis. He portrayed him as the embodiment of all a noble life should be. An Anglican, a graduate of Trinity College, Davis had the courage to enroll in O'Connell's Repeal Association and to declare for the "national cause." In doing this he never ceased to have regard and affection for his differently minded family, and to receive the same in return. Words were his weapons, but he was a solid worker endlessly studying and learning, wearing out his strength on the *Nation* newspaper. Whatever differences may have occurred between them, Duffy remembered Davis only as a steadfast, helpful, tender friend. He was modest and unselfish; he brought a fresh and exemplary fairness to Irish political discussion; he embodied, as a representative man, the hopes and capacities of the Irish generation of 1848. His friends carried his views with them into literature, into public life, into prison

10. Thomas Davis, *Letters of a Protestant on Repeal,* ed. T. F. Meagher (Dublin: Printed for the Irish Confederation by Wm. Holden, 1847), preface. Cited hereafter as Davis, *Protestant Letters.*
11. John O' Leary, *Recollections of Fenians and Fenianism,* 2 vols. (London: Downey, 1896), I, 2–5. Reprint, Shannon, Ireland: Irish University Press, 1968.

and exile. "It is easy enough now," Duffy wrote in his final eulo-
gistic paragraph, "to see that the work for which he was fittest was
to be a teacher, and he is still one of the most persuasive and
beloved teachers of his race; but beyond the thoughts he uttered,
and the noble strains he sang, the life he led was the greatest les-
son he has bequeathed to them."[12]

During his Australian years Duffy had some correspondence
with the historian Lecky on the subject of Davis. In a letter in
1873, Duffy, mentioning Lecky's *Leaders of Public Opinion in Ireland,* suggested that in any further revised edition of this work,
Davis should be included along with Swift, Flood, Grattan, and
O'Connell.[13] Later, in 1880, Lecky, acknowledging Duffy's presentation copy of *Young Ireland,* included in his note of thanks some
remarks on Davis which show a detachment that Duffy would
have found it hard to attain, and which coming from Lecky are of
great interest:

Your picture of Davis is very beautiful and interesting, but it is one
which required a personal friend to draw . . . owing to the whirl of excitement in which he lived, he hardly left any adequate expression of his
genius.[14]

Lecky goes on to speak highly of some of Davis's poems, and
of his essays on the Irish parliament of 1689, but continues: "his
writings have, I think, hardly that peculiar stamp which alone en-
dures. . . ." It is hardly surprising that the intellectual and critical
Lecky should have fastened on the fact that Davis had left no co-

---

12. C. G. Duffy, *Thomas Davis: The Memoirs of an Irish Patriot, 1840–1846* (London: Kegan Paul, 1890), 388. Cited hereafter as Duffy, *Davis.*

13. Lecky's *Leaders,* published originally in 1861, went through various revisions.
"Someday," Duffy wrote, "I hope you will complete your series of *Leaders* by a sketch
of Davis who was as remarkable a man as any in the series. Having to choose between him and O'Connell, I, an Irish Catholic . . . chose Davis as my leader. . . . One
of the pleasures I promise myself in the leisure we all hope for is to vindicate his
memory." Duffy to Lecky, September 7, 1873, Trinity College, Dublin, Manuscript Library, Lecky Correspondence.

14. Lecky to Duffy, Gavan Duffy Papers, Box 8005, National Library of Ireland.

herent, ordered body of writing. But how closely had Lecky examined his work? This we do not know.

Lecky's observations are significant, however. They point to the fact that there was much in Davis's writing, and therefore in his thinking, which had not been adequately sorted out. This was not surprising given the enormous activity he had crowded into his brief years. None the less, his life and his writing left the way open for later commentators to find their own Thomas Davis, to use him to validate causes of their own.

In 1890 there appeared a review of Duffy's *Davis* in the *Contemporary Review*. It was written by John O'Hagan, the Young Ireland friend of both Duffy and Davis.[15] A Catholic, O'Hagan had attended Trinity, had a distinguished legal career, and, versatile man that he was, had translated the *Song of Roland*. He has had no biographer, but the general regard in which he was held, his legal career, his reputation for fairness, his serenity of character, his wide and deep acquaintance with several literatures make one wish that someone would write O'Hagan's life. His review says nothing to suggest that Davis had been forgotten. Rather, O'Hagan observed that "in the far too scanty literary furniture of Irish households you are sure to find the verse and prose of Thomas Davis."[16] O'Hagan is revealing on the personality of Davis, and brings him to life. Wishing to show the qualities in Davis which drew so many people of varied character to him, O'Hagan uses the Italian word "gentilezza," which he translates as "a grace of nature and manner" which never fails to attract.

O'Hagan, however, as so many others were soon to do, brought Davis over to his own contemporary political views. Writing moving words about Irish nationality and the injustices of centuries, he came forth clearly as a Home Ruler and argued that Davis would have discarded the notion of Ireland "subsisting

15. John O'Hagan, "Irish Patriotism: Thomas Davis," *Contemporary Review* 58 (October 1890): 590–608. Cited hereafter as O'Hagan, "Davis."
16. Ibid., 593.

... as an independent nation as an impossible chimera. Rather union with England through the medium of Home Rule would have had no more enthusiastic supporter."[17] One can only reply "not proven." Davis's own words hardly support so drastic a retrospective conclusion. O'Hagan knew Davis very well, however, and may have remembered in him cautious and conservative attitudes not revealed in his *Nation* writings.

O'Hagan's review essay brought sharply into focus the contrasting ways of remembering Davis: his nature and character; his likely attitudes to contemporary Irish life and politics; his fairness on Irish issues as an example and an inspiration. What would continue to be missing, and what had been only partially achieved by Duffy in his 1890 biography, was a critical examination of Davis's ideas, a study of his sometimes contradictory writings. And just as necessary was a closer examination of the inner man who had become for so many merely a sainted patriot. It is not our purpose here to present a catalogue of all available pronouncements on Davis, but rather to mention a few of the more critical, significant, and various appraisals of his life, his work, and his personality.

In the Irish intellectual and literary ferment of the 1890s and during the early twentieth century, Davis continued to occupy a special place, a center around which much argument revolved. For instance, the young Yeats, in his well-remembered encounter with the old Gavan Duffy in the Irish Literary Society, struck out against Davis on the ground that literature must be separate from patriotism, must live of its own and not be judged by its Irishness.[18] In these arguments there was exaggeration on both sides, and later, in 1914, Yeats took a kinder view of Davis. Admitting his earlier hostility he still insisted that Davis was not a great poet,

17. Ibid., 608.
18. W. B. Yeats, *Memoirs: Autobiography-First Draft. Journal,* transcribed and ed. Denis Donoghue (New York: MacMillan, 1973), 64–65.

but "his power of expression was a finer thing than I thought. He had poetical feeling, but he saw that he had work to do which would not set him on that road, and he made himself the foremost moral influence of our politics." For in Davis Yeats had seen a corrective force in an Irish public life lacking "a tradition of restraint and generosity."[19]

Davis had, however, written extensively on nonpolitical subjects in his *Nation* essays on music, education, Irish archaeology, country life, study, temperance, adult education (public reading rooms), the writing of Irish history. For some Irishmen this kind of subject matter had great appeal. In May and June 1898 in the *New Ireland Review* there appeared two essays by Father Michael Hickey, S.J., originally delivered as a lecture to an undergraduate literary society at Maynooth. Father Hickey's thesis was that nations were nations whether or not fate and history had endowed them with political autonomy. Scotland and Ireland were, of course, examples. It had been Ireland's misfortune for the past one hundred years, he argued, that nationality had been so completely identified with politics. History had given Ireland its own traditions, experiences, ways of life, sorrows, joys, hopes, aspirations, which marked her off from England. Davis, Father Hickey believed, had expressed this nationhood both in his prose and in his poetry, and belonged in the company of such Irishmen as Ferguson, Stokes, de Vere, Petrie, and O'Grady, rather than in that of O'Connell or Parnell. It would seem that Davis's writings had an influence on this Jesuit father such as they had had on the Fenian O'Leary. For him, Father Hickey declared, it was one of the greatest pleasures of his life to deliver his lecture on Davis to the young students who would soon start out on their priestly missions. They would do well to carry with them a knowledge and memo-

19. W. B. Yeats, *Tribute to Thomas Davis,* With an account of the Thomas Davis centenary meeting held in Dublin on November 20th, 1914 (Cork: Cork University Press, 1947), 12–19.

ry of Davis, a great and lovable Irishman, and to remember his hopes and his work for Ireland.[20]

For T. W. Rolleston, who had published an anthology of Davis's writings in 1890,[21] Davis, despite his activities for the repeal of the Union, was also in part a nonpolitical figure. Rolleston's two essays, based on a speech he had given at the Irish Literary Society in London, were published in the *Irish Book Lover* in 1914.[22] His appraisal of Davis and his work, though little known, is one of the fairest, most knowledgeable that I have found. Rolleston saw Davis's gift of his personality as a moving inspiration to later generations, a judgment which followed that of Gavan Duffy. In his journalism, much as it was obsessed with Ireland, Davis did not forget Europe and kept the struggles and aspirations of the smaller European states before his Irish readers, giving a cosmopolitan note to his Irishness. Rolleston also emphasized that Davis was a scholar, though his work was not done "in the arena of scholarship." He was a popularizer, spreading his own wide historical knowledge by story, song, essay, and editorial among a wider public. Engaged in bringing all the peoples of Ireland into a sense of their common Irishness, he took note of their Celtic background as Wolfe Tone and Daniel O'Connell had never done. A Repealer, Davis had not thought the self-government issue through to the end, Rolleston believed. Noting the frequency with which Davis, despite his generally fair attitudes in political matters, expressed much vigorous and angry anti-English feeling, Rolleston, recalling how much reform needed doing in Ireland in the 1830s and 1840s, did not find this anti-English bias so surprising. Then like O'Hagan, he transplanted Davis to the later nineteenth century, and observed that the constructive legis-

20. Michael Hickey, "Nationality According to Thomas Davis," *New Ireland Review* (May 1898): 129–38; (June 1898): 206–15.

21. *Prose Writings of Thomas Davis*, ed. with an introduction by T. W. Rolleston (London: Walter Scott, 1890). Cited hereafter as Rolleston, *Davis* (1890).

22. T. W. Rolleston, "Thomas Davis," *Irish Book Lover* 6, nos. 4 and 5 (November and December, 1914): 50–52, 65–69.

lation which England had been carrying on in the later century would have seemed "to Davis and the men of his time something almost incredible . . . and he would undoubtedly have felt the aspect of the Irish question . . . altogether changed."[23]

Going back into Irish history, Rolleston saw Jonathan Swift and Bishop Berkeley at the headwaters of two streams of Irish thought: Swift, representing defense against enemies from without; Berkeley, efforts for improvement from within on the part of Irish people themselves. In Davis's life and work the two streams had combined. None the less, Rolleston saw Davis as most akin in spirit to men like Father Theobald Mathew, the temperance reformer, or Horace Plunkett, the leader of the Irish cooperative movement. Speaking of Plunkett's assistant in that movement, George Russell, Rolleston saw in his periodical, the *Irish Homestead*, a true lineal descendent of the aspirations and ideas which Davis had expressed in the *Nation*.

Ending his appraisal, Rolleston fell into a nostalgic Keatsian mood. Davis died just before the famine. Neither he nor his Young Ireland friends could hardly have done anything about this tragedy. Death had spared Davis the agony of seeing the wreckage of his work. "Let his image," Rolleston wrote, "remain with us, eternally young and bright . . . an image speaking of valor, and above all of unquenchable faith in high ideals, to all generations of his countrymen."[24]

In 1914 there appeared two collections of Davis's writings, markedly different in character: one edited by Arthur Griffith, and the other by D. J. O'Donoghue. First, let us look at the Griffith volume.[25] The 1890s had seen no more famous admirer of Thomas Davis than Arthur Griffith, whose journal, the *United Irishman*, was first published in 1898. Davis's influence on Griffith

23. Ibid., 52.   24. Ibid., 68.
25. *Thomas Davis, the Thinker and Teacher: The Essence of His Writings in Prose and Poetry*, ed. Arthur Griffith (Dublin: M. H. Gill & Sons, 1914).

is well known and if Griffith found in his writings a vigorous assertion of Irish identity and uniqueness, he saw also a message of reconciliation for Irishmen long divided by origin or religion. Called *Thomas Davis: the Thinker and Teacher*, the 1914 volume, in its prefatory remarks and in the arrangement of Davis's writings, was totally uncritical, dealing not with Davis the man, but merely with his words. Davis emerges as "one of the first men in Europe to resuscitate the doctrine of nationality." His love of country is described as "instinctive," but at the same time he is said to have been influenced in his doctrines by a Trinity tutor, Thomas Wallis. Davis is also described as the first man to see that the Irish nation must be rebuilt upon the Gael. Davis "would have wished," Griffith pronounced, that such of his writings as were ever republished would be chosen to intensify patriotism, and to create a nation of high-minded men and women. This collection, with all selections undated and with no sources indicated, with poetry and prose wildly mixed, with originally unified pieces of prose split up and juxtaposed with other pieces, is hopelessly unscholarly. The anthology is essentially a patriot's handbook. Widely read, it went through four impressions by 1922. From its arrangement of material, however, one can deduce what was in Griffith's mind when he arranged it as he had. In the larger sense it is evident that Davis was for Griffith a man of moderation and generosity, with a clear political sense of the possible. In the bitter Dail debates of 1921–22 when he pleaded for the ratification of the Treaty, which he and his colleagues had signed in London, Griffith returned to Davis, from whose principles, he said, he had never departed. He quoted one of Davis's famous essays:

Peace with England, alliance with England to some extent, and under certain circumstances confederation with England; but an Irish ambition, Irish hopes, strength, virtue, and rewards for the Irish.[26]

26. *Official Report. Debate on the Treaty Between Great Britain and Ireland, Signed in London on the 6th December, 1921.* (Dublin: Stationery Office, 1922), 23.

The men who had signed the Treaty, Griffith argued, had brought back a document which coincided in spirit with Davis's words of long ago. Later, as the angry debates were coming to a close, Griffith uttered his famous words: "Is there to be no living Irish nation? Is the Irish nation to be the dead past or the prophetic future?"[27] As we shall see, it was this way of thinking about Ireland which Davis shared with Duffy and Dillon when they founded their *Nation* newspaper in 1842.

Sharply different from Griffith's volume was the prose collection edited by D. J. O'Donoghue, librarian at University College, Dublin. Basing his choices on the essays in Duffy's 1846 volume, which had probably been cut in the interest of publishing a volume of limited size in the Library of Ireland series, O'Donoghue restored Davis's original texts from the *Nation,* indicating each by title and date. In addition, he included the text of Davis's 1840 *Address* to the Trinity College Historical Society, as well as a sketch of the life of John Philpot Curran which Davis had written as a preface to his collection of Curran's speeches. O'Donoghue's scholarly volume is a piece of work for which all later students of Davis and Young Ireland are indebted. Also, O'Donoghue's introduction, despite a few minor errors of fact, shows that he had studied and reflected on Davis and his opinions. He wrote: "Brief and partial extracts . . . would not do justice to the man . . . and might present him as an intolerant thinker, and, as far as his editorial articles are concerned, a little of a demagogue."[28]

A year after the Griffith and O'Donoghue volumes had appeared, Patrick Pearse, in 1915, completed two essays, one called *Ghosts,* the other *The Separatist Idea.* A third essay, *The Spiritual Nation,* was dated February 1916.[29] Davis in these essays, appears

---

27. Ibid., 338

28. D. J. O'Donoghue, ed., *Essays Literary and Historical by Thomas Davis,* Centenary Edition, preface and notes by D. J. O'Donoghue; also essay by John Mitchel (Dundalk: Dundalgan Press, 1914), xiv. Cited hereafter as O'Donoghue, *Davis Essays.*

29. P. H. Pearse, *Political Writings and Speeches* (Dublin, Cork, and Belfast: Phoenix Publishing, 1922), 223–329.

along with Wolfe Tone, James Fintan Lalor, and John Mitchel. All are imaginatively recalled as ghosts who must be appeased. Whatever else they may have said or thought, or whatever contradictions may be found in their ideas or actions, they are essentially at one in their adherence to the absolute separation of Ireland from England. Like others before him, Pearse is using earlier nationalists for his own purposes; Duffy could write of Davis's moderation, O'Hagan of his certain championship of moderate Home Rule, Griffith of his support for the Treaty of 1921. But Pearse, whose Irish rising lay just ahead, could summon Davis's words to his support for a protest in arms. And, of course, the necessary words were there—never mind others of a contradictory nature. In 1843, after Prime Minister Peel had made clear that he would stop at nothing to maintain the union, Davis in the *Nation* wrote that no matter what concessions England might make in lieu of independence, Ireland would maintain its claim to be a nation.[30] And there was Davis's poem "A Song for the Irish Militia," from which we quote a stanza:

> The tribune's tongue and
> poet's pen
> May sow the seed in
> slavish men;
> But tis the soldier's sword
> alone
> Can reap the harvest when
> tis grown.[31]

Finally, in *The Spiritual Nation* Pearse eulogizes Davis's character—seeing in his life a genius for sanctity. The real human being has disappeared.

All the writings on Davis which I have noticed differed in emphasis but shared one perspective: the relation of Thomas Davis's

---

30. Rolleston, *Davis*, 239–40. From *Nation*, 15 July 1843.
31. Pearse, *Political Writings*, 324.

life and work to the various national aspirations of Ireland. Except for Duffy's memoir in 1890, they were not biographical in any real sense. During the 1940s, the centenary decade of Young Ireland, and in 1945, the centenary of Davis's death, there were more reminiscences and eulogies in books, in periodicals, and in the newspaper press.[32] Among these commemorative pieces there appeared a brief biographical essay by Professor T. W. Moody, *Thomas Davis, 1814–45*, originally an address delivered in Trinity College on 12 June 1945. The appreciative tone of this study is not far removed from that of Gavan Duffy's biography, but does contain some significant critical comments. Noting that much of Davis's newspaper writing was done under the pressure of time, Moody judged that there were "distortions and crudities" amidst the excellence. Davis's "missionary enthusiasm," Moody wrote, overpowered his critical faculty and led him into "romantic extravagance of phrase." Concluding that Davis combined the mind of a scholar with the temperament of a nationalist evangelist, Moody saw a clash in which scholarship often yielded to political faith.[33] Two decades later, on the occasion of the celebration of the fiftieth anniversary of the 1916 rising, Moody delivered another address on Davis, an elaboration of his earlier study, which was published in *Hermathena, A Dublin University Review.* Appended to it was a bibliography of Davis's writings, published and in manuscript, and as well, a listing of secondary writings about Davis and Young Ireland.[34] During this same decade, in 1947, Professor Dudley Edwards published an essay, "The Contribution of Young Ireland to the Development of the Irish National Idea." In it there is an evaluation of Gavan Duffy's work and an examination of Duffy's sources, as well as a history of how he obtained his

32. K. B. Nowlan, "Writings in Connection with the Thomas Davis and Young Ireland Centenary, 1945," *Irish Historical Studies* 5, no. 19 (March 1947): 265–72.

33. T. W. Moody, *Thomas Davis, 1814–45* (Dublin: Hodges Figgis, 1945), 32.

34. T. W. Moody, "Thomas Davis and the Irish Nation," *Hermathena, A Dublin University Review* 103 (autumn 1966): 5–31.

materials from Davis's brother, who had been politically hostile to his younger brother's career as an Irish nationalist.[35]

That Theodore Moody and Dudley Edwards should have opened up to critical scholarship the life and work of Thomas Davis is hardly surprising, for it was they who were the first editors of *Irish Historical Studies*, the famous journal which had been founded in 1938, just a few years before the Davis centenary.

Since 1938 there has been an outpouring of critical writing on Irish history in books and articles which constitute an historiographical revolution. For a time, there was a heavy concentration in political and constitutional history, but more recently there has been deeper emphasis on economic and social history. All of this work is of course invaluable to any biographer. We mention here only a few of these critical works. For the Young Ireland era we now have new biographies of Daniel O'Connell,[36] and the eight-volume edition of O'Connell's letters.[37] For the broader political activities in which Thomas Davis was engaged there are a number of crucial books: Kevin Nowlan's *Politics of Repeal*,[38] Denis Gwynn's *O'Connell, Davis, and the Colleges Bill*,[39] and more recently, Donal Kerr's *Peel, Priests, and Politics*.[40] A new biography (1995) by the Australian historian John Molony appeared while this present work was in progress.[41] The study here presented will concentrate on what might be called Davis's inner world and the vision he had for his country's future. It will not repeat every detail of the political story of the 1830s and 1840s, but examine the issues and themes which have the most critical relevance to

35. In *Feilscríbhinn Torna*, ed. S. Pender (Cork: Cork University Press, 1947), 115–33. (Essays presented to Professor Tadg Ua Donnchadha)

36. Oliver MacDonagh, *The Emancipist: Daniel O'Connell, 1830–47* (New York: St. Martins Press, 1989).

37. Edited by Maurice O'Connell, 1972–1980.

38. London: Routledge, Kegan Paul, 1965.

39. Cork: Cork University Press, 1948.

40. Oxford: Clarendon Press, 1982.

41. Dublin: Geography Press, 1995.

Davis's life and ideas. Attention will be given to the modern research which has been offering fresh perspectives to the study of nationalism and its relation to the Irish story.[42]

We end this introduction with some words of Davis's own which perhaps speak to the aspirations that launched him into his brief but historic career as a national patriotic influence. Among the fragments of his manuscript regarding Wolfe Tone, all that is left to us of Davis's projected biography, we find a brief paper on which these words were written:

Some men are politicians because they are vain, some to gain a livelihood, some from malice. Others leave the gentler ways of love and literature and piety because they detest injustice, because they long to rectify the disordered . . . condition of society and are moved to realize some great ideal of national life.[43]

Written, probably, as a kind of meditation about Wolfe Tone, these words may reflect some of the inner impulses which drove Davis forward into that public life which would make him, despite his early death in 1845, a famously honored member of the European and Irish generation of 1848.

42. See especially D. G. Boyce, *Nationalism in Ireland* (Baltimore, Md.: Johns Hopkins University Press, 1982; 3rd ed., London: Routledge, 1995), and Robert Kee, *The Green Flag: A History of Irish Nationalism* (London: Weidenfeld & Nicolson, 1972). For wider European aspects see Miroslav Hroch, *Social Pre-Conditions of National Revival in Europe* (Cambridge: Cambridge University Press, 1985).

43. Davis Papers, MSS 1791, National Library of Ireland.

Chapter 1

Early Life, 1814–1842

❧❦❧

Mallow, once a popular watering place in County Cork, was the birthplace of Thomas Davis on October 24, 1814, a month after his father, James Thomas Davis, had died in England, in Exeter. Dr. Davis, a physician, and an inspector of military hospitals holding a commission in the British army, was on his way to Portugal to take up military duties at the time of his death. His family was of Welsh origin but had been long settled in England. Married in 1802 to Mary Atkins, he now had a family which included two sons and three daughters: Mary, Charlotte, and Anna Maria. Of the girls only Charlotte lived to grow up with her three brothers, John, James, and the posthumously born Thomas.[1]

Davis's mother, with four children on her hands, decided to remain with her family in Mallow. But soon after her mother's death in 1817 she left, and in 1818, when Thomas, her youngest

---

1. In his biography, *Thomas Davis: Memoirs of an Irish Patriot, 1840–1846* (London: Kegan Paul, 1890), Duffy gives Davis's birth date as October 14. The date on his tombstone in Mt. St. Jerome Cemetery is October 24. See also Kevin MacGrath, *Irish Book Lover* (June 1952), 12–15. MacGrath's article contains important facts about the Davis family, and Thomas Davis's correct birth date. See *Gentleman's Magazine* 74, pt.2 (November 1814): 505, which contains a notice of Davis's father's death. This notice indicates that Dr. James Davis had been for many years at Islandbridge, Dublin, in charge of the General Hospital of the Ordnance.

child, was four, she settled with her children in Dublin.[2] They lived at Warrington Place until 1830, and then removed to Lower Baggot Street, No. 61, now 67. It was there that Thomas Davis lived his brief life, and there he died in 1845.[3]

Davis's maternal ancestry requires some comment. We have considerable significant information about his mother's people, thanks to his older brother John, like his father a medical doctor, but also a famous genealogist, known in Dublin as "Pedigree Davis," and sometimes as "Who's Who."[4] Dr. Davis left behind many volumes of his work, telling everything he had learned about the families of County Cork, complete with elaborate charts. These can be consulted at the Herald's Office, now located in the National Library of Ireland. Davis's mother, Mary Atkins, traced her descent from a Cromwellian settler family, but in the 18th century there had been intermarriage with the Gaelic family of O'Sullivan Beare. Richard Atkins, who died in 1738, had married Anne, the daughter of Murtagh O'Sullivan Beare, and her granddaughter, Mary Atkins, was the mother of Thomas Davis. Further back on Davis's mother's side there was a remote English ancestor, Sir Jonathan Atkins of Yorkshire, whose wife was a Howard of Cumberland. The same Sir Jonathan, the great-grand-

2. Duffy, *Davis,* 4.

3. Ibid., 5, 6.

4. Ibid., 174. See also *Burke's Peerage: Landed Gentry of Ireland* (London: Burke's Peerage, 1958), 58, for "Atkins." Also Joseph Hone, "Thomas Davis, Family and Social Life," in *Thomas Davis and Young Ireland,* ed. M. J. MacManus (Dublin: Stationery Office, 1945), 5–13. According to Hone, Davis's middle name, Osborne, came from an ancestress on his father's side who had a Dutch mother, Susanna Van Doward. Davis's brother James married an Atkins cousin from County Cork and lived until his death in 1892 at the family home on Lower Baggot Street. His son was a Church of Ireland rector at Ettagh in County Cork. Hone also says that he had once met in London a Canadian, a Mr. Davis who was attorney general for Saskatchewan, who claimed to be descended from a brother of Thomas Davis. It is also interesting to notice Davis's collateral connections. For all the details see the genealogical volumes compiled by Davis's brother. For the O'Sullivan-Atkins line, see vol. 16, 120–121. (National Library of Ireland)

father, had been a governor of Guernsey in the 17th century. Davis's later preoccupation with the variety of Ireland's people had a solid basis in his own family. Did he and his genealogist brother talk about their forbears? Apparently they did. In a letter to Gavan Duffy from Cork on August 23, 1843, Davis wrote:

You seem to have a turn for genealogy. I wish you knew my eldest brother, who has the most extraordinary gifts in that way I ever met. There is no family in Munster but he knows the pedigree of; but alas, he is an English minded man.[5]

There is little solid information to be found on Davis's growing up years, between the time his family settled in Dublin in 1818, and 1831, the year he entered Trinity College at the age of seventeen. His family seems to have been happy and united, but we would give much to know what they talked about, what they thought of Daniel O'Connell, and to know in detail how Davis ultimately formed political opinions so different from those of his family. Indeed there is evidence in Davis's correspondence of the family's devotion to each other, and of his concern for the health of his sister, mother, and aunt; but there seems to have been no family break over Thomas's anti-Unionist political views. In Dublin, Davis attended the school of a Mr. Mungan on Lower Mount Street, and it is probably of that school that he was thinking in 1845 when he said that he was educated in a mixed school, meeting among students his fellow countrymen of different religions, whom he learned to know and love. Gavan Duffy, who later on gathered information about his friend's early years from a kinswoman in Melbourne, Australia, reported her saying that Davis was a dull child, and during his growing up years dreamy, self-absorbed, and quickly emotional. More than once, she told Duffy, she had seen him in tears listening to a common country fellow playing old Irish airs on a fiddle. Duffy mentions

5. Duffy, *Davis*, 174.

that prior to Davis's entrance to Trinity he was subject to fits of despondency which Duffy, in his Victorian language, attributes to "poetic temperament."[6] This diagnosis tells very little, but Davis himself, in 1842, told his friend Daniel Owen Maddyn that he found it necessary "to get involved in projects, otherwise my mind would fall into the old melancholy." Since we know nothing of what Davis is referring to, not much inference can be drawn. It is not unusual, however, for the depressive or melancholy temperament to seek release in excessive activity.[7]

It would also be interesting to know how early and how extensively Davis was familiar with Ireland outside of Dublin. References to his "dear, dear Munster" and the beauties of the Blackwater occur in his letters. Did the family make many journeys to their old home in Mallow? We do know that the Davis family had relatives in County Tipperary, and that an aunt, Mrs. Hastings Atkins, was the wife of the rector of Templederry, where Davis spent occasional holidays.[8]

Unfortunately, we do not have for Davis's pre-college or college years any source comparable to the revealing journal that the young Daniel O'Connell kept during his law student days in London, a journal briefly continued in the years after his return to Dublin (1795–1802). We know the books O'Connell read and his reactions to them; his observations on people and manners; his efforts at self-discipline; his strong sense that he must play a part "on the great stage of the world."[9] After Davis's graduation from Trinity, and his emergence from his book-reading, reclusive

6. Ibid., 5.

7. Ibid., 84, Davis to Maddyn, 24 July 1842.

8. See Dermot Gleeson, "Father Timothy Corcoran, S. J.," *Studies* 32 (June 1943), 153–57. Father Corcoran was interested in the obscurities surrounding Davis's boyhood. See also Gleeson, "Father John Kenyon and Young Ireland," *Studies* 35 (March 1946), 99–110.

9. Daniel O'Connell, *Daniel O'Connell: His Early Life and Journal, 1795–1802,* ed. Arthur Houston (London: Pitman Press, 1906).

undergraduate life, he was carefully observed by two people, Thomas Wallis and Daniel Owen Maddyn. To their recollections and reflections we shall return.

Davis entered Trinity College in 1831, taking his B.A. in 1836. Accounts which have survived suggest that he was a tremendous reader, precociously knowledgeable on many subjects, but unsure of his powers and capacities.[10] But like O'Connell before him, Davis was already thinking of suitable spheres of action for his own "great stage of the world." At some point in his Trinity years, Davis became friendly with a small group of Protestants, Thomas Wallis, Torrens McCullagh, and Francis Kearney, who were thinking about national politics and national independence. In 1844, in a memoir which was found among his papers long after his death, Davis had written that ideas of national independence and national policy had been developed in the historical societies of Dublin and belonged to Trinity College Protestants and a few Roman Catholics, also students at Trinity. Whatever influence these fellow students were to have on Davis's ultimate thinking, other ideas and feelings were also making their mark. John O'Hagan, also a graduate of Trinity but younger than Davis, knew him well, and remembered just before his own death in 1890 that Davis's first political views were Benthamite radical, "a class of opinion which he came afterwards heartily to detest"—"his deliverer from that barren coast was Wordsworth." In Wordsworth, O'Hagan recalled, Davis found "the ideal of pure and exalted love of country, an ideal that took full possession of him." These later recollections of O'Hagan's come as a surprise.[11] Is it possible that Wordsworth's famous poems "On the Extinction of the Venetian Republic" or "The Ode to Duty" may in some circuitous way have been part of

10. See Thomas Davis, *The Poems of Thomas Davis: Now First Collected*, ed. Thomas Wallis (Dublin: James Duffy, 1846).

11. John O'Hagan, "Irish Patriotism: Thomas Davis," *Contemporary Review* 58 (October 1890): 590–608.

the inspiration for Davis's patriotism or, at least, of his emotional patriotism?

In 1836, after receiving his B.A. degree from Trinity, Davis was in London keeping his terms as a law student. On his return to Dublin, he was active in Trinity's College Historical Society, founded in the eighteenth century, in 1770. Originally a society internal to the university, the "Historical" had been moved outside the college walls and continued as an extern society during the troubles of the 1790s. Only in 1843, after Davis was no longer active in its affairs, was it permitted inside the walls as an approved undergraduate organization. The records of the society survive, but with many gaps. With what remains, T. S. C. Dagg, himself a former College Historical Society member, published in 1969 a book which presents vivid pictures of the society over the whole period of its existence.[12] From Dagg's study we can watch in some detail the Historical Society as well as the emerging Thomas Davis between the years 1838 and 1840.

For the earlier 1830s we find many names of young men who were to have distinguished or useful careers in Irish political, literary, or professional life. There was Isaac Butt, frequently judged "best speaker" by his young colleagues, and Caesar Otway, clergyman, writer, editor, traveler around Ireland, well beyond undergraduate age in 1830 but still active in the society's affairs. Others were Thomas MacNevin, who was to become an important Young Irelander; Graves MacDonald, later to be a governor of Hong Kong; Sheridan Le Fanu, novelist and poet; John Edward Walsh, O.C., M.P., Master of the Rolls. Some of the topics of debate or discussion suggest the society's interest in the contemporary world outside Ireland: the significance of the American Declaration of Independence for England; the value of general

12. T. S. Dagg, "The External Society," in *College Historical Society, a History, 1770–1920* (Dublin: Privately Printed, 1969), 137–76.

education for the lower orders; the degree of freedom in the English and American constitutions; the impressment of seamen; emigration as a remedy for distress. Other public policies discussed were payment of members in the House of Commons, an absentee tax, repeal of the Corn Laws, and the introduction of a Poor Law into Ireland.

Isaac Butt, closing the first session of 1832–33, delivered a presidential address on "Oratory." Looking forward to the eventual return of the Historical Society within the college walls, he ended his speech, Tory in politics though he was, with patriotic thoughts on Ireland, when the condition of her people would be bettered and faction and division would have ceased.

Despite his Unionist political views, Butt was clearly hoping that his young colleagues in the Historical Society would in some way as yet unclear devote themselves to the service of their country. It is exactly the theme that Davis would elaborate more fully and more imaginatively in his presidential address to the society in 1840.

Between 1837 and 1839 it is difficult to follow Davis with any strict chronological account. After taking his B.A. degree, in 1836, he was called to the bar in 1838, after he had spent his required year of law study in London. Before his call, he was a member of another group, the Dublin Historical Society, made up of law students, to which he delivered in 1838 an address on the study of Irish history. But whatever direction his developing thoughts on Ireland and Irish history were taking, they did not keep him from publishing a pamphlet in 1837, now long forgotten, called *The Reform of the Lords*.[13]

This pamphlet, plainly but dully written in a style quite unlike that which Davis would later develop, has some slight interest as a

---

13. *The Reform of the Lords*, by a Graduate of the Dublin University (Dublin: Published for the author by M. Goodwin & Co., Printers, 1837).

key to the quality of his mind and his attitudes toward reform and change. Reformer Davis was, but no reckless radical. Gavan Duffy in his biography of Davis treated this diversion into British reform as a deviation from Davis's true path toward the Irish national cause. The work does suggest, however, that Davis believed, at least in 1837, that a different House of Lords might look more kindly on Irish reform. Dedicated to Lord Morpeth, his essay explores the place of the Lords in the British constitution since 1688, and examines their vast tentacles, which touch patronage, the crown, the army and navy, and, of course, the House of Commons itself. Addressing the English, the Irish, the Scotch, and the Welsh, Davis suggests that efforts for any kind of reform, whether in a Whig or a radical direction, would be useless so long as the Lords remained a graveyard for any reformer's hopes. To be sure, the Reform Bill of 1832 had been enacted, an omen for the future, but its passage had created a major constitutional crisis. Was it good for the stability of a country to have every serious political reform accompanied by crisis and popular demonstrations? "Responsibility" was Davis's key word and he proposed methods by which the government of the day might bring the Lords to heel. After a series of rejected reforms the Commons might pass a Lords Reform Bill, accompanied by a declaration that its rejection would mean the creation of one hundred liberal peers. If this were done, the legislative wars would end. Dissenters, radicals, Irish, and Scotch would all rally and the Lords would have to agree to their own reform. The logic is clear, but the essay is a youthful response to a complex reality. But how should the upper house be reconstituted? First the Lords should lose their judicial power, and a new Supreme Court set up. The present peers might continue for life, but new peers, chosen from men who deserved well of the state, should be created. The House, then, like the American Senate, should rotate by way of elections on a six-year revolving basis.

There were many aspects of reforming the House of Lords into which Davis does not go. It is clear, however, that he wanted both houses to be more representative. To his "reformed" House of Lords he wanted to leave an absolute power to reject bills. Hasty legislation in the hands of an omnipotent lower house would be a political danger. We see here a young reformer who has concern for tradition and stability.

If Davis appears in 1837 as a philosophical radical with reservations about pure democracy, he does make some slight references in this initial pamphlet to Ireland, which tell us tantalizingly little about his inner reflections. In one place he speaks of "looking for historic names in the cabin of the peasant," in another, of Ireland's "needing years of the gymnastics of political exercise" to develop political powers. Privately printed, the pamphlet attracted slight attention, but it did bring Davis to the notice of Daniel Owen Maddyn, who later was to become his close friend and confidant and play an important part in his life, leaving testimony about him for which all scholars are indebted.[14] Maddyn will have some part in our story, but it is sufficient here to note that, like Davis he was born in Mallow (in 1815, a year after Davis), was to pursue a literary career in London, and was to remain throughout his life a firm Unionist. One day in a Westmoreland Street bookshop Maddyn picked up a copy of Davis's recently published *Reform of the Lords.* Curious about its author, he learned from someone that Davis was "an odd sort of man, a great reader." Maddyn was to meet Davis himself some months later in the Historical Society, to whose affairs we now return.

The Trinity College Historical Society in 1840, like most undergraduate societies of similar character, had had its ups and downs. Exactly what the inner stresses were between its sessions

---

14. Duffy, *Davis,* 15 ff. Maddyn's memoir of Davis was written in 1847. Cited hereafter as Maddyn, "Recollections," in Duffy, *Davis.* Maddyn sent his recollections of Davis to Duffy in 1847 when he was first considering writing Davis's biography.

in 1837–38 and its reconstitution in 1839 the records do not reveal. In his chapter on this period of the society's life, Dagg speculates that arguments between members seeking the society's readmission to the college and those wishing to continue it as an extern society led to an informal reorganization meeting held in Francis Kearney's college rooms; the group was made up of ten liberals and ten conservatives, joining to redefine and reorganize the society. Davis was one of the twenty members present at the gathering on March 14, 1839. A search for a suitable meeting place followed, and soon after new members' names were put up for election, among them Michael Doheny, John Blake Dillon, and William Conor Magee. On March 26, 1839, Davis, already a member of the society's constitutional committee, was chosen auditor; Joseph Sheridan Le Fanu, president; and Charles Palmer Archer, vice president. Davis, the records show, was an active and well-regarded participant in the society's affairs; and if the college debating society was hardly "a great stage in the world" it served as Davis's introduction to a small measure of semi-public life.[15] Sometimes the society held formal debates, with speakers for the affirmative and the negative on the question before the group; at other times essays were read. On March 27, 1839, Davis spoke in favor of vote by ballot. On June 29, 1839, he read an essay called "On the Constitutions of England and America," receiving a unanimous vote of thanks for his "eloquent and audible address." It was at this same meeting that Davis was chosen president for the year 1839–40. During the course of his presidential year he read another of his American essays, "On some parts of the constitution of the United States" (November 5, 1839), and partici-

15. Dagg, *College Historical Society,* 158 ff. The constitution of the reorganized society permitted both graduates and undergraduates of the universities of the United Kingdom and members of the Society of Queens Inns, of the Queen's College of Physicians, and of the Royal College of Surgeons to be elected. Michael Doheny of the Queens Inns was at first rejected, then later, in April 1841, elected. Members of the public were admitted to the formal debates.

pated in several debates. He took the negative on the question of whether British rule was beneficial to India; the affirmative on the benefit of the Corn Laws; the affirmative on mixed education; the negative on the question of the beneficence of the Norman Conquest for England. Davis, it is clear from these debating subjects, was already reflecting on questions he would explore more fully three years later after he became a writer for the *Nation,* a journalist, and a public man.

His famous address of June 1840, given as outgoing president of the society, was called "The utility of debating societies in remedying the defects of a university education."[16] It was more than that, however, and has been seen by all students of Davis's career as his début as an Irish nationalist. True as far as it goes, this interpretation takes only a narrow view of Davis in 1840. He might better be defined at that point as a patriot, interested in all those elements that go to make up the health of any nation: the education of its people, the economic condition of the population, the civic virtue of the influential classes. Indeed, remembering him as he was in 1838, his friend Maddyn suggests that Davis's original bent was rather nonpolitical, and that the usual topics of political argument, the ballot, the extension of suffrage, and short parliaments, had little attraction for him. But in local government, in the reform of the corporations, and in all questions of education and social reform, he took the deepest interest. "From the first," Maddyn recalled, "he saw how little genuine and permanent popular improvement could result from mere political changes of the kind aimed at by the British radicals."[17]

---

16. *An address delivered before the Historical Society, Dublin, June 26, 1840* (Dublin: Printed for the Society by Webb and Chapman, 1840). Also in T. W. Rolleston, ed., *Prose Writings of Thomas Davis* (London: Walter Scott, 1890), 1–43. The address is also to be found in D. J. O'Donoghue, ed., *Essays Literary and Historical by Thomas Davis* (Dundalk: Dundalgan Press, 1914), 1–51. An original copy of the address is in the National Library of Ireland. Selections from the Historical Society address are hereafter cited as O'Donoghue, *Davis Essays.*

17. Maddyn, "Recollections," in Duffy, *Davis,* 21.

Davis's presidential address began with severe criticisms of the course of studies at Trinity, and a plea for the study of modern languages and for broad educational reform. He discussed ways in which students could educate themselves, their reading programs, and their study of oratory and history. That he was by now widely read in history and literature the address made clear. From his program for educational reform, Davis turned to the world outside and to the coming victories of political democracy, citing Alexis de Tocqueville, the first volume of whose *Democracy in America* had recently appeared (1835). It was good, Davis observed, that men everywhere were achieving greater freedom, but democracy when and if it was widely realized would be no necessary prelude to a golden age. Democratic quite as much as older monarchical or aristocratic power must be exercised with restraint, with respect for history and tradition, with regard for moral values. But let Davis speak for himself:

—on the shore of democracy is a monstrous danger;—the violence and forwardness of selfish men, regardful only of physical comfort, ready to sacrifice to it all sentiments—the generous, the pious, the just—till general corruption, anarchy, despotism, and moral darkness shall re-barbarise the earth. A great man has said [de Tocqueville] if you would qualify democracy for power you must "purify their morals and warm their faith"—But it is not the morality of laws, nor the religion of sects that will do this. It is the habit of rejoicing in high aspirations and holy emotions; it is charity in thought, word, and act; it is generous faith and the practice of self-sacrificing virtue. To educate the heart and strengthen the intellect of man are the means of ennobling him.[18]

Davis's concern for the civic responsibilities which should accompany the coming democratic age was inextricably intertwined with his developing patriotism. People everywhere, he was arguing, must be prepared for the exercise of power. The nineteenth century was not the time for ivory tower philoso-

18. O'Donoghue, *Davis Essays*, 45.

phies. Perhaps in earlier times of violence and unsettled government, withdrawal from the world was excusable, but now for the educated and the privileged, for the young men of Trinity, there was a compelling obligation not to hide their knowledge, not to wrap themselves in selfish unawareness, but to act for public ends. How could this be done? Davis's answer brought him to Ireland. Few could influence, at least in the short run, the world at large. One must act at home for the good of one's own people. He continued:

Gentlemen, you have a country. The people among whom we live, for whom, if our minds are in health we have most sympathy, are those over whom we have power, power to make them wise, great, good. Reason points out our native land as the field of our exertions—the country of our birth, our education, of our recollections, ancestral, personal, national; the country of our loves, our friendships, our hopes; our country; the cosmopolite is unnatural, base—Patriotism is human philanthropy.[19]

After Davis had become a public man, and long afterwards a significant figure in the history of Irish nationalism, he was seen as a Protestant who had gone over to the national, or as some saw it to the Catholic, side. To be sure he was to enroll in 1841 with his friend John Dillon in O'Connell's Loyal National Repeal Association.[20] But the position of Davis was not any simple one of changing sides. In his Trinity address he is talking to a largely Protestant student audience, middle and upper class, telling them that for the vocations they will follow in the years ahead their Trinity education has not properly prepared them. Given their positions in society they could normally count on influence, on family, on connections to advance their careers. But they will in the course of their lives face competition which their fathers and grandfathers never had, and he tells them they "must strip for the race." The middle classes are everywhere advancing, and in Ire-

19. Ibid., 46.   20. Duffy, *Davis*, 58.

land the national schools in existence since 1831 are creating literacy on a broad scale; from both will come some ambitious and
intelligent children who will seek further education and who will
ultimately rise in the world. "I tell you, gentlemen of Trinity college, the peasant boys will soon put to the proof your title to lead
them." One may surely ask here, what lay behind these thoughts?
What did they have to do with whatever vision Davis had of Ireland's future? As I have suggested, there is a theme all through
what Davis wrote of the importance of the active and intelligent
participation of his own Protestant people in the future life of the
country, minority though they were, and would be. So, what
should their sons be studying and learning in their college years?
To this question, a large part of the address is devoted, and is an
attack on the course of studies in Trinity, a curriculum which is
not preparing its students for the rapidly changing world of the
nineteenth century. Too much time is spent on the grammar and
prosody of the classical languages and not enough on the character of those ancient civilizations. Davis urged the serious study of
modern languages and literatures—French, German, and Italian.
He also pleads for English literature, and in doing so reveals his
own reading in Shakespeare, Milton, Lord Bacon, Bolingbroke,
Swift, and Hume, and in the oratory of Pitt, Fox, Sheridan, Burke,
Grattan, and Curran. He notes in passing that Carlyle and "the
rest of the Germanic set" are damaging the English language.

Much of what we would today call political science was not to
be found in the Trinity curriculum, and Davis urged the development of what he called the Lyceum System—more societies like
the Historical, formed by the students themselves for debate and
discussion. His catalogue of what students should be pondering is
a significant clue to his own thinking on life and politics: local
and central government, doctrines of representation, the limits
which monarchy and aristocracy should impose on democracy,
the basis of free government, the relation of social to political

equality, the free press, the jury system, the penal code. Beyond these subjects there were immediate and deeply controversial public issues: the Poor Law, the Corn Laws, absenteeism, colonies, and public finance. And why do the potential leaders, the young men who will participate in the life of the country need to study these subjects? In the coming democratic age, they cannot hope to win respect and regard from the people they would lead unless they know what they are talking about, political subjects in all their depth and consequences. Public issues had lights and shadows, and superficial advocacy of or opposition to any public measure was not enough to elicit the right decisions. Davis seems, in fact, to be thinking of some balance between tradition and progress, for improvements also had their dangers. Again he is considering the nature and perils of an approaching democracy.

The people are pressing on in a career certain of sweeping away every law and custom which impedes their physical comfort, though in doing so they may overthrow some of the barriers which protect their morals, and therefore guard their happiness.[21]

Historical studies were already a significant part of Davis's reading, and he would soon make his debut as an historian by publishing in the *Citizen* a scholarly study of the famous parliament of James II, held in Dublin in the spring of 1689. In his presidential address, he urges the claims of history on his young audience. It should be studied with a philosophical mind which examines facts in relation to political and social institutions, and as manifestations of human nature on great occasions. Its study must serve as a background to one's own life, and one's understanding of contemporary times. "Who," he asked, "can discuss the nature of each revolution which reformed England, convulsed France and liberated America without becoming a wiser man?"[22] He is aware that his young colleagues probably knew little of Irish

21. O'Donoghue, *Davis Essays*, 28.   22. Ibid., 34.

history, which he had been studying for some time. He tells them that he will not reprove their neglect of Irish history, but

I never heard of any famous nation which did not honor the names of its departed great, study the . . . annals of the land, and cherish the associations of its history and theirs. . . . The history of a nation is the birthright of her sons . . . who strips them of that . . . makes them poor indeed.[23]

The Historical Society arranged for the publication of the address, which appeared in October 1840 with a brief preface, essentially Davis's summary of his arguments. Significantly he writes: "How long will you sin against patriotism? Let no one dare to call me factious for bidding you act in union with any men, be they of what party they may, for our common country."

Davis sent copies of his address to Walter Savage Landor and to William Wordsworth, whose poetry, we have noted, he so admired. John Forster, in his *Life of Landor,* remarks that Thomas Davis had "qualities which would have made him incomparably the ablest politician produced by Ireland in our day; and his premature death before what was crude and immature in his opinions had time to ripen, was a great calamity." Landor, who had written sympathetically of Irish aspirations and grievances, was none the less opposed to O'Connell's Repeal agitation. To Davis he wrote acknowledging the gift of the address. Davis's reply, the earliest written evidence of his sympathy with O'Connell's activities, we print in full.[24]

61, Baggot Street. 17 December 1840.

Sir,—I have just received your kind note. When I sent you my pamphlet I wished . . . to express my respect for one whose books I loved. I

23. Ibid.
24. John Forster, *Life of Landor* (London: Chapman and Hall, 1869), 578–79. Davis's remarks about Father Mathew, the temperance reformer, are a reply to Landor's observations that he was doing more of value for the Irish people than O'Connell's Repeal agitation.

did not expect a reply, but as you were good-natured enough to send one, the least I can do is to thank you for it. . . . I am glad to find you have hopes for Ireland. You have always had a good word and I am sure good wishes for her. If you knew Mr. Mathew, you would relish his simple and downright manners. He is joyous, friendly, and quite unassuming. To have taken away a degrading and impoverishing vice from the hearts and habits of three millions of people in a couple of years seems to justify any praise to Mr. Mathew, and also to justify much hope for his people. And suffer me to say that if you knew the difficulties under which the Irish struggle, and the danger from England, and from the Irish oligarchy, you would not regret the power of the political leaders, or rather leader, here; you would forgive the exciting speeches, and perchance sympathize with the exertions of men who think that a domestic government can alone unite and animate all our people. Surely the desire of nationality is not ungenerous, nor is it strange in the Irish (looking to their history), nor considering the population of Ireland and the nature and situation of their home, is the expectation of it very wild. I have taken the liberty of saying this because of the last sentence in your note. And now, praying your pardon for this intrusion on your time, for I know you will forgive the freedom of what I have said,

I remain, sir, your most obedient servant,

Thomas Davis.

Walter S. Landor, Esq., Bath.[25]

Was Davis, in 1840, influenced in the patriotic ideas and feelings expressed in his address by the national and cultural movements in contemporary Europe—in Poland, in Italy, in the Germanies? In the address itself there is no mention of current continental political affairs, except that in the preface to its published version Davis compares the young Irishmen of 1840 with their contemporaries elsewhere and writes:

25. Wordsworth, like Landor, wrote to acknowledge Davis's *Address*. The text has been lost, but Davis told a friend that it was a cordial reply but critical of its "insular patriotism." Wordsworth had come a long way from his French revolutionary euphoria.

Are they [young Irishmen] like the young men of Germany, as students, laborious; as thinkers, profound and acute? like the young men of France, independent, fearless, patriotic? like the young men of England, Scotland, America, energetic, patient, successful?

He ends his short preface by urging his readers to act in concert for their common country and quotes Lessing: "Think wrongly if you will, but think for yourselves."[26] We have already taken note of Davis's private memoir of 1844 in which he wrote that ideas of national independence and national policy had been developed in the Trinity College Historical Societies by both Catholic and Protestant students.[27] Despite this, a succession of authors have written of Davis's visit to the continent sometime between 1838 and 1840, and have sought the seeds of Davis's brand of nationalism in his exposure to and reading of such German writers as Herder, Fichte, Lessing, and the Schlegels.[28] The romantic nationalism, thus engendered, it is inferred, would soon appear in its Irish incarnation in the pages of the *Nation* newspaper, which Davis was to share in establishing in 1842. The trouble with this interpretation is the lack of real evidence for so crucial a journey. But what evidence is there?

In the *Nation* for September 27, 1845, two weeks after Davis's death, there appeared the first of three long articles on his life— all unsigned as was the custom. The first article contains the simple, unadorned information that he travelled on the continent and studied modern languages.[29] This is presumably the origin of all the statements thereafter, one author repeating another. Davis himself never refers to such a journey, nor do his close friends in

26. O'Donoghue, *Davis Essays*, 4.

27. C. G. Duffy, *Young Ireland* (London: Cassell, 1880), 526–29.

28. Among others, Professor T. W. Moody, "Thomas Davis and the Irish Nation," *Hermathena* 103 (1966), 6. But Moody also notes the influence of the Trinity College circle.

29. *Nation*, 27 September 1845. It is only in the first of these three appreciations that any reference to foreign travel appears. The reference is not to Germany, but to the continent.

any of their correspondence with him or later memories about him.

The contrary evidence comes from Gavan Duffy's 1890 biography, which states simply: "He had never travelled."[30] Duffy, of course, knew Davis had been in England and Wales, and is clearly referring to continental travel. The statement was part of Duffy's account of Davis's wish both in 1843 and 1844 to write a history of Ireland and to take a leave of absence from the *Nation* for European travel. Some of this travel was to be spent in background investigations of Irish archives in European libraries. Duffy pictures Davis drawing up itineraries, carefully noting the time and the cost. Since Duffy and Davis were in close contact nearly every day for three years, discussing the European news which they regularly published in the *Nation,* this statement of Duffy's on Davis's never having travelled must carry weight.

How then did this presumably incorrect statement on Davis's travels get past Duffy's editorial eye in September 1845? The answer which suggests itself is that Duffy was not regularly present in the *Nation* office during the weeks after Davis's death. The reason was that his young wife had died almost immediately after Davis. "From the death-bed of my friend I passed at a stride to the death-bed of my young wife and was for a moment unfit for work," Duffy wrote. He tells us that Thomas O'Hagan, who was and was to remain a close friend, wrote the immediate article on Davis's death and burial, and presumably helped Duffy in other ways. The later Davis articles, and their authorship, Duffy does not mention, nor do we know to this day who wrote them. One can only conjecture that in the confusion of that sorrowful month much was overlooked and uncorrected.[31]

The more essential matter, of course, is what intellectual influences were stirring in Davis's mind and in the minds of his young Trinity friends. If the influences *were* German, he would not need

30. Duffy, *Davis,* 211.   31. Ibid., 371–72.

to have travelled to learn about current German writing, literary and political. He was an omnivorous reader, and in the Dublin of the 1830s there was much interest in things German, most particularly in the *Dublin University Magazine*, founded in 1833 by a group of Trinity College men of conservative political views, Unionists to a man.

To say that Davis might have read the *University Magazine* is not to say that he had. But if he had gone back to the earliest issues from 1833 on, he could have read translations of German literary works, articles on German schools and universities, and biographical notes on German authors.[32] Furthermore, Coleridge, in England, was influential in the spread of interest in German writing, and one of the more widely read books of the age was Madame de Stael's *De L'Allemagne* (1813). As for Herder, his monumental philosophical history had been translated into English in 1800.[33] Indeed, there is in the thought of Lessing and Herder much that is similar to Davis's own emerging ideas on national culture, literature, and language. It is too early in this study to discuss all the elements and influences that have been thought to be, or actually were, a part of Davis's thinking. Suffice it to say here that all were not German, if, finally, they were German at all. It seems clear that in one way or another, Davis and his young contemporaries were fully aware of the nationalism and romanticism that were reshaping Europe in the years after the Congress of Vienna. It was their historical milieu, the atmosphere in which they lived.[34]

But what of Davis the person in 1838? What was he like, beyond his Trinity reputation as a great reader of books? He now

32. On German literary influence in Ireland, see Patrick O'Neill, *Ireland and Germany: A Study in Literary Relations* (New York: P. Lang, 1985), 86–122.

33. Johann Gottfried von Herder, *Outlines of the Philosophy of the History of Man*, trans. T. Churchill (London: J. Johnson, 1800).

34. R. Dudley Edwards, "The Contribution of Young Ireland to the Development of the Irish National Idea," in S. Pender, ed., *Feilscribhinn Torna* (Cork: Cork University Press, 1947), 115–33.

had his B.A.; he had the experience of living in London while engaged in his legal studies; he had been called to the bar, but had taken no decisive steps toward an active legal career; he had resumed his contacts and activities in the Historical Society, and had created something of a stir with his 1840 address. Two friends of Davis, as we have noted, Daniel Owen Maddyn and Thomas Wallis, have left written impressions which give us some idea of Davis the person in the years 1838 and beyond.

Maddyn, meeting Davis in 1838 at the Historical Society, liked him at once for his plain speech, his simplicity of manner, his aura of frankness and sincerity. While remarking on his seriousness, a quality which made him impatient of some of the society's frivolities, Maddyn remembered as well that Davis despite his bookishness had a very social nature, and enjoyed the Historical Society because it brought young men together and prevented their intellectual stagnation. Ethical studies attracted him, but there was nothing fanatical in his nature, and he had a strong bias against anything savoring of religious zealotry. Common sense and rationality were marked characteristics. Reverent, averse to mockery, Davis was full of good spirits and more joyous than he was later to be, after he became immersed in practical politics. Maddyn says nothing of the occasional melancholia, which Davis himself, as we have noted, was to mention in a letter to him in 1842. Politically, Maddyn defined Davis as liberal but not radical. "He had no superstitious veneration for ancient things, but neither had he any of that sour antipathy to them which marked the narrow-minded radicals who were utterly incapable of appreciating immemorial usages and time-honored customs." Apparently, in 1838, Davis did not talk to Maddyn about his awakening interest in Irish affairs, for Maddyn makes the point that when he first knew Davis his political views were not patriotic nationalist, as they were soon to become. But in that same year, Davis was addressing a group of law students, organized as an historical society, on the study of Irish history.

Maddyn is informative on Davis's reading; history, modern travels, the biographies of authors, the text writers in politics, especially Bolingbroke, Burke, and Montesquieu, attracted him. Legal history and legal philosophy interested him far more than the case books of law. Never a directionless reader, Davis knew where he was going, what he was seeking, what studies he wished to master, and later he was to write the advice: "Study subjects not authors."

While Maddyn's recollections deal largely with character and intellect, they do not omit reference to Davis's lively temperament. Maddyn recalled that his friend was fond of what was "brilliant, rousing and exciting" and remembered Davis's accounts to him of his enjoyment of the more acrimonious debates in the House of Commons, which he was in the habit of visiting during his time in London. Maddyn chose to describe Davis's enthusiasms as thoroughly "Irish" and his solid habits of work "English"! In these informative recollections there is no reference to any continental travel. Maddyn left Dublin for London in July of 1838, and except for one letter was not in touch with Davis again until 1841.[35] After that, and during the *Nation*'s first three years, there was a lively and constant Dublin-London correspondence between the two young men. Later, Davis would appear as an idealized Young Irelander under the fictional name of Dormer in Maddyn's book, *Ireland and its rulers* (1844).

Thomas Wallis, whose recollections we now examine, was a tutor, sometimes referred to as a grinder who earned a slender living coaching students, and was apparently given to discussing politics and current affairs with them. Davis did not have with Wallis, ever, the close friendship he shared with Dillon or Maddyn, or later with John Pigot. But he liked Wallis, respected him,

---

35. Maddyn, "Recollections," in Duffy, *Davis*, 15–25. Originally, Maddyn spelled his name Madden. One story suggests that he made the change to distinguish himself from R. R. Madden, the historian of the United Irishmen.

and listened to him. And Wallis was one of the sponsors of the short-lived periodical the Citizen, in which Davis was to make his debut as an essayist. Wallis's recollections are found in two places: in his introduction to the volume of Davis's poems which he edited in 1846; and in three successive issues of Duffy's *Nation* in 1849, revived after the revolutionary year of 1848. These newspaper recollections are valuable because they go beyond Davis "before the *Nation*," and give later memories of him through the summer months of 1845, before his death in early September of that year. We learn from Wallis something of Davis's development from the reclusive student bookworm of the Trinity undergraduate days into the socially inclined public man with notable gifts for friendship. Wallis regarded this development as mysterious, and admits he cannot fully explain it, and regrets that Davis never lived to write his autobiography. Such a work, Wallis implies, would have been a document of the greatest value, not only for Davis's development but for students of Irish public life in the late 1830s and 1840s. Also, Wallis thought it would have necessarily explained how Davis became a nationalist. But it was not only Davis's political life which interested Wallis; in these recollections he expressed the hope that some future biographer would be able to unravel the mysteries of his inner life, for which there is even now scant evidence. Wallis's memories of the period 1838–39 do not entirely coincide with those of Maddyn. Wallis dates Davis's breaking into a more socially outgoing life about 1839, when his views began to have weight and his character and opinions were unfolding in a variety of ways. As we have seen, the new outgoing Davis had already begun a friendship with Maddyn in 1838, but there was probably a sympathy there which did not exist between Davis and Wallis. But of Davis's greatness of character, lively spirit, and rich promise, Wallis had no doubts. He wrote:

Had he been spared for a few years longer, the world would have known this well. As it is they must partly take it on trust from those who knew the man. For none of his writings either in prose or verse will enable them to know him thoroughly. . . . As indeed the richer and deeper, and more vital and versatile a man's character is, the more inadequate representation of his living self are his writings like to be.[36]

Wallis suggested that it was Davis's writing for the *Nation* which gave him an awareness both of his gifts and his varied abilities and suggested a true literary career to him, as novelist or historian. But he felt bound to the public political cause he had undertaken. Possibly, and again according to Wallis, Davis may have come to think of his activities in the Repeal Association as a personal sacrifice. If Wallis is correct, one can speculate as to whether there may have been serious doubts on Davis's part about the work he was doing as a journalist, and it may explain as well his wish for a leave of absence from the *Nation* for travel in Europe. Wallis recalls that just before his death in September 1845 Davis was collecting materials for a history of the Norman invasion of Ireland, which he hoped to make as "interesting as a romance." Since Davis was presumably at work on a biography of Wolfe Tone, which had an announced publication date but which was not completed at the time of his death, one wonders whether all of this activity was on the frantic side, obsessive in a word. All of it, Wallis argues, abridged Davis's repose and indeed Davis confessed to Wallis that he occasionally suffered from "nervous excitement," whatever precisely that may mean.

Finally we note Wallis's comments on Davis's sense of beauty, the combination of the poetic and practical in his nature, the union of sterling sense with kindness and versatility. But to the very end, in the third and last piece in the 1849 *Nation*, Wallis reiterates the changes that came over Davis in his short life and again laments the absence of biographical knowledge. He wrote:

36. *Nation*, 20 October 1849. (Essay No. 1.)

Such a piece of autobiography would have been the more valuable because the revolution he underwent was one of physical and mental constitution as well as aims, opinions, and preferences. It was his temperament above all things that in its outward demonstration . . . underwent a thorough transformation. The very geniality of character for which I have praised him and which was his passport to the confidence and good will of every man he came in contact with, distinguished him only in his later years. When I knew him first it was precisely the quality in which he was most singularly deficient. . . .[37]

Possibly Wallis is making too much of all this. Many young people, however aware of their abilities, talents, sensitivities, are slow to reveal them. And Wallis made the point that in the Irish society of the time, daring to be different, daring to break out of the class or rank or religion into which one was born, was very difficult, fraught with pain and perhaps ridicule.[38]

In the two years following his address to the Trinity Historical Society, Davis was moving forward in both literary and political directions. One of his first public activities was to join with members of the Dublin bar to protest the dismissal by the Whigs of the Irish Lord Chancellor, Plunkett, and his replacement by Lord Campbell.[39] The second was to write a spirited defense of the Royal Dublin Society against the efforts of the British government to interfere with *and* regulate its internal government. Today the Royal Dublin Society is known outside of Ireland as the sponsor of the famous summer horse show, as well as the agriculture show which used to be held each spring. Less widely known, especially to foreigners, is the Society's long and honorable history of education and practical benefaction to Ireland. Founded in 1731 by a group of Irish gentlemen, descendants of the English conquerors and settlers of the seventeenth century, it had done valuable work for Irish agriculture, for developing the natural resources of the country, for the fostering of arts and sciences. Its

37. *Nation*, 3 November 1849. (Essay No. 3.)
38. Ibid.   39. Duffy, *Davis*, 45.

story has been told several times by different authors, and their books will repay attention from students of Irish social and intellectual history.[40] Few visitors to Dublin who use the National Library or visit the National Museum, both on Kildare Street, realize that the collections of these famous institutions are in part offshoots from the Royal Dublin Society. And at the time of which we write, the Society's home, since 1815, was also on Kildare Street in Leinster House, now the seat of the Irish Dáil. The old Irish parliament had been generous to the society, but now, in the mid-1830s, its activities fell under the rationalizing and reorganizing eye of the British administration in Ireland. An unfortunate incident furnished unexpected support to the government's criticisms and intended reforms.

On November 26, 1835, at a meeting of the Society, a number of names were submitted for membership, among them Daniel Murray, the Catholic archbishop of Dublin. Already serving on the Board of National Education, Murray was known for his generosity of spirit and his conciliatory approach to questions which were dividing Irishmen at a time of intense religious bitterness. The seconder for Murray's membership, moreover, was a Protestant, the Rev. Dr. Sanders, a senior fellow of Trinity College. None the less, Archbishop Murray was blackballed. The Society had made itself a target, accused of prejudice and blind sectarianism, accusations which carried weight because of the sterling reputation and character of Archbishop Murray himself. No one, however, took these proceedings more calmly than he. In writing to his sponsor, he requested that he convey to the Society "my earnest solicitation, that in the future transactions of the Society, I may be wholly lost sight of; that the recent cause of momentary disagreement may be forgotten; and that the whole body may

40. The most recent history is James Meenan and Desmond Clarke, *RDS: The Royal Dublin Society, 1731–1981* (Dublin: Gill and MacMillan, 1981). See also Terence de Vere White, *The Story of the Royal Dublin Society* (Tralee: The Kerryman, 1955).

join in cordial union to promote the great objects of national improvement for which the society was established."[41] This letter attests the tolerance and grace of Archbishop Murray, and suggests the kind of member he would have become.

In the years between Archbishop Murray's rejection in 1835 and Thomas Davis's entry into public life in 1841, a lengthy struggle ensued between the society and the government regarding the intended reforms. Not surprisingly the charge of bigotry, because of the blackballing of Dr. Murray, lent support to the government's side. All the details of this quarrel need not concern us here; they have been thoroughly discussed in Terence de Vere White's *History*.[42] In 1841, six years after the start of the original quarrel, Davis entered the fray with a public letter in the *Morning Register* which looked at the whole matter from a fresh Irish perspective.

Davis, in his letter, urged the government not to deal harshly with the Dublin Society. Taking a position above the religious and party spirit inspired by Dr. Murray's rejection, Davis saw the question as rather one between the British government and an old and honorable *Irish* society which deserved well of the country. Actually, since 1836 it had finally responded to all the government recommendations except two. Addressing the British government in Ireland Davis wrote:

Was this the treatment due to an institution which has grown old in serving the interests of Ireland? . . . We ask, would the French government treat a public institution thus? Would the English treat an English society of old standing, great number, and respectability thus? No, they dare not. Verily, we are provincials. This society has existed over one hundred years; it contains eight hundred members; it maintains a body of professors of arts and sciences; it has schools, theoretical and practical for teaching; the agriculture, manufactures, the science, the literature of Ireland have been served by it; . . . It was founded by Irishmen; . . . an

41. White, *Royal Dublin Society,* 93–94.
42. Ibid., 92–106.

Irish Parliament, gave it, out of its scanty resources £10,000 a year—gave it generously and wisely. . . .

Davis went on to regret the blackballing of Dr. Murray, but saw this as a separate issue from the punitive measures and the reducing of its support, which the government was contemplating.

He concluded:

In fine, we ask the public not to look on quietly and see this old, useful Irish institution sacrificed to the rashness or caprice of an English minister. . . ."[43]

During this exchange Davis was in touch with his old school friend Robert Webb, a member of the Dublin Society, from whom he sought facts which would enable him to compare the government grants to the British Museum with those to the Dublin Society.

John Dillon had been close to Davis in this newspaper campaign and the owner of the *Morning Register*, Michael Staunton, decided to give Davis and Dillon a chance to write for his paper in an editorial capacity. Despite their lively articles in the *Register* on foreign politics, on Protestant nationality, and on national organization, the circulation of the paper had gone down, and Staunton courteously ended his contract with the young men.[44] But by July 1841, when their connection with the *Register* came to an end, Dillon and Davis had already become members of O'Connell's Loyal National Repeal Association, which they had joined on 19 April 1841. It was a pivotal year for the two friends; they had discovered journalism and entered the world of politics.

As for Davis the position he had taken on the Dublin Society was the one he had expressed in the Trinity address and in his letter to Landor, that beyond the divisions which history had created, beyond religious animosities, there was Ireland. Men and

43. Duffy, *Davis*, 49–50.   44. Ibid.

women born and raised there could understand their country as no outsider could. For patriotism as he saw it should transcend politics and religion, and was an emotion and an idea which Davis would have fully developed when he joined, a year later, with John Dillon and Charles Gavan Duffy to found the *Nation.*

O'Connell welcomed the young men into the Repeal Association and his correspondence suggests that he had already observed Davis's zeal in the cause, for in May 1841 he was advising his son John to tell Davis that the lack of funds was the reason for not pushing Repeal as vigorously as he would wish.[45] We have little in the way of detail for the remaining months of 1841. Dillon delivered a presidential speech at the College Historical Society, and Davis was writing for the *Citizen,* an activity which would continue after the *Nation* was founded. He was also writing his reflections and opinions in letters to his friend Robert Webb, some of which have survived.[46]

Dillon's speech to the Trinity Historical Society in 1841 should be noted. It was, in its way, an elaboration of Davis's now-famous earlier pronouncement, "Gentlemen, you have a country." Dillon's words were in the same vein. "The patriot revels in a thousand pure delights which the cold cosmopolite can never taste." Like Davis, he looked back to the events of the 1780s, arguing that great events brought forth great men.[47]

If we have little information on Davis's public life for the years 1841 and early 1842 we know that he was hard at work doing research and writing. His essays in the *Citizen* (later the *Dublin Monthly Magazine*) concerned Grattan's parliament, Afghanistan, and India. In these *Citizen* pieces Davis revealed himself to be a strong anti-imperialist, defending native cultures and their right

45. *Correspondence,* ed. Maurice O'Connell, 8 vols. (Dublin: Blackwater Press, 1972–1980), vol. 7, letter 2877, 78.

46. Duffy, *Davis,* 51, 74, 75, 76.

47. Duffy, *Davis,* 64–70. See also Brendan O'Cathaoir, *John Blake Dillon: Young Irelander* (Dublin: Irish Academic Press, 1990), 7–10.

to resist foreign interference. In short, he was an Irish Little Englander. Another essay, to which we have referred in passing, is on the Irish parliament of James II (1689). Here Davis appears as a careful historical scholar who for this essay would later, long after his death, win accolades from the historian Lecky. Lecky, in his *History of England in the Eighteenth Century,* had covered the same ground and could of course speak with authority.[48]

Probably the best known of these *Citizen* essays is "Udalism and Feudalism."[49] Divided into two parts, its raison d'être was a review of Samuel Laing's book *Journal of a Residence in Norway,* which had appeared in 1836. In Laing's work Davis found support for his developing views on the state of the Irish peasantry. Laing himself wrote many comparisons between Ireland and Norway, and his entire work is a defense of udal ownership, that is, peasant proprietorship and its wholesome social results. But it is only in the second part of his essay that Davis deals with Laing. The first part is a tract on the historical origins of the various land systems of Europe and on the onset of industrialism, and above all an attack on Irish landlordism. Here Davis emerges as an angry young man writing in uncompromising language. Quoting Sismondi,[50] he wrote that "the social order in Ireland is essentially bad, and must be changed from top to bottom." This essay, full of learning and rich with evidence of wide reading though it is, would not satisfy a present-day critical historian. What is missing is any analysis, such as modern research has been giving us, of the Irish land question. There is no attention to the European population explosion, no examination of the different kinds of land holdings, little attention to the variety within the word peasantry,

---

48. Lecky called these articles "the best and fullest account of this Parliament with which I am acquainted—the Acts of Repeal and Attainder are printed at length, and the extant evidence relating to them is collected and sifted with an industry and skill that leave little to be desired." W. E. H. Lecky, *The History of England in the Eighteenth Century* (New York: Longmans Green, 1878), II, 201n.

49. Reprinted in part in Rolleston, *Davis* (1890), 44–75.

50. Ibid., 55. From Sismondi's *Economie politique* (Paris: n.p., 1824), 273.

no notice of regionalism, no examination of differences of behavior among landlords. "The recollections, blood, and habits of the Irish landlords are utterly alien; they despise the people; the people hate them," Davis wrote.[51] "What are the evils under which the peasantry labor? Poverty. Give them land of their own to work on, they will then have motives to labor, and will soon cease to be poor," he concluded.

And how to bring all this reform about? His solutions are missing, and his final words do not match the anger of his feelings. He wrote that he was not going to point out the means by which "this great salvation" is to be worked out. Agitation on both the tenure and the national question must proceed hand in hand. Ultimately, such agitations will lead to the "opportunities of all redressing time."[52]

Finally, one of the leading intellectual interests of Davis during these formative years was the historical work of Augustin Thierry. Thierry's work on early French history, his study of the Norman Conquest of England, and his interest in the conquests of the Germanic tribes and their long-term social results made a strong impact on Davis and coincided with his own thinking about the fate of conquered peoples. Thierry had seen the current state of Ireland, political, social, and economic, as a kind of historical remainder, an outcropping recalling the social processes of medieval times on the continent. Davis did not write about Thierry in the *Citizen*, but his mature reflections on the French historian and the significance of his work for Ireland would appear in the *Nation* late in 1842. To these *Nation* articles on Thierry we shall return.[53]

At the end of these two years of tentative efforts, of thought and silent study, of the formation of feelings and opinions, Davis and Dillon late in 1841 met a new friend who was to change their

---

51. Rolleston, *Davis* (1890), 56.   52. Ibid., 75.
53. *Nation*, 26 November 1842 and 3 December 1842.

lives, as they were to change his. The friend was Charles Gavan Duffy, a young contemporary from County Monaghan who had been for two years editor of a Catholic journal in Belfast, the *Vindicator*. Like Davis and Dillon, Duffy had earlier done apprentice journalism for Staunton's *Register*. The first meeting of the young men was brief, but enough had apparently been said to suggest that they might have an interest in working together on a new journal. Returning for a short visit to Dublin in the spring of 1842, Duffy met Dillon and Davis at the Four Courts and together they walked to the neighboring Phoenix Park for a conversation about Irish affairs. The story of how this meeting led to the founding of the *Nation* newspaper has been many times told, but before we tell it, we must do for Duffy what we have done for Davis and relate something of his background and youthful thoughts, sympathies, and experiences.

We do not have to grasp at slender threads to find out about Duffy's beginnings. He has told the story himself in his two-volume autobiography, published in 1898 and called *My Life in Two Hemispheres*.[54] Unlike Davis and Dillon, Duffy was to have a long life, dying in 1903 at the age of eighty-seven.

Born in the town of Monaghan in 1816, Duffy was two years younger than Davis and Dillon. Unlike his two new friends he had not had a university education, but by 1842 he had behind him the practical experience of editing and managing the bi-weekly Belfast *Vindicator*, a Catholic-oriented newspaper.

Duffy's family was moderately prosperous. His father, a shop-keeper, had acquired some property and owned a share in a bleach-green, thus benefitting from the local linen industry. On his mother's side there was a Cromwellian ancestor, and so like Davis, Duffy could claim a mixed ancestry, Irish and English. The youngest of six children, Duffy was ten when his father died, and

54. C. G. Duffy, *My Life in Two Hemispheres*, 2 vols. (London: Fisher Unwin, 1898). See Introduction to this present work.

he pays warm tribute to the dedication with which his mother looked after the interests of her children. In these reminiscences we learn not only about his family life, but also about his education, his early friendships, his reading, and the trouble he took to get hold of books. But most of all we learn something of the social atmosphere in Ulster, how friendships between Catholics and Protestants existed side by side with deep antagonisms. He and his young Catholic friends felt their present wrongs keenly, "but we knew little of the remote causes from which they sprang. I had never seen a history of Ireland at that time."[55]

His education as the only Catholic boy at a Presbyterian academy was a solid one, and during his five years there he made friends and acquaintances across religious divides. Among these he singles out Matt Trumble, who was to become a lifelong friend. A quarrel with the headmaster, Mr. Bleckly, over what Duffy regarded as an unjust punishment brought these fruitful years of study to an end. He continued his education at home, however, reading with a student who was preparing for Maynooth. Other boyhood friends were Terence Bellew MacManus, later famous for his part in the Irish events of 1848, and Henry MacManus, already a student of the arts, who would become a well-known painter. Later, in the 1830s in Dublin, it was Henry MacManus who introduced Duffy to the Hogarths in Charlemont House, the historic portraits in Trinity College, the Grinling Gibbons ceilings at Kilmainham, and the famous buildings of Gandon.[56]

Duffy's reading, of the most various kind, depending on books that accidentally came his way, included *Gil Blas, Roderick Random,* and odd volumes of the *Spectator.* In his priest/guardian's house he found tattered volumes of Shakespeare, "but I did not know and was probably afraid to inquire if there were any more

55. Duffy, *My Life,* I, 13.
56. Ibid., 28–29.

of the same kind."[57] Later the major-domo of Colonel Westenra, brother of Lord Rossmore, lent Duffy books one by one from his master's library. This generosity provided him with *Blackwood's Magazine*. Its famous attacks on writers of an earlier time introduced Duffy to William Hazlitt, for whom he developed a lasting admiration, purchasing some years later a file of the *Examiner*. It was the *Examiner* which became in Duffy's youthful imagination the model for any journal he might one day edit. Its example was in his mind when he took on the editorship of the *Nation* in 1842.[58]

Among older citizens who had befriended him there was Charles Hamilton Teeling, a survivor of 1798. Planning a newspaper in Belfast, he asked Duffy to join him in soliciting prospective supporters in Monaghan. Teeling played some role as well in encouraging self-confidence in the ambitious adolescent, asking his opinions and treating his views with respect. Teeling's *Personal Narrative of the Transactions of 1798*, which he gave Duffy to read, was an introduction to events of which the young Duffy knew nothing. Later, he was to send scraps of prose and verse to Teeling's paper, the *Northern Herald*, which championed "the old fraternal spirit of 1798—the union of Catholics and Protestants for the national cause," a spirit Duffy noted, which had mostly disappeared from Ulster.[59]

After a year in Liverpool visiting his brother, Duffy's thoughts turned to a future in journalism. His guardian opened discussions with Michael Staunton, who again played a part in the early career of an ambitious young Irishman. He had no paid position for Duffy but agreed to take him on as a learner.

Duffy was not slow in proving himself, and before a year was out he was made a sub-editor of the *Register*, serving under Hugh

57. Ibid., 10.
58. Ibid., 22. The *Examiner* was a radical weekly, founded in London by Leigh Hunt in 1805 and to which Hazlitt contributed.
59. Ibid., 21.

Lynar, a Northern Unitarian who later emigrated to the Cape of Good Hope. Working obsessively, Duffy nearly ruined his health, but the society of new friends and long country walks restored his sense of proportion. It was during these hectic apprentice days in Dublin that he came to know the poet Clarence Mangan and made as well an acquaintance with Thomas Moore. Fate soon took Duffy back north where he accepted, after others had refused, the editorship of a new Catholic journal in Belfast, the *Vindicator*. In writing his youthful history, Duffy recalled his departure from the *Register* as a release from slavery. His realization of how burdensome work for a daily paper could be was a factor in his advocacy of a weekly paper when plans for the *Nation* were being made.

Duffy worked hard at his northern post, made the *Vindicator* a successful paper, and became a prominent figure in the civic life of Belfast. He mentions as his friends the Protestant newspaper editors James Godkin and James McKnight, and the distinguished physician Henry MacCormac. Closer to him were two young priests, George Crolly, later a professor of belles lettres at Maynooth, and Father Dorian, afterwards bishop of the diocese. Duffy participated in plans for O'Connell's famous visit to Belfast, and also played a part in bringing to the city Father Theobald Mathew, the temperance crusader, who would, over the years, become a cherished friend. Later, at a banquet in Newry in Father Mathew's honor, Duffy made a speech which he called the keynote of his later life. It concerned the moral, intellectual, and physical condition of the people after temperance had been attained. People needed, after all, recreation and society, and Duffy envisaged temperance societies widely diffused over the country which would become centers for promoting lectures, useful arts, and improved agricultural methods and for establishing exhibition rooms, gymnasia, and public baths. "Leisure," Duffy wrote, "is the poor man's right as much as food or clothes: leisure to think, to read, to enjoy. But without some friendly aid how are the people to attain these blessings?" This theme of character development at every level brings the Englishman Samuel Smiles to mind, and Duffy in due time and in his own way was to become an Irish earnest Victorian, and later a friend and correspondent of the famous author of *Self Help*.[60]

One feature of the *Vindicator* deserves especial notice. Duffy was persuaded, knowing something of what he calls "fragments of Celtic song in rude translations," that music was an "immense, though greatly underrated force." He encouraged the writing and publication of songs and ballads, and Clarence Mangan, whom Duffy knew from Dublin, became a contributor to the poetry pages of the newspaper.[61]

Something more must now be said about the third member of this founding trio of the *Nation*, John Blake Dillon. Born in 1814 in County Mayo, Connacht, Dillon had found in Benthamism a working political philosophy; with it, however, he was able to combine the patriotic romanticism of his Historical Society address. A recent biographer examining Dillon's social origins says he belonged to "that neglected class of Catholics who were neither landlords nor peasants."[62] His father, Luke Dillon, having been evicted from a Mayo holding, came to the town of Ballaghaderreen to another farm, and established as well a business, a large shop which would remain over time in Dillon family hands. One of seven children, Dillon was part of a family of whom he was proud and to whom he was devoted. In 1830, at his mother's urging, he enrolled in Maynooth, but left after two years, having realized that he had no priestly vocation. Entering Trinity in 1834, he met Davis and soon became part of that group

---

60. Duffy includes some of his speech in *My Life*, I, 53–54. Smiles, famous for his writings on thrift, self-improvement, and character, wrote a history of Ireland which he published in 1844 (London: W. Strange).

61. Duffy, *My Life*, I, 55.

62. O'Cathaoir, *Dillon*, 5.

of Protestant and Catholic students whom we have mentioned as dedicated to ideas of Irish national policy and independence. Like Davis, Dillon studied law, finishing his legal studies in London in 1838; also like Davis he had great gifts for friendship. All the young men around him would later attest to his kindness, good judgment, and good sense. We now have in the Dillon papers the letters he wrote during these early years; and in those he wrote to his wife, whom he was to marry in 1847, we see a man of broad humanity, tenderness, and good humor.[63] He went on to be, over time, an important influence on the *Nation* but less and less an active participant. Duffy has left an impression of him when he first met him in the *Register* office.

The sweet gravity of his countenance and the simple stately grace of his tall figure struck me at once . . . he was a man whom a casual observer could scarcely overlook.[64]

During the negotiations for their new journal, difficulties arose, Davis particularly thinking that a weekly paper might not carry enough weight. Wallis, always hovering about, was urging the reinvigoration of the failing monthly *Citizen,* for which Davis, as we have seen, was regularly writing. It was Dillon, finally, who carried the day for a weekly paper. Writing to Davis, he told him firmly that projects for reviving the *Citizen* were a waste of time. That journal was a losing proposition, "for you know a magazine which does not pay is not read." Dillon concluded: "Have you seen Duffy's letter in the *Vindicator?* It struck me as a first rate production. A weekly paper conducted by that fellow would be a valuable acquisition."[65]

Davis was won over, apparently convinced by Dillon, and a weekly was on its way. After much talk, the original name of *Na-*

63. Dillon Papers, Letters to Adelaide (Hart) Dillon, Trinity College, Dublin.
64. Duffy, *Young Ireland,* 46.
65. Duffy, *Davis,* 80. Letter from Dillon to Davis.

tional was abandoned, and *Nation* was chosen. The paper was to appear every Saturday. In the course of the preparations, Davis went north to confer with Duffy, who had provided the initial capital, and who was to take editorial command. Duffy resigned the editorship of the *Vindicator*, and before leaving Belfast was engaged to be married to Emily McLoughlin. She was fated to die early, in 1845, but her only child, John, would one day become a cabinet member in Victoria, Australia. Whatever success Duffy could look forward to as editor (and he was in no doubt as to his capabilities), he would always insist that "Davis was our true leader. Not only had nature endowed him more liberally, but he loved labour better, and his mind had traversed regions of thought and wrestled with problems still unfamiliar to his confederates."[66]

These summer weeks of 1842, of preparation and worry, found Davis in a whirlwind of activity. He visited Duffy in Belfast, and before starting on a holiday trip in Ulster with his old friend Robert Webb he left the *Vindicator* office as his forwarding address. Long letters of plans and ideas went off regularly to Daniel Owen Maddyn in London, the friend to whom he "opened his whole mind and heart," as Duffy remembered. But Davis still felt some responsibility for the *Citizen*, and urged Maddyn to contribute to it. He wrote:

Webb and I leave for the North on Tuesday next. After seeing the County Down, Belfast and Benburb, we mean to loiter around Antrim cliffs to Derry, and maybe to Donegal; and from either I shall return by the Fermanagh Lakes to Dublin, leaving him to close the autumn in the north with his wife and little ones—Webb is always asking for you.[67]

Another of these summer holiday letters to Maddyn has acquired a certain fame because of its frequent quotation out of context by various students of Young Ireland and of Davis's ca-

66. Duffy, *Young Ireland*, 49.   67. Duffy, *Davis*, 82.

reer. From it conclusions have been drawn regarding Davis's entire thought: his intellectual position on English-Irish questions and his political romanticism. I suggest rather that it represents a piece of Davis, feelings rather than full or final opinions, and views at some variance with those he later expressed. The letter is possibly the kind of emotional letting-off-of-steam which people write when they are not thinking very hard and unburden themselves to a trusted friend.

The July letter we quote in part:

The machinery at present working for repeal could never, under circumstances like the present, achieve it; but circumstances must change. Within ten or fifteen years England must be in peril. Assuming this much, I argue thus. Modern Anglicism [sic]—i.e. Utilitarianism, the creed of Russell and Peel, as well as of the Radicals—this thing, call it Yankeeism or Englishism, which measures prosperity by exchangeable value, measures duty by gain, and limits desire to clothes, food, and respectability,—this damned thing has come into Ireland under the Whigs, and is equally the favourite of the "Peel" Tories. It is believed in the political assemblies in our cities, preached from our pulpits (always Utilitarian or persecuting); it is the very Apostles' Creed of the professions, and threatens to corrupt the lower classes, who are still faithful and romantic. To use every literary and political engine against this seems to me the first duty of an Irish patriot who can foresee consequences. Believe me, this is a greater though not so obvious a danger as Papal supremacy. So much worse do I think it, that, sooner than suffer the iron gates of that filthy dungeon to close on us, I would submit to the certainty of a Papal supremacy, knowing that the latter should end in some twenty years—leaving the people mad, it might be, but not sensual and mean. Much more willingly would I take the chance of Papal supremacy, which even a few of us laymen could check, shake and prepare (if not effect) the ruin of. Still more willingly would I (if Anglicanism, i.e. Sensualism, were the alternative) take the hazard of open war, sure that if we succeeded the military leaders would compel the bigots down, establish a thoroughly national Government, and one whose policy, somewhat arbitrary, would be anti-Anglican and anti-sensual; and if we failed it would be in our own power before dying to throw up huge barriers against English vices, and, dying, to leave example and a religion to the next age.[68]

Some further thoughts are in order on this letter. In suggesting that England would be in peril in ten or fifteen years, Davis was probably thinking back to the concessions made by England to the Catholics, to the modification of the penal laws which came at the time of the American and French revolutions. Implicitly, he seems to be saying that agitation, though necessary, will not bring off Repeal. External circumstances must play a part. But he fails to pursue the subject. As for Utilitarianism, a philosophy he rejects, he sees it as shared by Whig and Tory and dominating the thinking of the British government in the 1830s. This official materialistic outlook threatens to corrupt the peasantry, whom he calls "faithful and romantic," words often quoted. Again he leaves this pronouncement undiscussed. Against materialism-utilitarianism he places the danger of a "papal supremacy," a surprising juxtaposition. Does it suggest that Davis was not unaware of the growing political influence of the Catholic church, and aware as well that his union of all Irish hearts, Catholic and Protestant, might not be easily attained? He goes on to envisage open war if the current materialistic "Anglicism" [sic] becomes a threat. Finally, he merely mentions English vices, leaves the whole subject, and goes on to talk about the *Citizen*.

This curious letter can hardly be taken to represent in any complete sense all that was going on in Davis's mind. Rather, as we have suggested, it was an emotional outburst of ill-defined feelings touching on subjects without following them through. One must guard against pulling out any one of Davis's writings and seeing in them his complete philosophy. There will be later contradictions. But to look ahead beyond his "faithful and romantic peasantry" of 1842: in 1845, reviewing in the *Nation* Carleton's *Traits and Stories of the Irish Peasantry*, Davis notes that Car-

68. Duffy, *Davis*, 83–84. Davis to Maddyn, 24 July 1842.

leton's work is preserving forever things that are going, but writes: "There is neither use nor reason in lamenting what we must infallibly lose . . . be it well or ill we cannot resemble our fathers. Let us be content to have the past chronicled wherever it cannot be preserved."[69]

In the course of these northern holiday wanderings Davis spent some time with Duffy in Belfast, where all the preliminaries were arranged for the Prospectus which was to be the public advertisement for the *Nation*. Whether Davis had any earlier experience of Belfast we do not know, but in his mind it had been the center of liberal movements of the 1790s and so possessed a romantic interest. The more practical Duffy warned him that all that history was over and that Belfast was as "sordid as Manchester." According to Duffy, his own northern friends, both Catholic and Protestant, found Davis an oddity, a southern Protestant taking up national opinions![70] The Belfast newspaper *The Northern Whig* would eventually take a strong line against both Duffy and Davis and their anti-Unionist editorials in the *Nation*.

The Prospectus was to have been written by all three founders. As it emerged, the text was the work of Davis, except for one sentence written by Duffy. The central theme of this famous pronunciamento was renewal: emancipation from old, tired themes and the direction of the popular mind and the sympathies of educated men to nationality and the blessings of domestic legislation. But most of all the new journal would work to bring all Irishmen of whatever historical origin to a love of their common country, and to convince them to act patriotically in its behalf. Essentially the Prospectus summed up what Davis had been saying and thinking since his Historical Society address. It was youthfully utopian.

The text of the Prospectus follows:

69. *Nation*, 12 July 1845. Included in O'Donoghue, *Davis Essays*, 356–61.
70. Duffy, *Davis*, 85.

On Saturday the 15th of October, 1842, will be published the first
number of a

DUBLIN WEEKLY JOURNAL,

TO BE CALLED

THE NATION

For which the services of the most eminent political writers in
the country have been secured.

IT WILL BE EDITED BY

CHARLES GAVAN DUFFY, late Editor of the *Vindicator*
Aided by the following contributors:

THOMAS OSBORNE DAVIS, Barrister-at-law;
W. J. O'NEILL DAUNT;
J. C. O'CALLAGHAN, Author of the "GREEN BOOK;"
JOHN B. DILLON, Barrister-at-law;
CLARENCE MANGAN, Author of "Anthologia Germanica,"
"Literae Orientales," & e.'
The LATE EDITOR of the LONDON MAGAZINE and
CHARIVARI;
A LATE EDITOR of the "TRUE SUN;"

And others whose names we are not at liberty to publish.

The projectors of the NATION have been told that there is not
room in Ireland for another Liberal Journal; but they think differently. They believe that since the success of the long and gal-

lant struggle which our fathers maintained against sectarian ascendancy, a NEW MIND has grown up amongst us, which longs
to redress other wrongs and achieve other victories; and that this
mind has found no adequate expression in the Press.

The liberal journals of Ireland were perhaps never more ably
conducted than at this moment; but their tone and spirit are not
of the present, but the past;—their energies are shackled by old
habits, old prejudices, and old divisions; and they do not and
cannot keep in the van of the advancing people.

The necessities of the country seem to demand a journal able
to aid and organize the new movements going on amongst us; to
make their growth deeper and their fruit more "racy of the soil;"
and above all, to direct the popular mind and the sympathies of
educated men of all parties to the great end of Nationality. Such a
journal should be free from the quarrels, the interests, the
wrongs, and even the gratitude of the past. It should be free to
apply its strength where it deems best; free to praise; free to censure; unshackled by sect or party.

Holding these views the projectors of the NATION cannot
think that a journal prepared to undertake this work will be
deemed superfluous; and as they labour not for themselves, but
for their country, they are prepared, if they do not find a way
open, to try if they cannot make one.

Nationality is their first great object—a Nationality which will
not only raise our people from their poverty, by securing to them
the blessings of a DOMESTIC LEGISLATION, but inflame and
purify them with a lofty and heroic love of country,—a Nationality of the spirit as well as the letter;—a Nationality which may
come to be stamped upon our manners, our literature, and our
deeds,—a Nationality which may embrace Protestant, Catholic,
and Dissenter,—Milesian and Cromwellian,—the Irishman of a
hundred generations and the stranger who is within our gates;—
not a Nationality which would prelude civil war; but which

would establish internal union and external independence;—a Nationality which would be recognized by the world, and sanctified by wisdom, virtue, and prudence.[71]

Duffy, in the course of their early acquaintanceship, had come over to Davis's view of nationality, namely that it should include all Irishmen of whatever origin. The old contests and antagonisms between Protestant and Catholic must be given up. Originally, however, Duffy had a different view of what constituted Irish nationality. And in his own words made this perfectly clear when he published *Young Ireland* in 1880.

When I knew him first [Davis] in 1842, I had lived nearly all my life in Ulster under the truculent domination of Orange officials; I was a strong Nationalist, but a Nationalist of the school of Roger O'Moore, who burned with a desire to set up again the Celtic race and Catholic church. Davis it was who induced me to aim, *ever after,* to bring all Irishmen, of whatever stock, into the confederacy to make Ireland a nation.[72]

The young men kept the promise of their Prospectus, and the *Nation* duly appeared on Saturday, October 15, 1842. Its motto was taken from a remark of Stephen Woulfe, later chief Baron: "to create and foster a public opinion, and make it racy of the soil." This first number was published in a quantity larger than most Dublin newspapers, but the editors' optimism was justified, for the paper sold out before Saturday noon. When Duffy was writing in 1880 he noted that this first number had become a collector's item and was selling for thirty to forty times the original price.

As was his custom when he had important news, Davis wrote off to Maddyn the same day.

71. The format and text of the Prospectus are included in Duffy, *Young Ireland,* 80.
72. Ibid., 528. This is part of a long footnote in which Duffy explains, after reading Davis's papers during his preparation of *Young Ireland,* his and Davis's relation to the *Nation* and to the doctrines it championed.

The *Nation* sold its whole impression of No. 1 before twelve o'clock this morning and could have sold twice as many more if they had been printed, as they ought to have been—but the fault is on the right side. The office window was actually broken by the newsmen in their impatience to get more.—The articles you propose will do admirably in your hands. Duffy is the very greatest admirer of the sketches of Brougham and Peel [written by Maddyn in the *Dublin Monthly Magazine*] that I ever met. Perhaps in a newspaper the points should be more salient and the writing more rough and uncompromising than in a magazine. . . .[73]

A bit later, in another letter to Maddyn he wrote:

Duffy and I are delighted at your undertaking the notice of Father Mathew. In your hands and with your feeling the article will be worthy of the man. . . . Four thousand copies to-day equal to the *Freeman* and double any other weekly paper. The country people are delighted with us if their letters speak true. . . .[74]

The paper was successfully launched and for the next three years its history was so intimately bound with Davis's life that it is difficult to separate the two. In Duffy's later account of these exciting early days, he leaves the impression that whatever there was of intellectual life or of literature and journalism in Ireland was unimpressive. The *Nation* came as a bringer of light to lift up the country and take it into new paths. Since the *Nation* resembled a magazine rather than a newspaper, dealing as it did with history, politics, literature, and economic life, it is necessary to have a look at Irish journals in the 1830s and early 1840s for some essential background to what Davis and his young colleagues were doing.

First, the *Nation*'s opening year was to be brilliantly successful, with a circulation at once higher than that of any other Dublin journal. Although Duffy was the editor and proprietor, the *Nation* was very much Davis's paper in its intellectual qualities and in the sheer number of essays, editorials, book reviews, and smaller

73. Ibid., 64.   74. Ibid.

pieces written by him. Between the first number and the end of the paper's first year in October 1843, Davis had written roughly 210 essays and editorials.[75] And between 1842 and 1845 he published about eighty poems. Duffy, despite his editorial responsibilities, was the second-heaviest contributor, and indeed there were times when he and Davis were writing most of the paper. For his work, Davis received £500 a year, a considerable sum for those days.[76]

What, then, of the *Nation*'s predecessors? Was its all-inclusive patriotism, its concern for Ireland's economic and social problems, its interest in Irish history and literature quite so unique as Duffy suggested? For perspective, for putting the *Nation* in a broader setting, we now have a recent valuable study written by Professor Barbara Hayley on the post-Union and pre-*Nation* periodical press: "A Reading and Thinking Nation: Periodicals As the Voice of Nineteenth Century Ireland." It is to this survey of Professor Hayley's that the following observations are in part indebted.[77]

In the shock of the various adjustments of viewpoint and political position made necessary after the Act of Union, there was little in the journalistic world that was original or creative. For the first three decades after 1800 the magazines which flourished were political or religious in content. Confrontational journalism held the day, with a *Union Magazine*, for example, opposing an *Anti-Union Weekly Magazine*. On the religions front it was the

75. Kevin M. MacGrath, "Writers in the Nation," *Irish Historical Studies* 6, no. 23 (March 1949), 189–223. See listings under "Davis." Articles identified go only through October 1843.

76. See R. R. Madden papers in Pearse Street Library, Dublin. Madden published only two volumes of his *History of Irish Periodical Literature* (London: Newby, 1867). The notes for the projected third volume contain an interview with Duffy on the *Nation* and its contributors.

77. Barbara Hayley, "'A Reading and Thinking Nation': Periodicals as the Voice of Nineteenth Century Ireland," in *300 Years of Irish Periodicals,* ed. Barbara Hayley and Enda McKay (Mullingar: Lilliput Press, 1987), 9–48.

same, with the *Irish Protestant and Faithful Examiner* in opposition to an *Irish Catholic Magazine.* By the late 1820s things began
to change. Two magazines which seemed at first sight to be continuing the earlier polemical spirit, *The Christian Examiner* and
Church of Ireland Gazette (1828), and the *Irish Catholic Magazine*
(1829), suggested some fresh beginnings. Caesar Otway, the editor of the *Christian Examiner,* published fiction and discovered
William Carleton, who became a regular contributor. Poetry,
travel, and topographical articles were also features of this magazine. Otway's resignation as editor was a blow to the *Examiner,*
which soon left Otway's paths to return to its anti-Catholic
polemicism. Otway himself went on to write for other nonsectarian, more liberal journals. But Otway's literary example could
be seen as well across sectarian barriers, in the *Irish Catholic
Magazine,* which contained literary criticism and gave attention
to poetry, to history, and to scholarship in various fields. In May
1829, in an editorial called "The State of Knowledge in Ireland," it
described the Irish as becoming "a reading and thinking nation."
The way seemed to be opening for journals which would abandon the fierce intolerant polemicism of the century's first two
decades. The *Dublin Literary Gazette* (1830) contained book reviews, news of forthcoming books, poetry, articles on famous
Irishmen, and essays on "the fine arts in Ireland." Its change of title in 1831 to the *Irish National Magazine* was explained by the editor as better representing a fresh national feeling: "As the *Irish
National Magazine,*" he wrote, "it will feature *Irishness,* adopt a
critical attitude, and give special attention to works of a clear national character." Banim's novels, Mrs. Hall's sketches, Otway's
travel writings, Petrie's *Views* were all noticed. Printed also from
time to time were papers read at the Royal Irish Academy and at
the Royal Dublin Society. Some of this content resembles what
will soon be found in the *Nation.* The magazine, however, ran
into trouble. Charles Lever, the editor, published an article sym-

pathetic to Shelley, who, it will be remembered, had once written in defense of atheism.[78] Angry subscribers brought about the editor's resignation. Under the direction of his successor, Philip Dixon Hardy, the magazine failed.

On the Catholic side after 1830, the *Irish Monthly Magazine of Politics and Literature* (1832–34) also declared its intention to encourage an Irish national spirit, supporting neither Whig nor Tory. Looking at these tentative efforts toward Irishness, and to a more generous spirit, Professor Hayley wrote: "Despite such failures it can be seen that the magazine world was almost ready for a new literary journal. The public interest needed to be caught just a little more. The financial side needed to go just a little better."

It was in 1833 that there was finally established a periodical that was a success, which indeed was to last until 1877—the famous *Dublin University Magazine.* Founded by young conservative Protestants connected with Trinity College, it was a true literary journal and spoke with what Professor Hayley calls "a distinct Irish voice." Caesar Otway, Isaac Butt, John Anster, the translator of *Faust,* and Samuel Ferguson were among its founders. Making no secret of its Protestantism, the *University Magazine* nevertheless had a confident "Irish voice," but could also look to the wider world, to England, and to continental Europe for its subjects. Speculating on why it succeeded where its predecessors had failed, Professor Hayley reiterates its general Irish tone, appealing to the new national spirit in Ireland and the "anthropological-sociological interest" of the general British reader. "Whatever its politics, it seemed to stand for and to speak for Ireland." Reviewing their first four years, the editors in 1837 called attention to a new spirit, to the intellectual excitement and the spread of knowledge in the country. These matters are intangible, of

78. P. B. Shelley, an unpublished set of arguments called "The Necessity of Atheism," written at Oxford. Shelley was interested in the wrongs of Ireland, writing in 1812 an address to the Irish people.

course, but there did seem to be a developing audience for what the *Nation* was about to do. The *Nation*, it might be noted, would regularly take note of the contents and significant articles which appeared in the *Dublin University Magazine*. These appraisals would be written for the most part by Thomas Davis.

Another journal, important for this decade, which also had a long and successful run was the *Dublin Review*, begun in 1836 in London. The leading Roman Catholic organ in Britain, the *Review* had numerous Irish contributors, many from St. Patrick's College, Maynooth: Dr. Murray, Dr. Russell, Dr. Kelly, and Father Crolly. As Davis was shortly to do in the *Nation*, Dr. Russell called attention to Irish history, and to its richness in subjects for literature.

In relating the story of these journals, one must keep in mind that their audience was for the most part among what one can only call the intelligentsia, who could afford to subscribe and indeed could understand most of what these magazines were saying. For the mass reading audiences there were also the penny magazines. One of the most distinguished and the first was the *Dublin Penny Journal* (1831–37), founded by Otway, who found collaborators in George Petrie and John O'Donovan. Its first year was its best. Petrie wrote on antiquarian matters and O'Donovan on Irish proverbs. There were articles on Irish language, Irish families, the fine arts, music, antiquities, and archeology, and original verse. At one point, the circulation reached 40,000. There were to be numerous other penny magazines, but the last and finest was the *Irish Penny Magazine*, which was to last only one year (1840–41). The editor emphasized that the contents would be Irish but would contain "no subjects tending in the remotest degree to irritate or offend political or religious feeling." Petrie wrote on the county seats of Irish families, O'Donovan on Irish family names, Carleton on the Irish peasantry. There were articles on Irish music and on Irish architecture; there were engravings and illustrations from Henry MacManus. None of this foregoing account is meant to denigrate or lessen the impact and success of the *Nation,* but it does suggest some questions. How deep, or how unspoken, was this new tolerant national mood reflected in these ephemeral journals? Did Davis read and consider how their work might be bettered and made more popular? We can only guess. But at least we can see that there were precedents for the work the *Nation* was to do, however Duffy would later dismiss his less successful predecessors.

Professor Hayley saw the *Citizen* (1839–43) as a transitional periodical, noting, as we have also done, Davis's contributions to it. Founded by Wallis and Torrens McCullagh, and heavily subsidized by William Eliot Hudson, the *Citizen* was not to enjoy the long success of the *Dublin University Magazine.* The tone of the *Citizen* might be called reformist-Whig. Short of any direct endorsement of O'Connellite Repeal it stood for intelligent social and political reform; it paid attention to Irish literature, and to Irish arts and artists; and every issue had a section on Irish music, one of the strong interests of Hudson. Many subjects to which it devoted long and often dull articles can be found again in the *Nation,* written up in brief and lively form. The *Citizen* had clearly been a training school for Davis.

We turn now to glance at the various worlds in which Davis, his colleagues, and the *Nation* newspaper existed: continental Europe, England, and Ireland. On all these subjects, domestic and foreign, the *Nation* would not merely report, but express opinions that were to have long repercussions. Always lively and readable, its views could be both fair and unfair, both rigid and flexible, both critical and supportive of O'Connell; and as some of their critics have noted, contradictory. But whatever their faults Davis and the Young Irelanders were to create a famous newspaper. Lecky, in the first edition of his youthful work *Leaders of Public Opinion in Ireland* (1861), has left memorable praise for the *Nation:* "What it was when Gavan Duffy edited it, when Davis, Macarthy and all their brilliant companions contributed to it, and when its columns maintained the cause of liberty and nationality in every land, Irishmen can never forget."[79]

79. W. E. H. Lecky, *Leaders of Public Opinion in Ireland* (London: Saunders Otley, 1861), 242. This appraisal was left out of later editions of the *Leaders.* For Lecky's changing views on Irish nationalism, see D. McCartney, *W. E. H. Lecky: Historian and Politician, 1838–1903* (Dublin: Lilliput Press, 1994). Also H. F. Mulvey, "The Historian Lecky: Opponent of Irish Home Rule," *Victorian Studies* 1, no. 4 (June 1958): 337–51.

Chapter 2

Backgrounds and Parallels

Continental Europe

European history after the political settlements of 1815 is a vast
subject which can only be suggested here as a contemporary
setting for the Irish story and for the life of Davis. Everywhere after 1815 there was a wish for quiet and stability after the upheavals
of the Napoleonic wars; but everywhere, as time elapsed, there
was also restlessness and a search for modifications of the political order fashioned in 1815 by the men of the Vienna Congress.
Everywhere there was growing wealth and technical achievement,
most notably in England. And everywhere in Europe there was
poverty and distress heightened by the spectacular growth of
population. William Langer, in his extensive and detailed survey
of the period 1832–52, has chosen Wordsworth's lines "the still sad
music of humanity" to mark the worsening condition of the lower orders.[1] For the upper classes, the bourgeoisie, and the intellec-
tuals it was the age of romanticism, itself an enormous subject.
But from Russia to Ireland, from the Baltic to the Adriatic, it was
an age marked by an interest in the past, in folklore, in the revival
of disappearing languages, in the exploration of moods and feel-

1. William L. Langer, *Political and Social Upheaval, 1832–1852*, Rise of Modern Europe Series (New York: Harper, 1969), xvii. This chapter is indebted to Professor
Langer's volume.

ings. It is in art, in prose literature, in poetry, in music that all this is manifest in the works of the men and women who came of age in the years after the French Revolution. If there were those after 1815 who thought in terms of more revolution, of reform still to be carried out, there were also those who, having seen the horror of the French terror and the long upheavals of the Napoleonic wars, were supporters of rational and peaceful change. Among these latter were Daniel O'Connell and his longtime opponent Sir Robert Peel. Davis, born in 1814 and growing up in the age of romanticism, would also be on the side of peaceful change, as we shall see. Since we shall be observing the political ideas, the literary tastes, the intellectual attitudes, and the reforming spirit of Davis and his Young Ireland colleagues, it seems useful to look at the general European scene for analogies and comparisons.

The national movements in the several European countries were either for separation and the restoration of lost political identity, the Poles, for example, pulling away from Russia, Prussia, and Austria, the great powers which had partitioned and annihilated the Polish state in the eighteenth century; or for consolidation, the Germans thinking of the unification of their thirty-eight separate entities into a large political Germany, or the Italians thinking of some kind of political union, but especially of the expulsion of the Austrians from Lombardy-Venetia. But there were also variations on the themes of separation and consolidation—certainly of interest to students of the Irish question. Some of the Czechs in Bohemia, under Austrian rule since 1620, were prepared to remain, with suitable autonomy, inside the multinational Austrian empire. These were the Austro-Slavs, whose well-remembered representative Francis Palacky brought out in 1836 the first volume of his *History of the Czech People,* giving an historical foundation to the rights of the Czech nation. Another Czech, a political realist, Charles Havlicek, as editor of the *Prague Gazette* rejected Pan-Slavism, emphasizing the linguistic variety and different historical experiences of the various Slav peoples. In Bohemia, the Slavs' true goal, he argued, should be to strive for equality with the Germans inside the Hapsburg monarchy, and to hope for the reorganization of that empire on a federal basis. A student of Daniel O'Connell's political methods, Havlicek founded in 1847 a Czech Repeal Club, copying O'Connell's constitutional and nonviolent approach to political action.

Some of these continental movements were social and cultural rather than political, and some were strongly linguistic in their emphasis. In Hungary, Count Széchenyi worked for reform and modernization, traveling in Western Europe and England for ideas and inspiration. England he enormously admired. One student of his career has written of him: "He appealed to every motive among his countrymen, public spirit, private gain, patriotism, the wish to be in fashion, the spirit of fun, the sense of *noblesse oblige.*" In 1825, he gave a year's income to help endow an academy for the Hungarian language, which the gentry had been gradually losing, talking German in Vienna, Slovak to their peasants, and, curiously, Latin in their representative Diet. Horse racing and a suspension bridge over the Danube, connecting Buda and Pest, were among Széchenyi's interests.[2] In Illyria, Louis Gaj (1809–72), rejecting the local dialect of Zagreb, and preferring the one used most generally by the Croats and Serbs, founded the literary language we know today as Serbo-Croatian, written though it is in two alphabets.[3]

In Denmark, in the 1830s and later, the most impressive figure in its cultural history was Nicholas Grundtvig. Like many of his Scandinavian contemporaries he was influenced by German phi-

2. For an interesting picture of Széchenyi and Hungary, see Priscilla Robertson, *Revolutions of 1848: A Social History* (Princeton: Princeton University Press, 1952), chap. 13.

3. Elinor Despalatovíc, *Ljudevit Gaj and the Illyrian Movement* (New York: East European Quarterly, 1975).

losophy, especially by Herder; he collected folklore and folk songs which exemplified the national spirit. *Northern Mythology,* published in 1832, was to demonstrate by way of these old tales the character of the Danish national soul. The achievement for which Grundtvig is best remembered is the founding of folk high schools, designed to build character and strengthen Danish national feeling through singing and the study of Danish literature and history. Grundtvig had visited and admired England. In Sweden, Erik Geijer not only wrote heroic poetry, but published between 1832 and 1836 a *History of the Swedish People.*

In Finland national and cultural issues were more complicated. Finland, before its annexation by Russia in 1809, had been for centuries a Swedish province, and the Finnish upper classes had become Swedish speaking; indeed, comparisons are sometimes made between these Swedo-Finns and the Anglo-Irish. But this extreme northern country was not to escape the romantic movement in its linguistic aspects. By 1828 there was a lectureship in the Finnish language at Helsinki University and a Finnish Literature Society in 1831, whose secretary was Elias Lönnrot. Traveling through the Finnish countryside, Lönnrot built up a corpus of folk songs (runes), stories, proverbs, and incantations. Rune singers never furnished him with exactly the same tunes or words, although the variations could be close. Believing that these runes were all part of a larger epic, he set himself the task of putting them together into a saga which in 1835 became the *Kalevala,* the Finnish national epic. (This collecting of tunes and their variants we shall find in Ireland in the work of John Pigot, Davis's close friend.)

Although Davis, as we have seen, was interested in Norway and its peasant proprietors, the *Nation* was to give little attention to Scandinavian affairs. Norway and Sweden, however, did have special interest for Ireland: they were under one king, the ruler of Sweden, Carl Johan Bernadotte, joined in a personal union brought about after 1815, when Denmark lost Norway to Sweden. Each country, however, had its own parliament, an arrangement that was to last until 1905, when Norway's full independence was peaceably conceded by Sweden. Comparisons with Ireland naturally suggested themselves.

No attempt has been made to analyze the wide variety and nuances of all these European national movements. To do so would involve a study of national histories, regional groups, class interests, and much economic and social history. We are only suggesting here the wider world in which the Young Irelanders lived and the parallels they found or thought they found with their own cause—the restoration of a native parliament to Ireland. There were two continental nationalists critical of Ireland's claims, however, both Italians: Giuseppe Mazzini and Count Camillo Cavour of Piedmont Savoy. What they had to say deserves attention.

Mazzini, republican, dogmatic, sure of his own rightness, but a central figure in the history of nineteenth-century nationalism, was in touch with its prophets everywhere in Europe. In 1847, two years after the death of Davis, engaged in founding a Peoples International League, Mazzini left Ireland out of his list of nationalities. Ireland, he argued, was asking merely for a better government—its own—not for any unique principle of life contrasting seriously with that of England.[4] In the Irish cause, he saw no high moral mission, in the Mazzinian coda a requirement for true nationality. Admittedly this "moral mission" could be nebulous. And if Mazzini could see no moral mission, surely he should have seen that Irish history was vastly different from that of England.

Both O'Connell and Davis, however different their emphases, would have answered Mazzini in historical terms: an Irish parliament, the creation of a conquering power, was none the less the possession by prescriptive right of the Irish people, narrow

4. For Mazzini and Cavour, see Nicholas Mansergh, *The Irish Question, 1840–1921*, 3rd ed. (London: Allen and Unwin, 1975), 88–102.

though its basis had once been. Restored, reformed, and democ-
ratized, it would speak for the Irish people as the Westminster
Parliament never could. But which Irish people would dominate
any restored parliament? The Protestant Anglo-Irish aristocracy,
gentry, and middle-class descendants of the earlier conquerors,
or the Catholic democracy, middle class, and peasantry? It was to
this question, to the historic internal divisions in Ireland that
Cavour turned his attention.

Writing in 1844,[5] after an eight-month visit to England and to
France, Cavour saw O'Connell and his Repealers as essentially on
the wrong track. Admitting and deploring the historical injustices
which Ireland had suffered at the hands of England, Cavour still
regarded the Act of Union as a wise measure, and in the long run
good for Ireland. Sweeping aside the Repealers' accusations that
the Union was a nullity because it had been enacted by corruption, in a post-1798 atmosphere of fear and intimidation, he made
a distinction between the long-term value of the measure itself,
and the means adopted to bring it about. The Irish Repealers'
leading idea that legislative independence was the key to Irish reform was in his eyes an illusion. In any revived Irish parliament
the predominant influence would be that of the Catholic democracy, all too eager to set right historic wrongs, with grievances
preventing impartial justice. The protestations of O'Connell that
no harm would come to the Protestant minority inspired no confidence in Cavour. Although his essay is addressed to O'Connell
rather than to the Young Irelanders, their argument that a patriotic union of Irishmen motivated by love of country would inspire
needed Irish reforms made little impression on Cavour. Rather,
he argued, an Irish parliament would be the scene of a war of interests without any mediator to compose and harmonize. Re-

5. His long Irish article appeared in the *Bibliothèque Universelle de Genève*. It was
translated into English in 1845. I use the translation and text of W. B. Hodgson,
Count Cavour on Ireland: Thoughts on Ireland, Its Present and Future (London: Trubner, 1868).

form, real reform, would best come from the British government. The Melbourne ministry had shown the way, and ministers of whatever party would have to continue on the path it had set. Observation of Great Britain, and a close study of its public and political life led Cavour to the conclusion that "it is probable that the present ministry and those which shall follow it, will continue to apply to Ireland the system of amelioration and of reform which Lord Melbourne was the first to adopt on a broad basis. . . . Its march will be measured and prudent; perhaps . . . slow; but it will be constant and nothing will make it turn back."[6] Real reform in the long run will compensate Ireland for the loss of "these brilliant dreams of national independence which she can never realize."[7] In one respect Cavour was correct: the imperial Parliament did reform Ireland.

Over the century before 1914, pushed on, to be sure, by Irish agitation, the British government was responsible for revolutions in land holding, in ecclesiastical privilege, in local government, and in education, all achieved before the political changes of 1920–21. Whether the Irish, in a parliament of their own, could have done all this themselves must remain for historians a highly hypothetical question. Thinking about Cavour's arguments does however bring perspective and reflection on the claims of O'Connell and Young Ireland.[8]

At this point, with the observations of Mazzini and Cavour in mind, we might note an essay of Davis's which he labeled "Sympathy" and which appeared in an anthology of *Nation* articles in 1844.

Whoever hears the cry of a nation for liberty longs to help them. Even the despot feels for all slaves but his own . . . let not Ireland, but Poland, Italy and Hungary, be glad at the progress which the foreign policy of

6. Hodgson, *Count Cavour*, 109–10.   7. Ibid., 110.
8. For perspective on the question of reform in an Irish or an imperial parliament, see J. C. Beckett, "Ireland under the Union," in his *Confrontations: Studies in Irish History* (London: Faber & Faber, 1972), 142–51.

Ireland is making. If Ireland be liberated by internal union and American and French sympathy . . . what people can be kept as an unwilling province? . . . We are battling for Ireland; if we conquer, it will be for mankind.[9]

Here, perhaps is some kind of Irish answer to Mazzini. A Repeal victory will also be a moral achievement, an example and inspiration to the "nations" of Europe.

Ireland and England

Davis may have written his essay on Sympathy as a kind of Irish identification with contemporary European nationalist movements. He was, however, not concerned with theories of nationalism, but with concrete issues of legal rights and the constitutional position of all the people of Ireland in relation to England.[10] As for the *Nation*'s Prospectus, it looked forward to creating a nation-state which might heal the divisions created by past history and to bringing all Irishmen of whatever class or origin or religion into a confederacy to make Ireland a functioning political nation. To understand all the implications of the *Nation*'s program and the history behind it one must take some notice of the life of Daniel O'Connell, his career and achievements before 1842.

The historian Macaulay, speaking in the House of Commons in 1843, called attention to the wide European interest in O'Connell's career. Traveling in Europe, an Englishman might expect to be questioned about O'Connell. What were his aims? Where was he going? What would he do next? For in post-Napoleonic Europe, with its Metternichian repressions, O'Connell's campaigns

9. *The Voice of the Nation: A Manual of Nationality,* By the writers of the *Nation* newspaper (Dublin: James Duffy, 1844), 47–48. When Davis speaks of an Irish foreign policy, he refers to Ireland's taking up attitudes opposed to official British policy, as in Afghanistan or China.

10. What I say is meant to suggest that Repeal as the Young Irelanders and Davis saw it was not part of any romantic movement, but a demand within the English-Irish constitutional tradition.

for civil and religious liberty had inspired wide admiration among liberals, liberal Catholics, and nationalists.[11] Born in 1775 in western Ireland in County Kerry, of a long-settled, landed Catholic family, O'Connell came into his early maturity in the political atmosphere created by the American and French Revolutions.[12] It was also the time when the old Irish parliament was acquiring greater independence from England, though remaining a subordinate legislature. Excluded from it by the penal laws, the Catholic majority was unrepresented; but O'Connell always saw the Protestant parliament as a long-rooted Irish institution capable of growth, reform, and development.[13]

Beginning in 1778, this Irish parliament, with prodding from London, had begun lifting the penal laws which had been enacted over several years after the Protestant victories at the end of the seventeenth-century wars of religion.[14] These laws had kept Catholics out of the legal profession, limited their land-holding rights and their educational opportunities, and made of them an underground society. They had not been barred from trade and business, however, and by the mid-eighteenth century there was a prosperous community of middle-class Catholics insisting on their loyalty to the British state and eager to get rid of the disability laws.[15] Various other forces were working in the same direc-

11. See Owen D. Edwards, "Macaulay's O'Connell," in *The World of Daniel O'Connell,* ed. Donal McCartney (Dublin and Cork: Mercier Press, 1980), 72–87. Also John Hennig, "Continental Opinion," in *Daniel O'Connell: Nine Centenary Essays,* ed. Michael Tierney (Dublin: Browne and Nolan, 1949), 233–69.

12. For the whole European background to Ireland in the eighteenth century, see R. R. Palmer, *The Age of the Democratic Revolution,* 2 vols. (Princeton: Princeton University Press, 1959). Also Maurice O'Connell, *Irish Politics and Social Conflict in the Age of the American Revolution* (Philadelphia: University of Pennsylvania Press, 1965), 25–36.

13. M. R. O'Connell, "The Eighteenth Century Background," in *Daniel O'Connell: The Man and His Politics* (Dublin: Irish Academic Press, 1990), 41–52.

14. Maureen Wall, *The Penal Laws, 1691–1760* (Dundalk: Dundalgan Press, 1961).

15. Maureen Wall, "The Rise of a Catholic Middle Class in Eighteenth Century Ireland," *Irish Historical Studies* 11 (September 1958), 91–115. For all of Wall's signifi-

tion. There were the military necessities of the British state: the recruiting of Catholics into the armed forces; there was the loyalty of the Catholics themselves, especially displayed during the Jacobite rising of 1745; and finally there was the new spirit of toleration associated with the European Enlightenment. By 1800, the penal laws were nearly gone: Catholics could enter the legal profession, take long leases on land, and attend Trinity College. By the Relief Act of 1793 the Catholic "forty shilling" freeholders were given the vote, but a Catholic could not as yet sit in the Protestant parliament. At this point, even dedicated reformers on the Protestant side hesitated about extending further rights to Catholics. To be sure, the number of Catholics in a reformed parliament would at first have been small, but given the great majority of Catholics as against the Protestants the future of Protestants might be at risk.[16] We cannot here discuss in any detail the decade of the 1790s: the career of Wolfe Tone; the Society of United Irishmen; the secret societies; the armed risings of 1798; the policies of the British government and its eventual decision for a parliamentary union of the two countries. This decision had as its background the French revolutionary wars which began in 1793 and were to continue to 1814. There had been invasion attempts, and one French landing in Ireland in 1798. Ireland's vulnerability was a worry to Britain as well as to Irish Protestants.

Despite their fears and reservations, many Protestants were none the less against the union; others saw it as a British protection, a safeguard against a rising Catholic democracy.[17] Prime Minister Pitt had envisaged a Catholic emancipation act as a

---

cant work on eighteenth-century Irish Catholic life, see Gerard O'Brien, ed., *Catholic Ireland in the Eighteenth Century: Collected Essays of Maureen Wall* (Dublin: Geography Publications, 1989).

16. The theme of a Protestant Ascendancy versus a possible coming Catholic Ascendancy, even if unspoken, hung over all political issues.

17. See S. J. Connolly, "Mass Politics and Sectarian Conflict, 1823–30," in *A New History of Ireland*, vol. 5, ed. W. E. Vaughan (Oxford: Clarendon Press, 1994).

companion piece of legislation to the Union, but was prevented from pushing it by the opposition of King George III. The promise of Catholic emancipation had led many Catholics to favor a Union, and when emancipation did not quickly materialize there was among them a widespread feeling of betrayal. As for the British government, with all the bitterness in Ireland engendered by the recent 1798 risings, it could hope that a Union might bring a more settled state of affairs in Ireland, given the background of the French wars and the dangers of invasion.

To return now to Daniel O'Connell and his reactions to the dramatic events surrounding him. He had been in France with his brother Maurice studying at St. Omer and at Douai. Interrupted in their studies by the revolution in France, the two young O'Connells left for home on the day in January 1793 that Louis XVI was executed. Young Daniel continued his education in London, and after a family conference it was decided that he should take up the study of law now that the profession was open to Catholics. Accordingly, with financial support from his Uncle Maurice,[18] Daniel enrolled at Lincoln's Inn and spent his next three years in London, returning to Ireland in 1796. We have already taken brief note of his *Journal*, kept during these early years in London and Dublin. No one interested in O'Connell's career, his personal life and opinions should overlook this *Journal*, published only in 1906.[19] It might be called "A Young Irelander in the Age of Enlightenment." We learn from it of the books O'Connell read, his opinions and reflections on them, revealing as they do the direction his own life was taking. His breadth of reading was remarkable. There was the literature of the French Enlightenment, Gibbon's *Decline and Fall*, Blackstone's *Commentaries on the Laws of England*, Adam Smith's *Wealth of Nations*, Paine's *Age*

18. Uncle Maurice, rich and childless, more or less adopted young Daniel as a son and heir.

19. See chap. 1, n. 8.

of Reason, Boswell's *Life of Johnson,* Henry's *History of England,* and Godwin's *Political Justice.* And there were many more.

It was Godwin's *Political Justice* which affected him most deeply, "more than any I have ever met with." It had, he wrote, "enlarged and strengthened my understanding," and "infused into my mind a serenity never before enjoyed."[20] From the reading of *Political Justice* O'Connell began that line of thinking which led to the belief that reform and necessary change in society could best be achieved by nonviolent means and by bringing mass public opinion to bear on whatever government needed reform. Implicit in all this was the necessity for the political education of a whole people, directing them away from secret societies and violent action. In 1796, contemplating the French naval expedition attempting to land in Ireland (with Wolfe Tone on board), O'Connell wrote in his journal:

. . . I love liberty. Liberty is in my bosom less a principle than a passion. But I know that the victories of the French would be attended with bad consequences. The Irish people are not yet sufficiently enlightened to bear the sun of freedom. Freedom would soon dwindle into licentiousness. They would rob, they would murder. The altar of liberty totters when it is cemented only with blood.[21]

Writing three years later he recalls a conversation with his friend Richard Bennett on the risings of 1798.

We talked much of the late unhappy rebellion. A great deal of innocent blood was shed on this occasion. Good God! What a brute man becomes when ignorant and oppressed! O Liberty, what horrors are perpetrated in thy name! May every virtuous revolutionist remember the horrors of Wexford.[22]

These emotions and the opinions to which they gave rise had been formed, and were to dominate O'Connell's career in the

---

20. O'Connell, *Journal,* 106–7.   21. Ibid., 154–55.
22. Ibid., 236.

public life of Ireland in the years before the appearance of Young Ireland in 1842. In joining the Repeal Association in 1841, Davis, Dillon, and Duffy had to subscribe to the doctrines worked out by O'Connell under earlier circumstances and brilliantly put to work in his famous campaign for Catholic emancipation in the 1820s.

Implicit in O'Connell's denunciations of 1798 was his awareness that liberty itself needed the underpinnings of education, moral and political, the abandonment of secret societies, and open political action for larger ends. His viewpoint was similar to what the *Nation* would expound between 1842 and 1845. Davis and O'Connell were not so far apart as they have sometimes been represented to be. There would be other differences, however, as we shall see.

In 1800, O'Connell was beginning the career as a lawyer which, in a few years, would make him an outstanding figure in the Irish legal world. From the start he was active in opposition to the Act of Union and, as well, was a leading figure in all Catholic activities keeping alive the claim of eligible Catholics to sit in the London Parliament. All proposals for Catholic emancipation conditional on British governmental supervision of clerical appointments he rejected, as well as proposals for the governmental payment of the Catholic clergy. A free church in a free state was his aim.[23] By 1823, O'Connell had made his mark and his public fame was established. As for familiarity with Irish public affairs, his law circuits had given him a thorough knowledge of Ireland and its people, good and bad. In that year a new Catholic Association was formed and put on a democratic basis, and its methods defined as strictly legal and constitutional. An associate membership fee of a shilling a year or a penny a month would draw in the poorest, giv-

---

23. "Religious Freedom," in Maurice O'Connell, *Daniel O'Connell: The Man and His Politics,* contains an extensive review of O'Connell's various statements on this subject.

ing them both a political interest and a stake in the movement. This famous "Catholic rent" brought, in the best of times, over a thousand pounds a week, serving many uses. Ultimately the organization could be seen as a kind of semi-legal political party. Underpinning the Catholic Association was the existence of the forty shilling freeholders, who had been granted the suffrage in 1793 and who normally would vote as their landlords directed. Could this be changed?

It turned out that it could. Actually there had already been cases where the freeholders, organized by the priests, had elected candidates who favored Catholic emancipation.[24] It was in 1826, however, in Waterford, very much under the eye of Thomas Wyse, a landowner and prominent Catholic citizen, that a candidate was put forward to challenge the one sponsored by the Beresfords, long powerful and influential landlords.[25] The Catholic Association showed itself master of the situation, and during the course of the election exercised a stern discipline over the voters' behavior. There was no drinking, no rioting, no Donnybrook Fair atmosphere.[26] The Association's candidate was victorious. Two years later there was a similar election in County Clare, and even though the official candidate, Vesey Fitzgerald, was in favor of emancipation, the Association put forward its own choice, and that was Daniel O'Connell himself. Elected, he could not take his parliamentary seat unless the law was changed, as well as the required entrance oath, which no Catholic could take. One scholar has put the situation succinctly: emancipation was not given, it was taken.[27]

24. Fergus O'Ferrall, *Catholic Emancipation: Daniel O'Connell and the Birth of Irish Democracy: 1820–30* (Dublin: Gill and MacMillan, 1985), 133. See especially his chap. 4.

25. A family vastly influential in Irish eighteenth-century politics.

26. A phrase often used to describe disorder.

27. See Thomas Bartlett, "The Catholic Question in the Eighteenth Century," *History, Ireland* 1, no. 1 (spring 1993): 21.

Wellington in the House of Lords, and Peel in the Commons, gave up their long opposition and made known to King George IV that the measure must pass into law. To the poor peasant who had given his penny a month, emancipation meant little that was tangible and would do nothing as yet to improve his condition. But for the Catholic body as a whole the right to sit in Parliament was a psychological victory, a coming into real legal equality in their own country, a matter of achievement and pride. But it also opened up for both the Catholic majority and the Protestant minority many questions about their future, their place and influence in an Ireland governed from Westminster.

O'Connell duly entered the House of Commons. The agitator became the lawmaker, and at the age of fifty-five showed himself adaptable to the ways of the House of Commons, becoming a great liberal statesman, and winning, if grudgingly, the respect of the House.[28] He and his Irish members supported the Reform Bill of 1832 and all the liberal measures of the 1830s, including in 1833 the abolition of slavery in the British empire—a cause O'Connell was to support for the rest of his parliamentary life, attacking slavery wherever it still existed, especially in the United States.[29] In 1834, he failed, not surprisingly, when he brought before Parliament a measure for the repeal of the Union. He knew his effort would fail, but the case was thoroughly if not convincingly made.[30]

At this point in our background history of the events of the 1840s, we must now say something of the economic and demographic situation confronting the advocates of a repeal of the

28. For O'Connell's parliamentary career see Oliver MacDonagh, "The Contribution of O'Connell," in *The Irish Parliamentary Tradition,* ed. Brian Farrell (Dublin: Gill and MacMillan, 1973), 160–69.

29. He was to differ with Young Ireland on accepting Repeal contributions from slave-holding Americans.

30. There had been British support for Catholic emancipation, but there was little support in Britain for repeal of the Irish Union.

Union. A crucial turning point was the year 1815. The years from 1780 to 1815 had in general been prosperous for Ireland. There was the demand for food, both for the army and navy fighting France, and for the growing urban centers in Britain, a consequence of the industrial revolution. Ireland itself in the later eighteenth century had a share of industrial development which would later collapse in the face of British competition. It was, however, in northeast Ulster that industrial development was strongest and which by 1840 would make that region more markedly different from the rest of Ireland than it already was.[31] Population had grown rapidly both in England and in Ireland; for Ireland the figures went from about three million in 1750 to what in the 1841 census would soon be about eight and one quarter million. After 1815 and the ending of the French wars, prices fell, some markets receded, and in the face of population growth there was growing unemployment and poverty at the lower levels of society. There were, of course, regional differences. After 1824 and the ending of special tariff protection for Ireland, many Irish industries, though not all, were unable to survive.[32] For many contemporaries the answer seemed clear: the Union was a major cause of worsening economic conditions. Modern historical research on Irish economic history, much intensified since 1960, has rejected these earlier *post hoc, propter hoc* political explanations, attributing instead to economic, demographic, and geographic causes the post-1815 poverty and distress so regularly reported by travelers, observers, and parliamentary commissions.[33]

31. See L. Kennedy and P. Ollerenshaw, eds., *An Economic History of Ulster, 1820–1940* (Manchester: Manchester University Press, 1985). Also J. C. Beckett and R. E. Glasscock, eds., *Belfast: The Origin and Growth of An Industrial City* (London: British Broadcasting Corporation, 1967).

32. Ibid. Also Eoin O'Malley, "The Decline of Irish Industry in the Nineteenth Century," *Economic and Social Review* 13, no. 1 (October 1981), 21–42.

33. For a recent discussion of the general economic situation after 1815, see R. F. Foster, *Modern Ireland, 1600–1972* (London: Allen Lane, The Penguin Press, 1988), 318–25.

Among the targets of many anti-Unionists, and later in the century of Land Leaguers, were the landed nobility—that is, the very top owners of the soil, as well as the gentry below them. Reinforcing the animus against landlords was a famous book by Gustave de Beaumont, *Ireland, Political, Social, and Religious* (1839).[34] Leaning heavily on upperclass landowners for fecklessness, absenteeism, and irresponsibility, de Beaumont was widely read, and at the time influential. Modern research, however, does not corroborate his extreme views, nor endorse his severities. Bad landlords there were indeed, but there were also others, and many who would qualify as well-intentioned and responsible. There were also some estates where the landlord rarely appeared, but which were well run by competent and informed land agents. Other landlords with estates in various parts of Ireland could not be resident on one estate at all times. Nor were the landlords as a whole without their own difficulties. Many bore a burden of heavy indebtedness, inherited from the extravagance of eighteenth-century ancestors; there were also mortgages and other charges on their estates, with obligations to widows and to various family members. If a landlord tried to clear overpopulated and subdivided holdings and create larger and more viable farms, he could face an angry tenantry as well as adverse public opinion, and worse, some kind of vengeance from a local secret society.[35] Recent students of the landlord class have their differences of interpretation, but none have endorsed the simplicities of the 1840 anti-Unionists. One historian, after an extensive examination of landlords, concludes that they were not central to

34. De Beaumont and his friend Alexis de Tocqueville had not only visited America, but were also interested in the social and economic structures in Ireland. De Tocqueville also wrote on Ireland. See Emmet Larkin, ed. and trans., *Alexis de Tocqueville's Journey in Ireland, July–August 1835* (Washington, D.C.: The Catholic University of America Press, 1990).

35. See T. Desmond Williams, ed., *Secret Societies in Ireland* (Dublin: Gill and MacMillan, 1973).

Irish history.[36] It is indeed an irony that the *Nation*'s program of bringing all Irishmen into a confederacy to make Ireland a nation should have printed so many anti-landlord essays. One of the first was "Aristocratic Institutions," written by John Dillon.[37] Davis, who could also judge severely, did however realize something of the complicated position of the landlord class.[38] In any restored Irish parliament, with an Irish House of Lords, they would have been part of a native government. How would they have acted? And how would they have related their own interests to those of the country at large?

A contributing factor in the Irish economic situation was the decline of Irish cottage industries, and their growing demise after 1825. Again, England's industrial revolution was the activating factor. Thousands of rural and partially urban workers, who were spinners and weavers of linen or workers in small related occupations, found their incomes drastically reduced. The only recourse was dependence on small plots of agricultural land, or worse, sinking down to the level of agricultural laborer. And of course for some there was emigration.

This demise of cottage industries was a Europe-wide phenomenon, and indeed its effects can be seen in England itself. The older textile home industries of East Anglia gave way to the Midlands, as steam power and the proximity to coal and iron gave the new cities of central England the lead in textiles, and indeed, ultimately, in other industries. Over Europe as a whole some regions went down as others went up.[39] And in this economic view, Ire-

36. L. Cullen, *The Emergence of Modern Ireland* (New York: Holmes and Meier, 1981), 253–56.

37. *Nation*, 15 October 1842.

38. *Nation*, 24 December 1842. Davis saw both peasant and landlord locked in a system from which there was no easy escape: "Bad examples, bad habits, and heavy debts." He could still write harshly about landlords, however.

39. See Joel Mokyr, *Why Ireland Starved* (London: Allen and Unwin, 1983, 1988), 279, 282–83.

land was less a nation than a distressed region sitting next to the most advanced industrial country in the world of that time.

As for agriculture, taken by itself it was not unprosperous. Before the famine output increased regularly, and landlords and middling farmers were the recipients of the profits. And, indeed, in some areas there was improvement in farming methods.[40] For the small farmer, cottiers, and laborers, however, among whom the population increase was greatest, the result was a potato diet, precarious income, and very bad housing conditions.[41] To write thus briefly of agricultural conditions leaves out the variety of regional circumstances. Enough has been said, however, to suggest that the very visibility of so much distress was a convincing argument for the reformer to concern himself with remedies. O'Connell, on the very eve of the Emancipation Act, was fully conscious of the social dangers of massive unemployment and poverty. He wrote to Pierce Mahony in 1829:

But, my dear Mahony, there must be a grant for public works. It will be repaid, every shilling of it, tenfold in revenue, in tranquility and in permanent utility. . . . The people will be taken out of our hands by Emancipation, as we took them from Capt. Rock by our agitation. They may fall back into Rock's hands unless the government has the common sense to take them into their own. . . . This can easily be done by giving them present employment.[42]

40. See Cormac O'Grada, *Ireland Before and After the Famine* (Manchester: Manchester University Press, 1988), chaps. 1 and 2. For the dilemmas of some landlords in County Cork, see J. S. Donnelly, Jr., *The Land and the People of Nineteenth Century Cork* (London and Boston: Routledge and Kegan Paul, 1975), 52–72.

41. In *Ireland Before and After the Famine,* O'Grada writes: "There is no denying the abject poverty of the neglected masses, nor the likelihood of impoverishment for a high proportion . . . of the total population. To that extent traditional accounts relying on the impressions of travel writers like Kohl, Inglis, or deBeaumont are correct. But poverty had strong regional and class components; and the island as a whole was less starvation-prone, less sickly, and less illiterate than often depicted"; 21–22.

42. O'Connell, *Correspondence,* vol. 4, letter 1544, 28 and 29 March 1829.

O'Connell's letter illustrates very well the dilemmas of laissez-faire economics and the plight of a backward country vis à vis a great and growing industrial neighbor. Whether O'Connell's campaign for emancipation slowed down agrarian violence is debatable.

Enough has been said in this necessarily brief summary of some of the leading factors in the Irish economy to suggest that a native parliament would have had its difficulties. As we have suggested, there would have been much self-interest on the part of a membership heavily upper class. But, knowing their country as Englishmen did not, would Irishmen have been wiser, more compassionate, more sympathetic? Thomas Davis hoped so. Dr. R. D. Collison-Black, in his *Economic Thought and the Irish Question* (1960), has remarked that Repeal "would not in itself have solved Ireland's economic problems."[43] He went on to say, however, that even with a strong landlord interest, any restored Irish parliament might have designed wiser policies than those devised in London. It could never have been easy to do so, however.[44]

Despite the *Nation's* later accusations of neglect and inadequacy, which it would direct against the British government, the accomplishments of that government between 1830 and 1840 were considerable and of long-range significance; and for these developments O'Connell was in part responsible. After losing his bid for Repeal in 1834, he decided in 1835 that much practical improvement could be achieved for Ireland by giving the support and the votes of Irish parliamentary members to the Whig ministry of Lord Melbourne. This informal arrangement, in return for legislation, administrative reform, and Catholic appointments to office for which, since 1829, they were eligible, is often

43. R. D. Collison-Black, *Economic Thought and the Irish Question, 1817–1870* (Cambridge: Cambridge University Press, 1970), 247.
44. Ibid., 248.

referred to as the Lichfield House Compact.[45] At the top of the Whig administration in Dublin Castle were three men who worked in harmony and cooperated to give Ireland the best government it had experienced since the enactment of the Union in 1800.

The Lord Lieutenant was Lord Mulgrave; the Chief Secretary, Lord Morpeth; and the Under-Secretary, Thomas Drummond. Mulgrave (later Lord Normanby) had an impressive, yet agreeable, friendly personality. Despite a formal military bearing, he was genial and cordial, enjoying great popularity among the people of Dublin, bringing drama, color, and good nature to his public appearances. For their political influence, these theatrical qualities are not to be discounted.[46] Lord Morpeth, who had to spend a half-year in London presenting Irish matters to the cabinet and the House of Commons, was more restrained in manner, but as dedicated as Mulgrave to the better government of Ireland. The third member of this intelligent and competent triumvirate was Thomas Drummond, who as Under-Secretary was the official closest to the day-to-day activities of Irish administration in Ireland. A Scotsman, Drummond had been for some years an engineer attached to the army ordnance survey, engaged in carrying out the mapping of Ireland. Taking him to every part of the Irish countryside, his survey work had given him a thorough knowledge not only of Ireland's geography but of its people, with whose condition and grievances he had come to sympathize. Possibly overzealous in his habits of work, he drove himself hard, and tragically died in 1840, mourned by a people he had served so well. The subject of two earlier biographies, Drummond and his work have more recently been critically and sympathetically ex-

45. See A. H. Graham, "The Lichfield House Compact, 1835," *Irish Historical Studies* 12 (March 1961): 209–25.

46. For a portrait of Mulgrave see D. O. Maddyn, *Ireland and Its Rulers Since 1829*, 3 vols. (London: J. C. Newby, 1843–44), vol. 2, chap. 15; vol. 3, chap. 1.

amined by Professor O'Tuathaigh. Drummond's rebuke to the Tipperary magistrates is often quoted: "Property has its duties as well as its rights. . . ."[47]

Before noticing the reforms of the O'Connell-Melbourne collaboration, we should mention that even earlier there had been significant administrative action on the part of the British government. In 1805, provision had been made for public health with the establishment of dispensaries equipped to give free medical attention to the poor. By 1840 there were at least six hundred of these spread across the Irish countryside. How effective in practice they all were we cannot be sure, but there was at least a recognition that there were responsibilities for public health which a government must face.[48] As well, building on eighteenth-century parliamentary activity, there was in every county one infirmary and one fever hospital supported by local taxation. For the treatment of insanity, neighboring counties were grouped for the establishment of regional mental hospitals and brought under a national system of inspection. Professor MacDonagh writes: "If one takes policy and structure as the criteria, Ireland had one of the most advanced health services in Europe in the first half of the nineteenth century."[49] Professor MacDonagh notes as well that of thirty Dublin hospitals in 1840, twenty-one specialized in one branch of medicine. He goes on to suggest that this combination of governmental activity, private support, and medical specialization may account for the years 1830–50 becoming a period in Irish medical history marked by fresh discovery and significant research.[50]

In 1831 the government tackled the problem of elementary ed-

---

47. G. O'Tuathaigh, *Thomas Drummond and the Government of Ireland, 1835–41,* O'Donnell Lecture (Dublin: National University of Ireland, 1978).

48. Oliver MacDonagh, *Ireland: The Union and Its Aftermath,* rev. ed. (London: Allen and Unwin, 1977), 37. (First published in the United States in 1967 by Prentice-Hall.)

49. Ibid.   50. Ibid.

ucation, setting up a national nonsectarian system but providing for separate religious instruction. Into the difficulties that surrounded the system and its administration, and the quarrels over it by different religious groups, we cannot enter here. The system failed to bridge Ireland's bitter sectarian divisions; but what it did do, and probably its greatest achievement, was to make Ireland highly literate in the English language. In 1841, the proportion of people five years and up who were unable to read or write was 53 percent; in 1851, it was 47 percent; in 1861, it was 39 percent; in 1871, 33 percent. Though Irish history was excluded from the curricula of these schools, a fact which Thomas Davis was to deplore, the students emerging from them were able to read the books, newspapers, and pamphlets which pleaded the national cause.[51] Over the century, spoken Irish was steadily receding. This trend toward English, enhanced by the schools, had begun long before.[52] We shall return to the subject of education, in which Thomas Davis took the deepest interest.

In 1831, a new Board of Works had been established, superseding weaker but similar bodies existing in the late eighteenth and early nineteenth centuries. Intended as a standing body the Board was to organize works that would be tied to a larger national plan. It would both recommend and carry out, and would be staffed by experts, especially engineers, who would serve also as inspectors of the projects which they had studied and recommended. At first the Board was concerned with roads, ports, and harbors, but almost immediately its jurisdiction expanded, and before the decade ended its activities involved inland navigation, fisheries, and land reclamation and drainage. It also played a role in the recommendations of the Irish Railway Commission, which in

51. D. H. Akenson, "Pre-University Education, 1782–1870," in *A New History of Ireland,* vol. 5, ed. W. E. Vaughan (Oxford: Clarendon Press, 1989), 536–37.

52. Maureen Wall, "The Decline of the Irish Language," in *A View of the Irish Language,* ed. Brian O'Cuiv (Dublin: Stationery Office, 1969), 81–90.

1838 presented a plan for an Irish railway system. Over the decade the Board had been responsible for extensive grants and loans for various constructive purposes. We are noticing here responses to necessities despite current doctrines of laissez faire. If there was also similar "government growth" in England there was more of it in Ireland.[53]

To return now to the Melbourne ministry. During the entire decade there was a tithe "war," a violent resistance to its payment, and as well the violent actions of secret peasant societies.[54] Drummond turned his attention to these problems of law and order, and in 1836 there was established, building on already existing peace preservation arrangements, a new body which would become the famous Royal Irish Constabulary. Catholics were encouraged to join, and the force, nonsectarian and efficient, won trust and respect and played its part in the better public order which began to prevail in Ireland by 1840. Tithe itself was reordered, but not abolished. Commuted to a rent charge, lessened in amount but payable by landlords who could obtain reimbursement from their rents, it brought an end at least to the violent disturbances of the earlier decade. The poorest tenants were exempt from charges, and arrears for the years 1833 to 1837 were excused by the state. Interestingly, Peel and O'Connell had supported this solution. Tithe, payable by a Catholic population to support an Anglican church, was widely felt to be unjust even by many Protestants.

The year 1838 also saw the enactment of an Irish Poor Law. Earlier, an Irish Poor Law Commission under the chairmanship of the Anglican Archbishop Whately suggested, among its recommendations, measures that would have required extensive state

---

53. MacDonagh, *Ireland*, 39–40. The phrase "government growth" is Professor MacDonagh's, the title of one of his books: *A Pattern of Government Growth* (London: MacGibbon & Kee, 1961).
54. Williams, *Secret Societies*.

intervention: reclamation of waste lands; drainage and other agricultural improvements; agricultural instruction for farmers to acquaint them with improved methods of cultivation; state loans for general improvements; large-scale assisted emigration. As Whig politicians saw it this report was a vast scheme of social engineering which they were not prepared to undertake and which would lead they knew not where. It is most interesting, however, that at that point there were people who, on the basis of their impartial inquiries, had arrived at a deeper, more thoughtful view of what needed to be done for Ireland, so different from England in its history, class relationships, and economic circumstances.[55]

The Whig ministry threw out the recommendations of Whately's committee, a report which had been three years in the making. Instead they despatched to Ireland one George Nicholls, who delivered the report expected of him: that a Poor Law for Ireland, similar to the English law of 1834, be enacted despite Ireland's special circumstances so clearly set out by the Irish commission. Work houses were set up over the Irish countryside and, as one scholar puts it, "just in time to face and be overwhelmed by the catastrophe of the Great Famine in the late 1840s."[56] For the government of these workhouses there were to be boards of Poor Law guardians, partially elected, with both Catholics and Protestants eligible for membership. The guardians brought a degree of democracy to local government. As time went on, various local necessities would enlarge their spheres of action, until the passage of the Irish Local Government Act of 1898.[57]

As for Irish municipal reform, that issue was sharpened by the

55. Even Sir Robert Peel had now and again to remind the House of Commons that Ireland was not England.

56. K. Theodore Hoppen, *Ireland Since 1800: Conflict and Conformity* (London: Longman, 1989), 24.

57. The Act of 1898 was to have a revolutionary effect on Irish local affairs.

enactment of the English act of 1835. The final but much delayed Irish act of 1840 was far less democratic in its provisions and it had behind it five years of opposition from the House of Lords; as finally enacted, it was a compromise and a disappointment. Many older Irish town corporations were abolished, only ten surviving with reduced functions. A ten pound household franchise and a high property qualification for corporation membership meant the dominance of upper- and middle-class membership. The Whig alliance was bringing reform, slow and inadequate. One can see, however, why Count Cavour, viewing it all from Europe, was hopeful for the future. Things could not go backward. As for Davis, the inspiration for his 1837 pamphlet, which we have examined, had been the obstructive tactics of the House of Lords. The majority of the corporations turned out to be strongly nationalist and sympathetic to the campaign for Repeal which O'Connell would soon reactivate. As for O'Connell, he became Lord Mayor of Dublin's reformed corporation in 1841, an office he was to administer efficiently and impartially.[58]

The Melbourne ministry's initiatives were not, however, all to be realized on the political level. Different possibilities were open when it came to administration and the power to make appointments, and so to bring Catholics into positions of legal significance. Immediately after 1829 little was done, but during the Melbourne ministry, serious changes began. The Irish executive in Dublin Castle, often with the recommendation and advice of O'Connell, began to appoint Catholics to legal and judicial offices. I cite here two interesting examples: Michael O'Loghlen became solicitor general in 1835, attorney general the same year, and a Baron of the Exchequer in 1836. David Pigot, another O'Connell friend, moved up the same ladder to become Chief

58. Oliver MacDonagh, *The Emancipist: Daniel O'Connell, 1830–1847* (New York: St. Martins Press, 1989), 202–9. O'Connell was the first Catholic since 1688 to be Lord Mayor of Dublin.

Baron of the Exchequer in 1846.[59] Both these distinguished Catholics were graduates of Trinity, and their respective sons, Colman O'Loghlen and John Edward Pigot, were also graduates of Trinity who later became close friends of Thomas Davis and his colleagues in Young Ireland affairs. The point to note here is that many Catholics of property and education, seeing no immediate hope of Repeal, were prepared to accept office and make their way in the world while retaining, if quietly, nationalist political views. As we shall see, Young Ireland was to turn against what it called "official expectations," that is, office under the crown. O'Connell himself had been offered political office in 1838, Mastership of the Rolls. Tempted, he refused.[60] He would stay out of office and continue to agitate for Ireland.

Between 1838 and 1841, the year the Melbourne government went down before Peel's motion of no confidence, O'Connell was puzzling over his next step. His letters to his financial manager, P. V. Fitzpatrick, reveal worry, depression, and a sense that his Whig alliance may have been alienating him from the Irish people.[61] His policy of cooperation had indeed brought reforms but not enough, and the Catholic rent so necessary for his political work was falling off. Outwardly O'Connell's concerns were revealed in his founding of three successive societies directed to Repeal: the Precursor Society, the National Repeal Association, and finally the Loyal National Repeal Association. One letter to Fitzpatrick suggests his worry that the violent forces in Ireland were simmering still, and would break forth again if he were not, by resuming full control of national politics, in charge of another great movement. Action of some sort must be taken in the face

59. For brief biographical notices of these men see J. S. Crone, *A Concise Dictionary of Irish Biography* (Dublin: Talbot Press, 1928), 192, 206.

60. MacDonagh, *The Emancipist*, 175. Also O'Connell, *Correspondence*, vol. 6, O'Connell to P. V. Fitzpatrick, 18 June 1838.

61. O'Connell, *Correspondence*, vol. 6, O'Connell to Fitzpatrick, letters 2645 and 2646, 7 and 8 August 1839.

of a new ministry headed by his old antagonist, Sir Robert Peel.[62]

Here, we should take note of another famous contemporaneous cause, Father Theobald Mathew's temperance crusade, which had its origin in 1839 in Cork. While praising and admiring Father Mathew's work and influence, O'Connell had some reservations. In January 1843 he would tell a Dublin gathering held in the good friar's honor that the temperance movement, admirable as it was, passed too heavy a censure on the condition and character of the Irish people.[63]

It is important to notice this movement, however, which Davis and the Young Irelanders regarded as a strong support in the campaign for self-government. Political progress in their eyes was related to the moral elevation of the Irish people; political freedom and moral regeneration went hand in hand.

The question, finally, presents itself: could Davis, Duffy, and Dillon have sponsored some kind of nonpolitical movement independent of O'Connell? Long years later, in 1898, John Kells Ingram,[64] writing to Duffy, suggested something of the sort: if the *Nation* had kept out of politics, and confined itself to social teaching and the reconciliation of classes, avoiding both cooperation and conflict with O'Connell, real results might have been achieved. My own answer to Ingram is negative. In the climate of the early 1840s, and with O'Connell a dominating force in Irish public life, it seems hard to imagine any movement that could have ignored him. He gave the Young Irelanders their stage. Their newspaper, however, was their greatest achievement, and indeed, was a social as well as a political teacher.

---

62. Ibid., vol. 7, O'Connell to Fitzpatrick, letter 2905, 17 July 1841.

63. See Elizabeth Malcolm, "Temperance and Irish Nationalism," in *Ireland Under the Union: Essays in Honour of T. W. Moody,* ed. F. S. L. Lyons and Richard Hawkins (Oxford: Clarendon Press, 1980), 78–79.

64. Ingram to Duffy, 30 April 1898. Gavan Duffy Papers, National Library of Ireland. As a young man, Ingram had written the poem "Who Fears to Speak of '98"; in 1879–87, he was a professor in Trinity and its librarian. A disciple of Auguste Comte.

Statue of Thomas Davis (1852) by John Hogan. Dublin City Hall.

Used by permission of Dublin City Council.

Chapter 3

Journalism: Personal and Public Life,
October 1842–1843

🦋

The three years from the founding of the *Nation* to Davis's death in September 1845 were filled for him and his colleagues with passionate activity. The first year, coinciding as it did with O'Connell's huge outdoor meetings for the repeal of the Union, was filled with hope and optimism. Whatever secret misgivings O'Connell or the *Nation*'s staff may have had about the chance of winning repeal of the Union, they could for the moment act as if their own aim was attainable, as if O'Connell's earlier successful campaign for Catholic emancipation might be repeated for this different, though more difficult, goal. Wellington and Peel had capitulated in 1829; Peel, now the Prime Minister, might, they sometimes let themselves believe, capitulate again. Davis, as we shall see, was less sure of this possibility, and indeed he had good reason to be doubtful. Like its sister nationalist journals, the *Freeman* and the *Pilot,* the *Nation* carried accounts of the weekly meetings and debates at O'Connell's Loyal National Repeal Association, and in the late spring, summer, and early autumn of 1843 reported in much detail on O'Connell's "monster meetings" held throughout the countryside.[1] But this kind of re-

1. The *Nation* carried frequent editorial comment on O'Connell's meetings and speeches.

porting on immediate contemporary affairs would never have made the *Nation*'s fame nor given it the place it was to win in Irish historical memory. For it was a publication with a double identity, both a newspaper and a magazine of opinion, interested in a wide variety of subjects, not necessarily contemporary or political, but giving special attention to Irish history and literature, and indeed to all things Irish. Lively editorials were inspired by current issues, but they were also exhortations to patriotic behavior, and to each person's responsibility, however small, for the condition of Ireland. The theme of the Prospectus was developed with infinite variety: the healing of old wounds, the internal union which would lay the foundation of the new Irish nation that had never yet existed.

In 1844, Davis and Duffy brought together and published what they regarded as the most significant writings of the *Nation*'s first year. This little volume, called *The Voice of the Nation*,[2] is an invaluable guide to Young Ireland's thinking. It was Davis who wrote the final essay called *A Year's Work*. Nationality, the breaking down of barriers among Irish people, bringing to light Irish history, promoting a tolerant public spirit in social and political matters—these were his major themes. Urging the settlement of the tenure question, Davis called for the enactment of prospective laws which would tend "by natural and easy stages" to reduce great estates and create a body of small proprietors over the whole country. "But," he wrote, "we are not ready to jump into servile war for this purpose."[3] Also, during this first year, Davis had advo-

2. The *Voice of the Nation* (Dublin: James Duffy, 1844). The articles in *Voice* represent what the editors considered the best and most representative of their work in 1842–43. Twenty-six of the essays were Davis's. In a preface the authors stated that the *Nation* was "less a paper of news than of education . . . indifferent to sect and independent of party." Their word "nationality" was the name for many things, among them "a literature made by Irishmen, and coloured by our scenery, manners and character." The writers are identified by initials, making the volume useful to scholars. A second volume bringing together literary and historical papers was planned but never published.

3. *Voice*, 187–93.

cated what he called a foreign policy for Ireland. And in this summary essay he urged it again. For him such a policy meant dissociating Ireland from any approval of the British wars of conquest in India or Afghanistan or elsewhere, and seeking as well the good opinion of countries with whom Britain might be at odds, winning from them sympathy and support for Ireland, even though the support was merely that of their public opinion. The Irish must learn about France, the German states, America, or India from sources not necessarily British. Public awareness of significant Irish issues and viewpoints and intelligent participation in the wider movements of public life would be promoted by the establishment of local reading rooms, by public lectures, and by the public's patronage of Irish art and literature. Like O'Connell, who had drawn a whole people into his Catholic emancipation campaign, Davis was aware of those intangibles by which even the humblest individual could feel himself to be part of a larger political movement. One piece of his 1843 manifesto is worth quoting:

Let no one forget that he who gives one favorable or instructive national fact to his circle—that he who saves an air, a relic of antiquity, a tradition, an old custom from loss—he who makes a temperance band play, or a friend sing an Irish instead of a foreign tune—who gives or teaches a book on Ireland, or its literature or history, instead of one on England or the English—that he who promotes to the value of a farthing Irish trade or agriculture, or helps in the least our knowledge, commerce, and respectability, does his duty and does what the half of us must do, or Ireland cannot be a nation. . . .[4]

As he ended his retrospect on the *Nation*'s first year Davis noted that the newspaper's success had been attributed to its participation in the Repeal movement. His own answer was different. "We succeeded," he wrote, "because we were in earnest."[5]

Earnestness, however, can be dull, and dull this early *Nation* seldom was. Written in a lively style, whether in short or long ar-

4. Ibid., 193.   5. Ibid.

ticles, weighty subjects came out simply and clearly. Also, the newspaper was witty, although the wit often led to exaggeration and unfair generalizations. For example, an Englishman was characterized in one article as a boastful "great Briton" without sensitivity or imagination. On the other hand, the English people, if not their government or aristocracy, could sometimes be depicted with kindness and sympathy. Despite lapses, the *Nation* did exhibit an attractive generosity of tone.

The three young men did not, of course, come to their task unprepared. All had done apprentice journalism under the tutelage of Michael Staunton of the *Morning Register*. Duffy had been the editor of the *Vindicator* and had a sharp eye for what makes a good paper; Davis had stores of learning and a rich background of reading directed to subjects which interested him, and which he was able to put into brief, arresting, readable form. Dillon's articles, fewer in number, were especially concerned with agrarian questions, but he was to write far less than his two friends, compelled as he was by circumstances to devote himself to his profession as a lawyer. But he was always there, a supporter and friend "whose advice was always sought in trouble." As for Davis, his *Nation* style, direct, vivid, commanding the reader's attention, had come a long way from the circuitous and involved writing of his address to the Trinity Historical Society and his serious essays in the *Citizen*.

Some further words are in order on the *Nation*'s content. It had amusing answers to correspondents; letters from Irishmen who had emigrated to America, to Canada, or to Newfoundland; accounts of travels on the European continent, especially to France; experiences of Irishmen who had visited or settled in various English cities. Particularly interesting were the biographical sketches of famous Irishmen, poets, soldiers, artists, politicians, all directed to the theme of Irish achievement. There was something for everyone. And then there was the poetry.

Duffy, during his editorship of the *Vindicator,* had published poetry, songs, and ballads, which had proved a most successful part of his newspaper. Not surprisingly, he was eager to repeat this success with the *Nation.* Responding to Duffy's appeal, though he had never published any of his own youthful poetic attempts, Davis appeared one day with his "Lament for the Death of Owen Roe O'Neill," published in the sixth number of the *Nation.*[6] Later, and regularly, under the pseudonym of the Celt, Davis, as we have noted, was to write and publish many more songs and ballads. His poetry, popular then and later, and still often quoted, has become the subject in recent years of scholarly criticism, its spirit and subject matter often at odds with the message of internal union and harmony among Irishmen which so largely characterized his prose essays. His harshest verses, it should be noted, were directed against the "Saxon" English and their historic cruelties in Ireland.[7] But many poems also carried the message of the prose: conciliation, harmony, and cooperation among Irishmen.[8] In 1843, the editors collected the *Nation's* poems, publishing an anthology, *The Spirit of the Nation,* which went through many editions in both Ireland and abroad during the nineteenth century.[9]

Contemporary newspapers both in Ireland and in England were very much aware of the *Nation* and the impact it was mak-

6. This famous ballad can be found in *The Poems of Thomas Davis: Now First Collected,* ed. Thomas Wallis (Dublin: James Duffy, 1846), 133–35.

7. For the contrasts between Davis's prose and poetry and the conflicting messages they contain, see Maurice O'Connell, "Thomas Davis, a Destructive Conciliator," *Irish Times* (Dublin), 6 August 1974; also Alf MacLochlainn, *Irish Times,* 20 November 1973.

8. See "Orange and Green," "A Nation Once Again," "My Land," "The West's Asleep," "Celts and Saxons." All are in the collection edited by Thomas Wallis.

9. *The Spirit of the Nation* (Dublin: James Duffy, 1843). And later, *The Spirit of the Nation, or Ballads and Songs by the Writers of the Nation,* reissued in Quarto form with Music, and an Artistic page by Frederick Burton, with illustrations and preface by Thomas Davis (Dublin: James Duffy, 1845). This volume (1845) reached a fiftieth edition by 1877.

ing in O'Connell's Repeal campaign. The *Warder,* the Protestant paper wrote:

We regard . . . the *Nation* newspaper as the most ominous and formidable phenomenon of these strange and menacing times. No less than nine thousand copies of that paper are regularly issued . . . a circulation more than three times as great as the largest conservative press in Ireland, a circulation, too, multiplied indefinitely by the eager transference of each copy from hand to hand. . . . *The Nation* is written with a masculine vigor and an impetuous singleness of purpose, which makes every number tell home.[10]

The *London Times* noticed not only the newspaper, but especially the poetry published by the editors in *The Spirit of the Nation.* The *Times* observed:

One invention of the agitator for talking treason without being hung for it they have very much bettered . . . poetry is one of the most convenient instruments in the world for saying what you please. Nobody has a right to know exactly how much you may or may not mean. Let a man make his thoughts rhyme, and there is hardly any amount of treason and iniquity he may not utter without giving anybody a right to say positively that he intends it. . . . Mr. O'Connell has been charging the Irish mind with Wexford massacres and Clontarf victories (with the most unreserved parenthetical recommendations of tranquility). . . . But even his mischievous exhortations are as nothing compared with the fervor of rebellion which breathes in every page of these verses, disguised under the very penetrable mask of an allusion to other times. The writer seems to think his pen absolutely unfettered if he does but put in 1641 or 1782 at the head of his poems. . . .[11]

Leaving out for the moment any final appraisals on the language and political intent of both Young Ireland and O'Connell in 1843, we take note of the judgment of Brian Inglis, author of *The Freedom of the Press in Ireland, 1784–1841,*[12] who has paid warm tribute to the high character of the *Nation.* He has written:

10. Reprinted in an appendix to *Voice of the Nation,* "Notices of the Journals," 7.
11. Ibid., 5.
12. London: Faber and Faber, 1959.

When I began to work on the newspapers of the early 1840s I was half afraid that it might become clear that the *Nation's* influence had been inflated, exaggerated, expanded into myth and legend. Not at all. Its impact was astonishing. . . . it caught the public imagination as no other paper has done before or since. Why? If I had to sum up its virtue in a word, I would point to its integrity. Gavan Duffy, John B. Dillon and especially Thomas Davis were men of honesty of purpose. . . . They would not trim, either to ascendancy on the one side or O'Connell on the other, out of expediency.[13]

The *Nation* office, located first on Trinity Street just off Dame Street, was a short walk from Trinity College and within sight of the old Irish parliament house which had now become the Bank of Ireland. It was the center for an informal group of friends and contributors to the paper who soon came to be called Young Ireland, a name, as we have seen, which the founders of the *Nation* never invented themselves but finally came to accept. From many sources we know about the *Nation* group, but the most solid information comes from Gavan Duffy's *Young Ireland,* where he brought to life in overwhelming detail all the enthusiasm, the vitality, the bright hopes of his comrades of forty years before. But we also have Davis's correspondence, MacNevin's letter on Young Ireland, Doheny's *Felon's Track,* and the reminiscences and reflections of the many people who had known and admired Davis. Something needs to be said about the leading young men who attached themselves to the three *Nation* founders; some of these, inspired all their lives by their Young Ireland days and their friendships with Davis, were to have later interesting careers, some in the public life of both England and Ireland. The two earliest associates were John Pigot and John O'Hagan, both the same age, and both eight years younger than Davis. They had met as students at Trinity, had belonged to the Historical Society, and

13. Brian Inglis, "The Press," in *Social Life in Ireland, 1800–1845,* ed. R. B. McDowell (Dublin: Colm O'Lochlain, The Sign of the Three Candles, 1957), 110–11. This essay is useful for newspapers preceding or contemporary with the *Nation.*

were soon to go to London to complete their legal studies, sharing law chambers in Southhampton Row in Bloomsbury. Like Daniel Owen Maddyn, Pigot was a regular correspondent of Davis, who wrote many letters to this younger friend telling of his activities, his doubts, and his hopes. Pigot's family connections are interesting, and despite their solid respectability he can be seen as a classic young man in rebellion. His father, also a lawyer, was a close friend of Daniel O'Connell, and would become in 1846 Chief Baron of the Exchequer, a post he would hold until his death in 1873. The family belonged to the Catholic middle class, emerging into public life in the post-penal years of the later eighteenth century. The grandfather, Dr. John Pigot, was a physician of solid reputation in County Cork. Both the elder Pigot and his son were deeply interested in Irish music, and the younger Pigot's musical enthusiasms were a bond between him and Davis. Before knowing Davis, Pigot had been thinking along lines similar to those Davis had set out in the Prospectus for the *Nation*. After Davis's death, Pigot would confide to his diary that all his thoughts and plans for Ireland had included Davis as his collaborator.[14] Dark, handsome, engaging in manner, Pigot looked the very image of the romantic patriot. Not surprisingly, he became a model for the hero of Marmion Savage's satirical novel, *The Falcon Family, or Young Ireland* (1845). Disguised as Tigernach MacMorris, Pigot is pictured as the champion of impossible projects, among them the return of Stonehenge to Ireland, in his view its original home. The novel is exaggerated and unfair, but even the Young Irelanders had to laugh.[15]

14. For an extensive essay on Pigot, see Denis Gwynn, "John E. Pigot and Thomas Davis," *Studies* 38 (1949): 144–57. Also, the entry in J. S. Crone, *A Concise Dictionary of Irish Biography* (Dublin: Talbot Press, 1928), 206. Cited hereafter as Crone.

15. Duffy Correspondence, MS 5756, National Library of Ireland, O'Hagan to Duffy, n.d. O'Hagan had only dipped into *The Falcon Family,* but he and others agreed that the hero was modeled on Pigot. Admitting that "we all laughed," O'Hagan went on to write that it was a disgraceful thing for Savage to have done, seeing that he was a friend of Pigot's father.

John O'Hagan, whose later tribute to the work of Davis we have earlier mentioned, was a northerner born in Newry to a prosperous Catholic merchant family. Serving as a municipal counselor, his father, the elder O'Hagan, had won the high regard of his fellow citizens for his integrity and public spirit. In their obituary, the editors of the *Newry Examiner* observed that though Arthur O'Hagan "was warmly attached to his own religious and political opinions . . . he never allowed his sentiments on either of these subjects to interfere with the ordinary intercourse of society."[16] It is easy to see how the influences of O'Hagan's early life would lead him toward the purposes and plans, and the tolerant spirit, of the Young Irelanders. Educated by the Jesuit fathers in Dublin at their school in Hardwicke Street, O'Hagan completed his education at Trinity, receiving his B.A. in 1842. Although these two young men remained devoted friends throughout their lives, they were, superficially at least, quite unlike. Duffy notes O'Hagan's agreeable smile, his general good nature, and then tells us: "But behind these lay a judgement and sagacity, notable at any age, and marvelous in one so young."[17] Duffy continues: "He was safest in council, the most moderate in opinion, the most considerate in temper of the young men; and after a time, any of them would have recourse to him, next after Davis, in a personal difficulty needing sympathy and discretion."[18]

By the end of the first year there were others in the inner circle: Thomas MacNevin, Michael Joseph Barry, Denny Lane, and Denis Florence McCarthy, all Catholics and of whom something must now be said. Born and living in Cork, Barry and Lane were in touch with Davis through visits and correspondence with the

16. For O'Hagan, see Matthew Russell, "Poets I Have Known, John O'Hagan," *Irish Monthly* 33 (1908), 71–84. Also, Russell, "Judge O'Hagan, Some Notes on His Life and Letters," *Irish Monthly* (August 1912): 419–28.

17. Charles Gavan Duffy, *Young Ireland: A Fragment of Irish History* (London: Cassell, 1880), 292.

18. Ibid.

group in Dublin. Lane would be involved all his long life in his family's business interests but also in the cultural and philanthropic activities in his home city.[19] From the few letters which remain to us we can deduce that Lane had the kind of friendship with Davis that gave him freedom to criticize, for he wrote to Davis with surprising frankness, but always tactfully, about his political conduct.[20] Lane was a cousin to Daniel Owen Maddyn, whom we have noted as Davis's close friend and confidant; it was perhaps through him that Lane came to know Davis so well. A graduate of Trinity, Lane may also have met Davis at the College Historical Society. More than Lane, Barry was a participant in the work of the Repeal Association. Later, he would edit the *Cork Southern Reporter* and publish *The Songs of Ireland* (1845), for which Davis would write an introductory essay. His most outstanding Young Ireland achievement would come in 1845 when he won first prize in the Repeal Association's contest for a plan for a new constitution for Ireland. Barry envisaged for Ireland a form of government similar to what Canada was on the way to achieving during the 1840s and 1850s: ministerial responsibility and local independence under the British crown. Davis was one of the three judges who awarded Barry the prize, another clue, probably, to the constitutional lines along which Davis, in 1845, was thinking. Ironically, after the debacle of 1848 Barry abandoned his Young Ireland faith and decided against any further agitation for Irish self-government.[21]

MacNevin, also a graduate of Trinity, and exactly Davis's age,

19. For Barry, MacNevin, and Lane, see entries in Crone.

20. Lane was a close observer of the proceedings of the Repeal Association and of Davis's style and manner. He wrote sensible but diplomatic letters of advice to Davis. Some can be found in Davis Correspondence, MS 2644, National Library of Ireland.

21. Barry's Repeal Prize essay has been mostly ignored by later students of the period. In view of contemporary constitutional developments in Canada, it holds great interest for Young Ireland's thinking. See *Repeal Prize Essays* (Dublin: James Duffy, 1845).

had begun to write for the *Nation* only after Dillon was unable to keep up his original pace as a contributor. Inspired by Davis, MacNevin would write two historical works for the *Nation*'s Library of Ireland: *The Confiscations of Ulster* (1846) and *The Volunteers of 1782* (1843). Witty, sparkling in conversation, MacNevin was often erratic in behavior, and sometimes tactless in ways of which his young colleagues disapproved. In November 1844 he was to publish in the *Nation* an open letter to the Belfast *Vindicator* explaining what the Young Irelanders were about, and defending them from charges of religious infidelity.[22] MacNevin did not share Davis's enthusiasm for the Irish language, nor did he approve too much dwelling on Ireland's ancient history. To Duffy he wrote:

I think . . . our task is to work the virgin mine of nationality; but not, I submit, the nationality of Ollam Fodlah and other gentlemen before or after the Flood. . . . Our task is to elevate the character of the people, raising up, in fact, their bumper of self-esteem and suppressing the bumps of servility and fury. . . . We must be cosmopolitan, and deviate occasionally from our native bogs. We shall have a better chance of success by being less Irish. . . .[23]

McCarthy, devoted in friendship to all the Young Irelanders, was less politically inclined than they. Like most of the leaders a Catholic graduate of Trinity, he planned a legal career but, as Gavan Duffy tells us, "he was essentially a poet and a man of letters," charming in society, but never thoroughly at home in the courts, in the council room, or on the platform."[24] A contributor both to the *Nation* and to the *Dublin University Magazine*, McCarthy would later make a literary career as a scholar and translator of Spanish literature, especially of the works of Calderon. He would in his later years write centenary odes for Daniel O'Connell and

22. *Nation,* 2 November 1844.
23. Duffy, *Young Ireland,* 563.   24. Ibid., 293.

Thomas Moore. With his special friend, John O'Hagan, he maintained a lifelong correspondence.

Every Saturday after the weekly *Nation* was safely out, this inner group would celebrate with evening suppers held in rotation at their various houses. Sometimes there was a Sunday excursion as well, to historic places in or near Dublin. Conversation centered around the currently issued newspaper, on accomplishments so far, and plans for future issues. To these weekend gatherings sympathetic friends were often invited, some of them finally moving into the inner group, or closer to it.[25] Among these were John Gray, Richard D'Alton Williams, Michael Doheny, and Father C. P. Meehan. A Protestant, the same age as Duffy, Gray had studied medicine in Edinburgh, but was to turn his talents to journalism, becoming in 1841 part proprietor of the *Freeman's Journal,* and sole owner in 1850. Later, as a Dublin town councillor, he was to devote his energies to obtaining for the city a proper water supply. After the success of this project he was awarded a knighthood in 1863. As a parliamentary representative for Kilkenny City, Sir John advocated the disestablishment of the Protestant Church of Ireland, reform of the land laws, and free denominational education. Chosen as Lord Mayor of Dublin in 1868, he declined the offer.[26] Williams, a Catholic exactly the age of Pigot and O'Hagan, had come to Dublin from Carlow to complete his medical education. Only in 1848, after his earlier association with the *Nation* as a writer of verse, did he come into public notice. In that revolutionary year, he joined with Thomas Antisell to found the rebel paper the *Irish Tribune.* Williams emigrated to America where he found a teaching position in Alabama, at the Jesuit College at Springhill in Mobile. After his marriage he settled in New Orleans where he practiced medicine until his early death in

25. Ibid.
26. For Gray, see Henry Boylan, *A Dictionary of Irish Biography,* 2d ed. (Dublin: Gill and MacMillan, 1988), 134.

1862.[27] Educated at the Irish College in Rome, Father Meehan was ordained in 1834, beginning as a curate in a Dublin parish the Church of Saints Michael and John. He published in 1846 *The Confederation of Kilkenny*.[28] Michael Doheny, born in 1805, was somewhat older than the average Young Irelander. Self-educated, he was the son of a small Tipperary farmer but managed to become a barrister. Writing occasional pieces for the *Nation* he came to know Davis and prized his friendship. He is remembered for his *Felon's Track,* an account of the events of 1847–48, and for his later role in the Fenian movement. Doheny fled to the United States after 1848, living there until his death in 1863.[29]

Here, perhaps, it might be useful to explain this excursion into these brief Young Ireland biographies. I have made it for the reason that in nearly all general histories, Young Ireland has been generalized into a movement, into a collective portrait of a younger generation rebelling against the older O'Connell, with serious political differences from him and with ideas deriving from German romanticism. Their individualities we notice. With the supposed German influences on Davis I have already dealt.[30] For the rest, nearly all these young enthusiasts were members of the Repeal Association, and were in full agreement with O'Connell on the necessity for a native Irish parliament. Events and policies would create strains, but Young Ireland would be inflexible in regarding nationhood as an absolute. Any temporizing, any future alliance with a British political party such as O'Connell had arranged with the Whigs in the 1830s, was not to be considered. Nevertheless, as we shall see, Davis was prepared to take gradual steps toward the goal, if to do so was all that was possible. As for his colleagues, they differed in the emphasis they placed on various political and cultural questions. Fated to live under the

---

27. See entry in Boylan.   28. Ibid.
29. Ibid.   30. See chap. 1.

Union which they had failed to break, they made lives and careers in different ways. They were united in their youth, in their enthusiasms, in their wish to escape from old and narrow rigidities of class and religion into a fresher, freer atmosphere. In the end, they had to become something besides nationalist agitators.

Close as he was to Davis, MacNevin, as we have noted, was intent on not being "too Irish," and was opposed to doctrinaire notions about language. Lane had to give priority to his family's business interests, and reminded his young friends that there was life outside Dublin. Gray would, like Lane, live a life of civic usefulness, and even as a Protestant advocate the disestablishment of the Church of Ireland. A successful career as an equity lawyer did not change O'Hagan's Young Ireland belief in a national parliament, a cause he championed to the end. Contemplating these viewpoints and the later lives of the Young Irelanders, one again reflects on Davis's life and direction had he not died in 1845. As we shall see, a friend would tell him that his talents lay beyond mere agitation.[31]

The Young Irelanders were mostly Catholic. To us, in our secular world, it may not seem surprising that Davis, who shared with so many of them a Trinity College education, should be so confident that other Irishmen of differing religions could be brought together under the secular banner of a common Irish patriotism. Just as interesting is how he kept up his political activities and lived in peace with his family, his mother, brothers, and sister, who all shared a common home on Baggot Street. Did any of the *Nation*'s Saturday suppers ever take place there? There is no evidence, but I surmise not. But Davis could never for a moment have been unaware of the strong anti-Catholic feeling among Protestants, with its long history and its reinforcement after Catholic emancipation in 1829. If Davis accompanied his family

31. Maddyn, in a letter of 27 September 1843 to Davis.

to Sunday church services, he would hear among other com-memorative prayers one of thankfulness for deliverance from the Irish Catholic uprising on October 23, 1641. Only in 1859 was this prayer removed from the liturgy.[32] Nothing in his surroundings would have led him to underestimate Protestant fears of a Catho-lic ascendancy, however misguided he might regard them. He would learn in 1845, in the discussion on Peel's Colleges Bill, how tenacious as well were Catholic views or prejudices, even though many Catholics supported Peel's bill.

But we now return to Davis's place among his Young Ireland friends in this early happy first year of the *Nation*. Duffy, both in his *Young Ireland* and in his *Davis* biography, paints in joyous if sometimes superabundant detail all these behind-the-scenes ac-tivities of the friends of his younger days. Nor does he leave any doubt that these were among the happiest years of his life. Davis he portrays as the soul of all the Young Ireland gatherings, inside and outside the newspaper office. Simple, unpretentious, and cheerful in manner, Davis was always ready to share his stores of knowledge. "Whatever subject one of us was studying," Duffy wrote, "we could count upon Davis to suggest the essential books and furnish more serviceable help from the library of his memo-ry and judgement."[33] When he was averse to some newspaper project presented to him, crude or extravagant though it might be, he never failed in courtesy. When he disagreed with anyone his invariable phrase was, "Do you think so?" in a tone that invit-ed agreeable reconsideration.[34] Duffy, in writing all this, was aware that Davis's wide knowledge could have invited dislike or even envy, but such was not the case. His good humor, his always

---

32. On October 23, 1641, see T. C. Barnard, "The Uses of the 23 October 1641 and Irish Protestant Celebrations," *English Historical Review* 106 (1991): 890 ff. See also Brian Cuarta, S.J., ed., *Ulster 1641: Aspects of the Rising* (Belfast: Institute of Irish Studies, 1983).

33. Duffy, *Young Ireland*, 294.   34. Ibid.

thoughtful kindness, and his obvious sincerity in the work he was doing won all hearts.[35]

Reading Duffy one thinks back to Thomas Wallis, whose puzzlement over Davis's evolution from a cloistered Trinity scholar, shy and unsure of himself, into a friendly, outgoing public man we have earlier discussed. Is this development all so mysterious, as it was to Wallis, or did Davis give some thought to his manner with his co-workers and make a more conscious effort toward leadership and its requirements? There is no real evidence except some undated, badly scribbled words among his papers now in the Royal Irish Academy, which lead us to a bit of highly tentative speculation. Davis is writing about how to come at possible auxiliaries to his cause, and how to hold them in hand for Repeal. He writes of classes, passions, quarrels to excite, and how to purchase alliances by not appearing to seek them.[36] What all this means one cannot know, but it does suggest that Davis's friendly, gracious manner, so clear to those who were his colleagues, would be useful in getting his views a respectful hearing from the other side. In other words, don't antagonize the opposition. On the opposite side of the scribbled page are the words (undated): "Write only one side of anything in future."[37] Does this mean he was criticizing himself for having been perhaps too generous to those who opposed his views? One has in all this many questions but no answers. Possibly one can only suggest that there were strains going on all the time between the private and the public Davis, with Repeal and how to win people to it always his foremost concern.

During his first year of journalism there are three significant pieces among his *Nation* contributions that deserve special attention. The first, an essay on Augustin Thierry presented in two

35. Ibid.
36. Gavan Duffy Papers, P15 no. 2, Royal Irish Academy.
37. Ibid.

parts in late November and early December of 1842; the second, *Letters of a Protestant on Repeal* extending over several issues; the third, two essays in 1843 on the Irish language.

First Thierry. The French historian's work will form a part of a later chapter on Davis's study and writing of history. These two *Nation* articles, however, provide us with an illustration of how Davis could use his wide knowledge for popular education, and use it as well to illustrate his never-neglected theme of the necessary union of all Irishmen into a nation. Taken together his two *Nation* essays provide a brief sympathetic biography of Thierry: his historical interests; his researches in many libraries and archives conducted often under great difficulties; his advancing blindness and his determination to continue work with the help of his friends Fauriel and Armand Carrel. Thierry's work on the *Norman Conquest of England,* his investigations into the city republics of Europe and into the history of France, are all briefly described. To Thierry's collection of essays published in 1834 as *Dix Ans d'Etudes Historiques,* Davis gives particular attention, quoting at length from the essay "On the National Spirit of the Irish in Relation to the Melodies of Thomas Moore." Davis and Thierry were as one in their admiration for the beauties of Irish music and for Thomas Moore's poetry. Even though most of its original words had been lost, the ancient music "which paints the insides of souls" had played a great part in preserving the national spirit of the Irish, Thierry believed. Davis's own enthusiasm for Irish music, as we have noted, was shared by John Pigot, but also by that other collector of Irish music, William Eliot Hudson, a friend of Davis and a major financial supporter of the *Citizen,* the journal for which Davis first wrote, and for which in 1842 he was still writing.

Thierry's obsession was the history of conquests and the part they had played in the extinction of local liberties in Europe and elsewhere. For Thierry, Ireland had become a visible living exam-

ple, still going on, of what had happened in the past in the building of European monarchies. There in Ireland exposed for all to
see were the consequences of conquest in the lives of conquered
and conquerors. Davis, however, fascinated as he was by the
French historian's theories and ideas, could still be critical, noting
Thierry's too-exclusive attention to distinctions arising from race
(conquered and conquerors) and "attributing to alienage in
blood differences arising from legal or personal incidents." Translated, this would seem to mean that if conquests explain something, they do not explain everything. There were complexities in
Irish history beyond any single explanation. Imbedded in these
two interesting lively essays was Davis's political sermon:

However closely we study our history, *when we come to deal with poli-*
tics, we must sink the distinctions of blood as well as sect. The Milesian,
the Dane, the Norman, the Welshman, the Scotsman, and the Saxon,
naturalized here, must combine regardless of their blood—the Strong-
bonian must sit with the Ulster Scot, and him [sic] whose ancestor
came from Tyre or Spain, must confide in and work with the Cromwellian and the Williamite. This is as much needed as the mixture of
Protestant and Catholic. If a union of all Irish born men ever be accomplished, Ireland will have the greatest and most varied materials for an
illustrious nationality and for a tolerant and flexible character in literature, manners, religion and life, of any nation on earth.[38]

We come now to Davis's *Letters of a Protestant on Repeal,* five
letters which appeared in the *Nation* over a period of several
months in 1842–1843.[39] The form chosen is an indirect one. The
Letters, supposedly, are not written from the *Nation*'s editorial
office, but rather by "a Protestant" from the outside who claims
he represents patriotic Protestants in sympathy with the *Nation*'s
aims. The first letter begins by urging on all sects mutual forgive-

38. *Nation,* 26 November, 3 December 1842.
39. These letters appeared from time to time in the *Nation* over 1842–43. They
were collected and published as a pamphlet, *Letters of a Protestant on Repeal,* ed. T. F.
Meagher (Dublin: Printed for the Irish Confederation by Wm. Holden, 1847).

ness. All, in the past, had injured each other, and among all these were men who, according to their lights and loyalties, had acted nobly for Ireland. Only a recognition of these facts could point the way forward. Protestants, though an overall minority, are to be found in every class: peasants, artisans, merchants, gentry, and nobles. Among all these is a widespread belief that Repeal and a Catholic ascendancy would be one and the same thing. They must be convinced, this Protestant insists, that such would not be the case. Protestants must involve themselves in Ireland's political life if they would play any role in their country's future. For, indeed, there *is* a danger, namely a possible pact between the Roman Catholics and one or other of the English parties without the approval or participation of the Protestants. But our Protestant argues that, if they are to be won over, "you must address their reason, their interest, their hopes, and their pride. I, for one, a Protestant—intimately knowing them—think it possible to effect this object."[40]

In Letter III, Davis's Protestant paints a picture of an Irish Senate, unencumbered by imperial problems, turning its attention to the condition of the peasantry, to the concerns of merchants and manufacturers, to internal economic development, to educational and cultural matters. In all these concerns the new Senate's strength would rest on the fact that its members were Irishmen, living in the country, familiar with its problems as an English assembly could never be. It would have a true national voice. If this idealized version of an Irish parliament invites skepticism given the huge problems of the Irish 1840s, it might be noted that Davis was no unrealistic fanatic. He wrote: "This would not make Ireland an Elysium. We should still have our faults and sorrows. . . . Ireland (whether nation or not) must endure such storms as blow over every land."[41]

---

40. Davis, *Protestant Letters,* 11.   41. Ibid., 19, 20.

In Letter IV, Davis turns to Europe and compares Ireland with other small states in terms of population, resources, and local institutions. Small states could aspire to greatness, and here examples were to be found in Holland and in the trading city republics of the Middle Ages. But small size only succeeds if there is something else: national or civic spirit. "Ireland has the bulk of a nation and the physical power of independence; but the higher power—knowledge, and the highest power—resolve, she hath not. . . . Body hath she, but where—where is the soul."[42]

The final letter praised both the Protestants of 1782 and the Catholics who had won emancipation in 1829. In both cases there was resolve, determination, and union. Could these successes be repeated for a whole Irish nation? Such was the prayer of an Irish Protestant.

Now, to the language question. Davis's two 1843 essays, republished together in O'Donoghue's anthology as *Our National Language,* appeared at intervals, the first in April and the second in December, 1843. Different in tone but alike in enthusiasm, they raise questions as to why the second is more moderate than the first.[43] Perhaps Davis's colleagues, MacNevin for example, had urged him to rethink and moderate his views. The first essay, ignoring the progress which English had been making over a long period as a widely spoken language,[44] suggested that Irish was the "natural" language for Irishmen to use. "To lose your native tongue," Davis wrote, "and to learn that of an alien is the worst badge of conquest—it is the chain on the soul." Or, "nothing can make us believe that it is natural . . . for the Irish to speak the speech of the alien, and to abandon the language of our kings and

42. Davis, *Protestant Letters,* iv.

43. *Nation,* 1 April and 30 December 1843, reprinted in D. J. O'Donoghue, ed., *Essays Literary and Historical by Thomas Davis* (Dundalk: Dundalgan Press, 1914), 97–107.

44. Maureen Wall, "The Decline of the Irish Language," in *A View of the Irish Language,* ed. Brian O'Cuiv (Dublin: Stationery Office, 1969), 81–90.

heroes." In concluding this first essay Davis seems to be dealing in historical improbabilities. "Had Ireland used Irish in 1782," he wrote, "would it not have impeded England's conquest of us?" All this could not have been reassuring to the Anglo-Irish had they been reading the conciliatory Protestant *Letters*. What *did* the *Nation* stand for? they might fairly ask. Davis began his second essay in a less crusading tone. "Now reader, don't be alarmed. . . . For you, if the mixed speech called English was laid . . . on your child's tongue, English is the best speech of manhood." But, he went on, to be entirely ignorant of Irish was none the less unfortunate. Geographical and place names, however Anglicized, were of Gaelic origin. Some knowledge of this fact every Irish citizen should have. Davis went on to argue that using the sources for early Irish history required a knowledge of the old language; nor could any serious student of Irish literature be without such knowledge. To the argument that there was no modern literature in Irish he replied that one could be created. As for scientific words, they could be adapted into the Irish language just as they had been into German. To the argument that reviving Irish could not succeed he replied:

If an attempt were made to introduce Irish either through the national schools or the courts of law into the eastern side of the island, it would certainly fail. . . . But no one contemplates this save as a dream of what may happen a hundred years hence. It is quite another thing to say, as we do, that the Irish language should be cherished, taught, and esteemed, and that it can be preserved and gradually extended.[45]

Toward the close of his essay Davis makes his famous and often quoted generalization.

About half the people west of a line drawn from Derry to Waterford speak Irish habitually, and in some of the mountain tracts east of that line it is still common.[46]

45. O'Donoghue, *Davis Essays*, 105.   46. Ibid., 106.

Finally, he takes note of bilingualism or even trilingualism in North and South America, and in many countries of Europe: Denmark, Holland, Switzerland, Poland, and Hungary. One language in these countries may be a medium of commerce, another "the vehicle of history, the wings of song, the soil of their genius, and a mark and guard of nationality." These two language essays illustrate a point we have discussed in an earlier chapter, namely, the contradictions which often appear in Davis's writings: extreme statements, often modified by a more thoughtful consideration of realistic possibilities. Could we suggest analogies with some of O'Connell's speeches, which often sounding violent were not actually urging violence, as in the famous Mallow Defiance? None the less the reader or listener could pick and choose.

We must now look outside the *Nation*'s office and examine Davis's relation to the public events of 1843, O'Connell's famous Repeal year: to the Dublin Corporation's debate on the Repeal question; to the monster outdoor meetings held over the spring, summer, and early autumn; to the Council of 300, another of O'Connell's devices for dramatizing Repeal.

First, the Corporation debate. Lord Mayor of the reformed Dublin Corporation from 1841 to 1842, and now a member of its Board of Aldermen, O'Connell had suggested to his colleagues a public debate to be followed by a petition to Parliament pleading that the repeal of the 1800 Act of Union be considered. The debate, lasting for three days, was held in late February in the Assembly Rooms in William Street, with O'Connell himself the star of the occasion. Speaking nearly the whole first day, O'Connell made, as Gavan Duffy would later recall, a "masterly and exhaustive statement of a great case."[47] O'Connell's arguments dwelled

47. Duffy, *Young Ireland*, 193. For the full text of the debate see John Levy, ed., *A Full and Revised Report of the Three Days Discussion in the Corporation of Dublin on the Repeal of the Union* (Dublin: James Duffy, 1843).

on Ireland's natural advantages, her geographical position, her population, her size, greater than five independent European kingdoms, her earlier legislative history. The arguments which later Irish nationalists would use, contrasting the prosperity of Ireland between 1782 and 1800 and the economic decline after 1815, were presented in detail. Any economic analysis of the deeper causes of Irish prosperity before 1815, and decline after that, was missing. The explanation lay in the Union. We know now more thoroughly from more recent scholarship how much the long French wars and their ending in 1815 had to do with developments in the Irish economy before and after the Union. The political structure alone was not a major explanation.[48] As for the Union, carried as it had been by coercion and corruption in the tense atmosphere following the rebellions of 1798, it should not have happened at all; it could, therefore, never be binding in the hearts and minds of those Irishmen who disputed its validity. This point of O'Connell's would have a long history.

O'Connell made comparisons between the ethnically mixed independent Belgium and Ireland; he made mention of Sweden and Norway, with Norway enjoying substantial local government under the Swedish crown. Replying to Protestant fears of a Catholic ascendancy, given Catholic numbers, O'Connell was reassuring but necessarily evasive. Missing was any exact statement of how such a restored parliament would be reconstituted and the suffrage basis on which it might rest. O'Connell, of course, knew that his nonviolent agitation must persuade as well as threaten the British government, and as Professor MacDonagh has argued, all O'Connell's words were an "invitation to treat," an opening for the British government to negotiate some kind of

48. See R. F. Foster, *Modern Ireland, 1600–1972* (London: Allen Lane, The Penguin Press, 1988), chap.2; also Cormac Ó Gráda, *Ireland Before and After the Famine: Explorations in Economic History, 1800–1925* (Manchester: Manchester University Press, 1988), chaps. 1 and 2.

settlement.[49] Rigid details at the outset could block the road.[50] At the end O'Connell said:

... a Parliament inferior to the English Parliament I would accept as an installment if I found the people ready to go with me, and if it were offered me by competent authority. It must first be offered me—mark that—I will never seek it ... but I will not give up my exertions for an independent legislature until from some substantial quarter that offer is made. ... Upon this subject I must not be mistaken, I will never ask for or look for any other save an independent legislature, but if others offer me a subordinate parliament, I will close with any such authorized offer and accept that offer.[51]

Leaving for the moment O'Connell's statements of the absolute and the contingent, let us turn to Isaac Butt's response and examine Davis's reaction to both. Butt brought sharply into focus all that was involved in the "restoration" of the Irish parliament as it stood between 1782 and 1800. A leading young Irish Protestant conservative,[52] Butt would eventually embrace in 1870 the Irish domestic government that he had attacked in his youth. Getting down to the particulars which O'Connell had evaded, Butt asked: what real powers did the Irish possess under the Constitution of 1782? It was true that the Irish parliament could pass laws without British parliamentary interference. But those laws once passed must receive the sovereign's assent, which would have to be given under the Great Seal of Britain, not that of Ireland. But under whose advice would the British sovereign act? As the British constitution had developed, the king's decision would be given under the advice of his *British* ministers. From 1782 to 1800, an Irish executive under British authority still sat in Dublin

49. Oliver MacDonagh, *The Emancipist: Daniel O'Connell, 1830–1847* (New York: St. Martins Press, 1989), 84.

50. Ibid., 84–85.

51. Levy, *Full and Revised Report*, 191–92.

52. For Butt, see Terence deVere White, *The Road of Excess* (Dublin: Browne and Nolan, 1945), 65–73.

Castle. Who, then, would constitute the Irish executive under a restored Irish parliament? Were the Repealers facing those questions of the relation between an undefined Irish executive and an Irish legislature? Furthermore, Butt continued, beyond constitutional matters there was the social and political program of the Repeal Association: complete abolition of tithes, the establishment of fixed land tenures, manhood suffrage, vote by ballot, three-year parliaments, equal electoral districts, and the abolition of property qualifications for parliamentary members. Reciting all this, Butt declared that Repeal was revolution, not a return to anything that had existed before. Finally, how could the imperial Parliament be compelled to enact a Repeal statute without the coercion of a physical force which did not exist?[53]

To Daniel Owen Maddyn in London Davis wrote on March 3, 1843:

I know that much good has already followed from the explanations, the good temper, arguments, and concessions which came out during the discussion. O'Connell's two speeches were greatly superior in style and argument to those in St. Stephen's in 1834. I sat out the whole affair. Staunton's [54] was the next in real worth. His statistics were mature and unanswerable. Butt was very clever, very fluent, and very ignorant. . . .[55]

Davis's judgment on Butt is curious. Why did he call Butt ignorant? Butt's points are unanswerable. Indeed they brought out issues that Davis himself had undoubtedly been considering, reflections deepened by his knowledge of recent events in Canada. Davis had written articles for the *Citizen* on Grattan's parliament which clearly showed his familiarity with late-eighteenth-century Irish history. In January 1843, just seven weeks before the Corporation debate, there was another *Citizen* article entitled "Recent Events in Canada," unsigned, as was the custom. But did Davis

53. Ibid.
54. Duffy, *Young Ireland,* 208. Davis to Maddyn, 3 March 1843.
55. Ibid.

write it? The style, in places, suggests he may have done so. But if he did not write it, he surely read it. He was close to the *Citizen's* editors, and in the Royal Irish Academy there is his own complete and signed set of that periodical. The article comes to grips with nationality and with events in Canada in 1837 and Lord Durham's mission a year later. Responsible government in Canada was not to be firmly rooted until Lord Elgin's Governor Generalship, but the *Citizen* article surmised what was probably coming.

. . . a great principle has been formally conceded in the government of Canada, and by inference, in that of all countries similarly situated with respect to Britain. That principle, as laid down very candidly by Sir Charles Bagot himself is nothing less than this—that the executive must be responsible to the representative control over the community over whom it presides, and that without such sanction, no constitutional executive can subsist.[56]

These constitutional observations are followed by remarks on the blessings of any local government in the hands of men who know the local situation. The conclusion has clear reference to Ireland.

We only wish that every other tributary of empire were half so far advanced on the safe and clear road to practical self-government as the comparatively youthful Canada; or as well circumstanced for the steady assertion of the inalienable right of every land on earth, to be ruled by its own children, and according to its own sense of what is lawful and true.[57]

If Davis and his *Citizen* friends were delighted with the Canadian drift toward responsible government, they could hardly have envisioned in 1843 the Commonwealth of Nations to which Canada and the other British colonies of settlement would move in the later nineteenth and twentieth centuries; nor envisioned either the role which that same Commonwealth would play in

56. See *Dublin Monthly Magazine* (previously *The Citizen*), January 1843.
57. Ibid.

the creation of an Irish Free State in 1921–22. Davis, despite his patriotic poetry, his overall language enthusiasms, and his nationalism, was basically concerned with Ireland's separate identity and his belief that all the Irish people, native and settler, Protestant, Catholic, and Dissenter, had more in common than economic and religious divisions might suggest. With an Irish government of their own, they could learn to work together and the responsibilities of freedom would turn a dependent, degraded, and powerless province into a nation. It was a faith, but as we recognize it we do well to recall and ponder the forebodings and warnings of Cavour.[58]

This belief in the magic of self-government led Davis from time to time to face the possibility of accepting something less than what he hoped for. On March 11, 1843, we find him writing, ". . . *even* were we to get the constitution of 1782," Ireland would be better off than she now was under the Union.[59] This language suggests that Davis was hoping for a great deal more than what had existed between 1782 and 1800. But imperfect as that constitution had been it had given Ireland a political identity.[60] The language also suggests that whatever O'Connell's ambiguities, he and Davis could agree that the Repeal agitation could have *some* results, however unforeseen. The British government might, just might, be driven to some sort of offer.

Closely tied to Davis's ideas and feelings about Irish home government was his animus against centralization, a view which brought him close to Mazzini's thinking on the Italian question.

. . . centralization, when there are no independent powers to check it, creates an official despotism. . . . Europe's interest, Europe's hope is not to raise its oligarchies from their tombs, not to plunge into despotism;

---

58. For a recent study on the Irish constitutional question, see Alan J. Ward, *The Irish Constitutional Tradition: Responsible Government and Modern Ireland, 1782–1992* (Washington, D.C.: The Catholic University of America Press, 1994), 30–49.

59. *Nation*, 11 March 1843.   60. Ibid.

no! it is to repeal centralization—to create as many separate nations with separate governments, laws, manners, characters as possible . . . to give back their separate heart and independent will to the old states which the wars of kings and the treachery of nobles have forcibly united.[61]

If someone had pointed out to Davis that centralization, the growth of larger units of government, had often brought good as well as bad results, he might have admitted it, but for him the true test of any government was a moral one—the effect it had on its people of high or low estate. And the character of a citizen was not improved if government was in the hands of officials and foreigners; the soul of a country needed citizens proud of their national inheritance and alert to their responsibilities for their country's welfare.[62] A *Nation* article by Davis also expressed concern for Scotland, which had received from the Union of 1707 benefits which had not come to Ireland since 1800. Despite the benefits, Scottish national treasures, precious and intangible, were being lost.[63]

It was not, obviously, with the nuances of government in Canada that O'Connell and his outdoor audiences were concerned. For him, the Repeal agitation served many purposes, not least the waking up of England to Irish grievances and necessities. For his audiences, Repeal was an all-purpose panacea for national ills as well as a hope and a promise for the future. Davis and his Young Ireland companions did suggest some of the historical symbolism inherent in the carefully chosen places where these meetings were held. Recent research, however, is making clear how much O'Connell, personally and directly, despite his

61. *Nation,* 18 March 1843. Compare Davis's statement with Joseph Mazzini, *Italy, Austria, and the Pope* (London: Albanesi, 1845), 421: ". . . there is little or nothing to hinder the unification of Italy: unification, I say, not centralization such as it seems to be too often understood, pushed to those furthest limits where it passes into despotism."

62. There were frequent references in the *Nation* to Englishmen holding Irish offices.

63. *Nation,* 18 March 1843.

sixty-eight years, had to do with the management of these meet-ings. And as in the earlier agitation for Catholic emancipation, the Irish Catholic parish clergy played a central role in the organ-ization of local meetings, giving Repeal a more Catholic cast than Davis possibly would have wished. Those interested in all the vivid detail of these famous gatherings should read the excellent recent study of Professor Gary Owens to which the following brief account is indebted.[64]

First of all, huge though they were, these Repeal assemblages were never as large as contemporary newspaper reports asserted. None the less they touched the political consciousness of large numbers of people—even those who were not present. "Given the number of people and location of the monster meetings," writes Professor Owens, "it was theoretically possible for almost everyone in Leinster, most parts of Munster and Connacht, and portions of South Ulster to attend at least one of them."[65] Even if the reality was somewhat different, news of the meetings spread far and wide, and the speeches of O'Connell were always printed in local newspapers. As one historian has said, they were "hedge schools" in which the masses were educated in nationalist poli-tics.[66] Actually, these meetings had antecedents in rural assem-blings at markets, festivals, and fairs, at outdoor political gather-ings in the later eighteenth century, and in the meetings in support of Catholic emancipation. The temperance movement of Father Mathew and the nonviolent political teaching of O'Con-nell had much to do with the good order which prevailed. Ballad singers were banned lest their songs arouse passion and anger. Provocative banners were forbidden; O'Connell himself ordered

64. Gary Owens, "Constructing the Repeal Spectacle: Monster Meetings and Peo-ple Power in Pre-Famine Ireland," in *People Power: Proceedings of the Third General Daniel O'Connell Workshop*, ed. Maurice O'Connell (Dublin: Institute of Public Ad-ministration, 1993), 80–93.

65. Ibid., 83.

66. Ibid. The phrase is from Donal McCartney, *The Dawning of Democracy in Ire-land, 1800–1870* (Dublin: Helicon Limited, 1987), 153.

the removal of a banner on which was written: "Ireland Her Own Parliament or the World in a Blaze."[67]

British officials from the Prime Minister on down had, of course, to react in some fashion to these meetings. Were they treasonable or simply legitimate expressions of public opinion, similar in some ways to the anti-Corn Law demonstrations then going on in England? Peel was inclined at the beginning to let them be, but the Lord Lieutenant de Grey and some members of the cabinet took a sterner view. Finally Peel, on 9 May 1843, did make a statement in the Commons that the Union must be preserved, and that civil war would be preferable to the dissolution of the empire.[68] Whatever O'Connell was actually thinking, he replied in a speech to the Repeal Association on May 18 that Peel was the very man to concede Repeal. He assured his audience that he would observe the law, but continue his legal nonviolent procedures.[69] But Peel, in mid-May, was not playing the role O'Connell was projecting and prophesying. On May 23 the government, represented by Sir Edward Sugden, the Irish Chancellor, removed from the Commission of the Peace thirty-four magistrates who had attended Repeal meetings. Presumably their removal could be on a conflict of interest theory. Other magistrates, in a protest of sympathy against this move of the government, resigned their commissions. Among them were Lord Cloncurry, Henry Grattan Jr., and William Smith O'Brien.

During these same months of frenetic public activity, O'Connell planned for a meeting of what could be considered, and might look like, an alternative Irish parliament, a Council of 300. The projected body must have, however, an innocent face, for it could be considered outside the law by the terms of the 1793 Con-

67. For the background of these public assemblages see Thomas Bartlett, *The Fall and Rise of the Irish Nation: The Catholic Question, 1690–1830* (Dublin: Gill and MacMillan, 1992), 311–19.

68. Kevin Nowlan, *Politics of Repeal* (London: Routledge and Kegan Paul, 1965), 45–46.

69. *Nation,* 20 May 1843.

vention Act, which declared that any assembly of representatives outside parliament was illegal.[70] O'Connell's delegates, however, were not by his definition representatives, but rather bearers of Repeal contributions from their localities. Who, however, could predict what such a gathering might become? Davis gave much thought to this project, and there is evidence in his correspondence that he had both enthusiasm and misgivings, even though he planned to become one of the 300. While traveling in the south of Ireland he wrote to Duffy:

If O'Connell would prearrange, or allow others to prearrange a "decided" policy, I would look confidently to the Three Hundred as bringing matters to an issue in the best way. . . . we must not postpone it until Parliament meets, for the Three Hundred will not be a sufficiently brilliant thing to shine down St. Stephens and defy its coercion. Yet we must not push it too quickly, as the country, so far as I can see, is not braced up to any emergency. Ours is a tremendous responsibility, politically and personally and we must see where we are going.[71]

Plans went ahead for Davis to bring one hundred pounds to the Council of 300 as a delegate from County Down. There were pressures on him, however, to stay out of the whole project, or at least play no part beyond that of simple delegate. This major negative pressure came from his friend Daniel Owen Maddyn, whose letter of advice to Davis we quote.

Very Private

London Sept 27 [1843]

My dear Davis,

In your last letter you ask my advice about your going into the Council of 300 that some persons suppose O'Connell will assemble in Dublin.

---

70. Passed in 1793, the law forbade public assemblages acting outside legal legislative boundaries. It was prompted by the action of representatives of an informal Catholic Convention going directly to London with their reform program, bypassing the Irish parliament.

71. Duffy, *Davis*, 173.

Assuming that the Three Hundred will meet ought you to join in it? It may be difficult for one like me to answer such a query, but I think I know your position sufficiently to offer an opinion.

Were I in your position—with your aims and resolutions, your profession as a Barrister, and as a politician, I would in standing by the colours which I had myself hoisted, endeavor at the same time to keep myself as unclogged as possible. If, therefore, I consented (as T. O. Davis) to enter the Three Hundred, I would at the same time accept no office such as secretary—Committee member. Your acceptance of an office in it, could not possibly increase your personal or political power in any way, and it might only expose you at great disadvantage to attacks of various kinds, as well from your own side as from the Government. *Believe me you would have a responsibility cast upon you, while at the same time, you would not be permitted to think and act upon your own views of affairs.*

It will be an O'Connell Council, if it even be allowed to meet. You must all say *ditto* to your leader, and not dare to oppose him rigorously, even where you think him weak and vacillating. *You* are not an O'Connellite—your views of public matters are taken from other sources— You would not be allowed to retain your independence, and as Secretary, Deputy Chairman or Committee man, you would be compelled to register many an edict of which your moral conscience and political judgement disapproved.

Besides, are you not—for a very young man—sufficiently committed already? Have you not manifested your politics sufficiently plainly, and is not your influence through the Press greater than you could achieve on your legs in the Council? It has struck me as strange that you have never "come out" more at the Corn Exchange than you have done. Whatever be the causes that prevented your making yourself very prominent at the Corn Exchange, would also operate against you in the Council. Whether it be a manly aversion to popular artifices—a dislike of [unclear]—imputations—or a consciousness that your own ideas and thoughts on Irish Patriotism were not understood or sympathized with by the mere agitators—you have never figured at the Association as one would have expected. I believe in my heart and soul, that such a spirit as yours, could never find genuine utterance in Agitation. And the council will be a mere body of Agitators.

But, the government will never permit it to assemble. They will put it down, and challenge the country to resist it, and all reasonable men of the Whigs, Conservatives, and Moderates, will approve of the Government's resolution. By the 1st of March, 1844—it will be seen that no man will have lost more reputation than O'Connell and no man gained more than Sir. R. Peel.

I would strongly advise you not to fetter yourself more than you are at the moment. Do not shackle yourself by assuming impossibilities, while you will not be allowed to retain your *own right of decision.*

You say that "conscience and policy urge you."

But does not Conscience suggest that you have already done a vast deal for your party. What other young man of your talents and class have given up more than you have done? Conscience ought to suggest that there is a difference between gallant maintenance of *your own* Irish views and submitting to have your hands tied to a stake which others will drive. Conscience must whisper that you ought not make the rest of your life suffer for unguarded exposure in 1844. If you join the Council—accept a place in it, work in it, get indicted with the rest of them, and are finally let off with an inglorious binding over to keep the peace and see what a *tack* will be to your name for the rest of your life! You will always be looked on as mistaken. You will be chalked off as a mere agitator of the O'Connell School.

As to policy, firstly, does it not ask what influence or permanent power would you acquire by your becoming a leading member in a Council which will never dare to do anything great. What more could you do for your ideal Ireland than you can now achieve? It is pretty plain, that you must have either a pen or a pike in your hand, and is the Council the place for you to work with such implements?

2ndly—Does not Policy suggest that your most influential post would be as a public censor of the Council of Three Hundred? If *you* will praise it while you are yourself a prominent actor in its proceedings you will be only glorifying yourself and friends, and how could you freely comment on the deliberations while you would yourself be one of the actors in it? It is a question between your power as a public writer and as an individual in the Council. *Both* you cannot have.

3rdly—the Government would pounce upon you—namely even as an inactive but *known* member of the Council. *You,* who have written

so much against the government will be placing yourself completely in
its power. . . .

On the whole, looking at it from the side of mere policy, it will be a
rash step for a man of your peculiar opinions, character and talents to
go prominently into the Council. If you will, be *one* of the 300, but be
nothing more amongst them. You must not tie yourself up too much,
and you are evidently too ready to believe in the protestations of the
Agitator. Leave yourself as much as possible as free agent for the future
and consider that all Irish history is not to be acted in the next six
months. . . .

This is all that I can say on the subject—we both differ very widely
in politics, but still I understand your position. . . .

Always, sincerely yours

D. O. Madden[72]

As things turned out the Council of 300 never met. It is hardly
surprising, given Maddyn's Unionist views, that he saw the Council as he did. The most interesting observation in the letter is his
comment on Davis's future: "I believe such a spirit as yours could
never find genuine utterance in agitation."

During the summer days of O'Connell's meetings, Davis made
plans for a holiday, leaving Dublin in August to attend the sessions of the British Association for the Advancement of Science,
which was meeting in Cork.[73] After the sessions he conferred
with Denny Lane, by this time a close friend, on the progress of
Repeal in the south. He enjoyed a visit to Bishop Murphy of
Cork, delighting in the chance to inspect the prelate's huge and
famous private library. Sailing along the Cork coast, he wrote
home that he preferred the wilder shores of Donegal. Most of the
travel letters from which Gavan Duffy quotes have disappeared,
but the excerpts included in his Davis biography reveal a zestful

72. Maddyn to Davis, 27 September 1843. Davis Correspondence, MS 2644, National Library of Ireland.
73. Another example of Davis's wide interests.

young man, thoroughly alive, responding to people and the incidents of travel with warmth, humor, and imagination. Nor was
work left behind, for Davis regularly wrote to the *Nation* office
about prospective articles and future editorial policy. He made
some travel notes, but these had faded with time and when Duffy
tried to use them forty years later for his biography, he found
them hard to decipher. Single words or phrases which would
bring recollections to Davis were a mystery to Duffy.

Bishop John Murphy interested Davis. His cosmopolitan
background, his large library, and the saga of his long life cap-
tured Davis's imagination. The old bishop had been educated in
Lisbon, had begun to study Irish in his fortieth year, and had collected a store of Irish manuscripts. He had known the sculptor
Canova in Rome, and was an early patron of the Irish sculptor
John Hogan. Living and working in Rome, Hogan made occasional visits to Ireland, and in fact was in Dublin during Davis's
visit in Cork. Bishop Murphy's great library would eventually be
sold in London, except for the Irish manuscripts, which went to
Maynooth.[74] Interested in the large landed estates in County
Cork, Davis learned what he could about their ownership and
history, and also about the working of the penal laws on these
landed properties. He noted the geography of the coast, the castle
strongholds on the headlands, and the piracy which had once
flourished. Nor did he forget to notice and mention the beauty of
the country women, their heights, their coloring and bearing. To
John Pigot he wrote of his visit to Mount Melleray, where he
learned of O'Connell's earlier severe retreat. He had a sharp eye
for the monastery lands and gardens, and their agricultural management. Apparently, he hit it off with his monastic hosts, who
pressed him to make a return visit.

Pigot's reply is full of interest; although he had not been at

74. For Bishop Murphy, see entry in Crone, 163–64.

O'Connell's meeting at Tara Hill he had learned of it from John O'Hagan, who had called it a "transcendent sight." Pigot's letter also reported on a day he had recently spent in Dublin with the sculptor John Hogan, who had been chosen to do the statue of O'Connell commissioned by the Repeal Association. Pigot wrote of his alarm that the Association might try to interfere with the sculptor's work. Speaking for the full freedom of the artist, Pigot wrote: "Hogan must be left to himself. . . . Surely this, of all, must be our national statue of O'Connell, let it be worthy of the country forever."[75] Hogan had told Pigot that the figure would be at least ten feet high, expressing all the power and grandeur of Ireland, a figure of pride and command.

The holiday went on into September and on the eighth, from Bantry Bay, Davis was writing to his old friend Webb for a letter of introduction to William Smith O'Brien, whose wife, Lucy, was a kinsman of Webb's. In Limerick Davis met the brother of Gerald Griffin, the author of *The Collegians,* who had died in 1840. Davis learned from the brother of the hardships the novelist had undergone in London, his later success, his abandonment of literature, and his entry into the monastic life.

The correspondence with Duffy reveals the two journalists collaborating and thinking ahead. Davis had agreed to write an anniversary article for the October issue of the *Nation,* which would celebrate its first and successful year. By the time Davis had arrived in Galway he had finished the essay, and as he was mailing it off to Dublin, he told Duffy to throw it in the fire if he did not like it.[76] Some of their correspondence had to do with the projected Council of 300. Davis wrote to Duffy about what he could and could not do in the 300; a letter probably written be-

75. This Munster journey is described in detail in Duffy's biography, with many letters included and with references to the Davis-Pigot correspondence. For Hogan, see the entry in Crone, 96.
76. Duffy, *Davis,* 176.

fore he received the letter on the subject from Maddyn, which we have already noticed.

I am not, nor shall I try to be, an orator, I would, if possible, to my limited powers be a politician. If your friends think such a man fit for their purposes, I shall do their work as cautiously, firmly and honestly as I can. . . .[77]

In another letter to Duffy, he shows editorial discretion and reveals as well why he was winning a reputation as a conciliator. MacNevin had written a *Nation* article on the Irish Whigs which had given offense. Davis asks Duffy to explain in the *Nation* that the article did not refer to Smith O'Brien nor men like him. "We have need of tolerants as well as allies for awhile," he wrote.[78]

Davis's leisurely holiday came to an abrupt end in early October in Galway where he heard the news of the Peel government's action against O'Connell. The last projected Sunday outdoor meeting, to be held at Clontarf on Dublin Bay, had been prohibited, and O'Connell decided instantly to obey and cancel the meeting. He would stay within the law, however unjust he thought the government's decision to be. According to Duffy, writing in retrospect, Davis believed that O'Connell was pledged to resist any violation of the right of public meeting. Apart from interpreting O'Connell's words, Davis was also thinking of the Volunteers of 1782, who had stood for the greater liberty of their Irish parliament. In short, the voice of a united people should again have had a powerful and persuasive effect. But one must free one's self, in examining the expectations of the Repeal movement, from any undue reliance on Duffy's account of Clontarf and its aftermath. We have already noted that both O'Connell and Davis probably had their doubts about what could be gotten out of the British government. O'Connell especially, with his long and close observation of public life and particularly of the British Parliament and

77. Ibid., 175.   78. Ibid., 176.

of the slowness of obtaining any reform, could hardly have seriously believed that Sir Robert Peel would imperil his political life in 1843 by coming out for any kind of change in the Act of Union. He had the Corn Laws with him day and night, not to speak of his own stern intention to retain the Union. Both Davis and O'Connell were fully aware of how long it had taken to win Catholic emancipation, even with numerous Englishmen in favor of it. There was no wide English opinion in 1843 in favor of Repeal. There was reality and there was fantasy. And O'Connell, always a realist, was writing to Lord Campbell a month before the scheduled Clontarf meeting: "Our Irish movement has at least the merit that it has roused the English nation from slumber. There can be no more dreams about Ireland. Our grievances are beginning to be admitted by all parties and by the press of all political opinions to be afflicting and not easily endured."[79] The next few sentences of his letter suggest that he was already thinking about parliamentary action as once more a field for his political agenda.

I ask why the Whig leaders are not up to the level of the times they live in? Why do they not propose a definite plan for redressing these grievances? Why does not Lord John Russell treat us to a magniloquent Epistle declaratory of his determination to abate the Church nuisance in Ireland, to augment our popular franchise, to vivify our new corporations, to mitigate the statute law as between landlord and tenant, to strike off a few more rotten boroughs in England, and to give the representatives to our great counties? In short why does he not prove himself a high-minded, high-gifted statesman capable of leading his friends with all the advantages to be derived from conciliating the Irish nation and strengthening the British Empire?[80]

Davis hastened from Galway to Castlebar to discuss the proclamation with John Dillon; he then sent to his mother in

79. O'Connell to Lord Campbell, 9 September 1843. O'Connell, *Correspondence*, vol. 7, letter 3034.
80. Ibid.

Dublin instructions to burn papers which might incriminate his friends. He returned hurriedly to Dublin, "painfully discomposed," according to Duffy; his first thought was to quit the Repeal Association forever, "and serve Ireland in some other field."[81]

Davis, however, along with Duffy, soon decided on calmer behavior and both turned their energies to preparing for the future. Agitation must give way to education, to exhortation, to propaganda for the national cause. For the moment, however, the Repeal cause was receiving a further blow. On October 11, 1843, O'Connell and his son John, Thomas Matthew Ray, secretary of the Repeal Association, Thomas Steele, Charles Gavan Duffy, John Gray, Richard Barrett, and two Catholic priests were charged with conspiracy—acting unlawfully to change the constitution and government of the country.[82] The trial ran from 15 January to 12 February, 1844, and ended in a verdict of guilty. On 30 May 1844, O'Connell was sentenced to a year's imprisonment and a fine of two thousand pounds. A comfortable imprisonment for O'Connell and his indicted companions in Richmond Bridewell lasted until 6 September. The Law Lords, the judges of appeal for the House of Lords, finally reversed the judgment against them.

Duffy's trial and imprisonment combined with Davis's decision to stay with the Repeal Association and the *Nation* meant a year of hard, responsible work from which Davis tried to free himself with a leave of absence to write a history of Ireland. In the event he gave up the project, feeling committed to staying with the patriotic agitation which he had joined. Something of his divided self is revealed in two poems, both published in the *Nation*. We quote some verses from "We Must Not Fail":

81. Duffy, *Davis*, 186.
82. Duffy, *Young Ireland*, 379 ff.

I.

We must not fail, we must not fail
However fraud or force assail;
By honour, pride, and policy
By Heaven itself!—we must be free.

IV.

We called the ends of earth to view
The gallant deeds we swore to do;
They knew us wronged, they knew us brave,
And all we asked, they freely gave.

V.

We took the starving peasant's mite
To aid in winning back his right,
We took the priceless trust of youth;
Their freedom must redeem our truth.

VIII.

But—calm, my soul!—we promised true
Her destined work our land shall do;
Thought, courage, patience will prevail
We shall not fail—we shall not fail! [83]

The path was marked out: to struggle for an uncertain and as yet invisible end.

The second poem, "O'Connell's Statue," written almost simultaneously, was inspired by the work on which the sculptor Hogan was now engaged, the statue of O'Connell. The poem indicates an affection and feeling for O'Connell that Duffy was never to share. We quote a few lines of Davis's poetic message.

Chisel the likeness of The Chief . . .

But would you by your art unroll
His own, and Ireland's secret soul

83. *Poems of Thomas Davis.*

And give to other times to scan
The greatest greatness of the man?
Fierce defiance let him be
Hurling at our enemy.
From a base as fair and sure
As our love is true and pure,
Let his statue rise as tall
And firm as a castle wall;
On his broad brow let there be
A type of Ireland's history;
Pious, generous, deep, and warm,
Strong and changeful as a storm;
Let whole centuries of wrong
Upon his recollection throng.[84]

84. Ibid.

Chapter 4

Public and Private Life, 1843–1845

O utwardly, in the late autumn of 1843, Davis was still with the Repeal cause, but possibly in something of a turmoil over the direction of his life and career. In fact, he raised again with Duffy in 1844 the possibility of a leave of absence from the *Nation* for travel and research on his projected history of Ireland. Later there would be rumors emanating from his elder brother that Davis had been "coerced" into remaining with the Repeal cause.[1] He stayed, however, and gave up for the moment the writing of his dreamed-of Irish history.[2] His decision may have become more acceptable to him as he joined with William Smith O'Brien in the months after Clontarf in giving fresh vitality to the Repeal Association. The two men became congenial collaborators, never failing, however, in loyalty to O'Connell. For O'Connell, in his necessary absences during the hectic months of 1844, had charged O'Brien with a kind of sub-deputyship of the Association. First, O'Connell and his associates were tried and found guilty of con-

---

1. Pigot to Duffy, 26 May 1846, Gavan Duffy Papers, 5756, National Library of Ireland.

2. The frequent scrawled notes among Davis's papers suggest how much this project was on his mind. Eventually, Duffy would suggest a series of histories on special subjects. These became The Library of Ireland. Duffy's *Ballad Poetry of Ireland* was to be one of the series.

spiracy; while awaiting sentence O'Connell visited England, attending public meetings and hearing addresses from English sympathizers. Finally, as we have noted, there was his imprisonment lasting three months before his release on appeal to the House of Lords. The judgment was to be reversed in early September 1844 by the Law Lords' vote of 3–2. Taking his new responsibility very seriously, O'Brien, with Davis and other young men attached to the *Nation* group, embarked on a program of extensive political education and public information. Davis and O'Brien drew closer, becoming good friends, and from the correspondence between them we learn in some detail of the internal affairs of the Association, its strains and stresses during 1844 and 1845.[3]

O'Brien, a member of a famous Clare family with a history of Irish political involvement extending back over several generations, had been in Parliament since he was twenty-six, entering in 1828. The O'Brien family had a reputation as good landlords and as men of patriotism, with a record of constructive public service. Over many years an O'Brien had sat either for the borough of Ennis or for County Clare. Earlier, in Grattan's Parliament, Sir Lucius O'Brien had participated in the events leading to the constitutional revolution of 1782, and Edward, Sir Lucius' son and the father of William Smith, had opposed the Act of Union. It was a patriotic heritage, shared by other Irishmen, who over the years in their different ways had come to terms with the Union of 1801. Smith O'Brien had supported Catholic emancipation, but with the rest of his family had opposed the intrusion, in 1829, of O'Connell into the politics of County Clare.[4] O'Brien's adherence to Repeal was a startling reversal, but even without the govern-

---

3. These letters, part of a huge O'Brien family archive, were given to the National Library by Denis Gwynn, a grandson of O'Brien.

4. Denis Gwynn, *Young Ireland and 1848* (Cork: Cork University Press, 1949), 19–20.

ment's action in suppressing the Clontarf meeting he might well have become a Repealer. In early July 1843 he had made a passionate speech in the House of Commons on Ireland's grievances, followed by a petition asking for redress.[5] Losing his motion, he soon left Ireland for a summer journey to the continent to study and compare conditions in Europe with those in Ireland. He returned gloomier than ever about the state of his homeland. Clontarf was the trigger. He joined the Repeal Association in October 1843.[6]

The Young Irelanders were of course delighted at this turn of affairs. Combination of classes had been one of their central hopes and here was a Protestant landlord who had put Repeal patriotism, as they saw it, above all other considerations. As for O'Brien himself, he has not had much sympathetic appreciation in general accounts of this period, seen later on as the failed rebel he was to become in 1848. English-educated (Harrow and Cambridge), O'Brien has always been described as reserved and formal in manner. But almost nothing has been written about his interests or his beliefs. His Commonplace Book, now among his letters and papers in the National Library of Ireland, contains interesting and critical appraisals of historical and literary works; a long section on Alexis de Tocqueville presents thoughtful reflections on the governments of France, England, and America.[7]

Welcomed into his new position in the Association, O'Brien began by setting up a parliamentary committee from among the Association's membership. Its purpose was to study issues which were politically significant in themselves, or those which might come up in the imperial Parliament. Such studies would also be a preparation for the day, however distant, when there would be a parliament in Dublin. Davis found all this solid work a dream

5. Hansard's Parliamentary Debates, Third Series, vol. 70, 675–77.
6. Gwynn, *Young Ireland,* 20–21.
7. O'Brien Papers, Commonplace Book, MS 455, National Library of Ireland.

come true; and indeed Duffy in writing of it later compared the collaboration of O'Brien and Davis to that of Washington and Alexander Hamilton, one of Duffy's numerous if somewhat exaggerated parallels between Irish and American history.[8] O'Brien encouraged all the Young Irelanders to contribute to these studies and reports, which were presented at meetings of the Association. Published in three volumes in 1844–46, the reports repay study. We turn to the first, which was O'Brien's.[9]

O'Brien began by affirming the main object of the Association, which must forever remain central: repeal of the Union.[10] Pursuit of this goal must not, however, mean neglect of the wider general interests of the country. The intelligence and patriotism of the Repeal Association should be directed to mastering subjects which might, in due course, be considered at Westminster. A body of informal opinion in Ireland itself would be of unquestioned value, supplementing and supporting the work of Irish MPs in London. Courteously referring to the Irish members, his parliamentary colleagues, O'Brien none the less felt that they inadequately represented the variety of opinion in Ireland. As for the English members, O'Brien was more severe, saying that five-sixths of them were utterly ignorant of everything concerning the internal condition of Ireland. Moving quickly to his major point, he asserted that if neither the Irish representatives in London nor the Repeal Association could make a case for Ireland "we shall . . . be furnished from the committee's studies with strong additional arguments in favor of domestic legislation."[11]

The original subjects for special study would be the land question, the franchise, the bank charter, and the estimates for the

8. Duffy makes many references to the experience of America in its revolutionary and constitutional era.

9. *Reports of the Parliamentary Committee of the Loyal National Repeal Association of Ireland,* 3 vols. (Dublin: J. Browne, 1844–46). Referred to hereafter as *Repeal Reports.*

10. *Repeal Reports,* vol. 1, 1–3.   11. Ibid., 2–3.

public services. In the event, the topics studied went far beyond O'Brien's original list. Over the next year, and into the summer of 1845, Davis played a major part in preparing these reports, writing first on the Ordnance Memoir, on the Irish Arms Bill, on the hurrying of Irish bills through Parliament, and on the attendance of Irish members at Westminster.[12]

Seen in later years as a poet, journalist, and youthful agitator, Davis in these Association documents reveals himself as a very practical man indeed, capable of drafting state papers which were serious, thorough, and diplomatically courteous. His concern with parliamentary action and the character of the Irish members led to a correspondence with the Earl of Wicklow, who had taken issue with the arguments of the parliamentary committees. Why, asked Wicklow, if the Association members considered the Westminster Parliament worthy of critical scrutiny, did they not insist that Irish members scrupulously attend its sessions? Wicklow, in his letter, noted the paradoxical nature of the Association's position. Some members are urged to attend in London; others, declared Repealers, are urged to stay in Ireland working for the Repeal Association. Where lay the difference?

Davis, in his reply to Lord Wicklow, covered all aspects of attendance and nonattendance. Recurring to O'Connell's compact with the Whigs in the 1830s, Davis argued that with the exception of the inadequate Municipal Reform Bill, Ireland got little from Parliament. "We got coercion bills, arrears bills, disfranchising bills, stipendiaries,—special commissions,—and fraudulent juries."[13] At present the efforts of the Repeal Association were directed to the diffusing of social and political information, the better to qualify the Irish people for self-government. "Believe me, my lord," Davis wrote, "a short apprenticeship on one of our

12. Ibid., Davis, April 17, May 27, August 19, August 24, September 2, 1844.
13. Ibid., 354; correspondence between Lord Wicklow and the Loyal National Repeal Association.

committees would disincline you to Westminster. How glad we should be to see your lordship seated with us in our . . . noble occupation of educating, nationalizing, and binding in closer union the whole people of Ireland. . . ."[14]

Continuing his remarks to Wicklow, Davis pointed out that most Irish MPs were not Repealers. Their place was in London, but: "These papers if attentively considered ought, we think, to convince the readers of them that Repeal is the only honorable, safe, permanent, and practicable remedy for the miseries of our country."[15] At home and in England under present circumstances, both Repealer and non-Repealer could serve their country.

Replying to Davis, Wicklow affirmed his still unclouded confidence that there existed in the British people a desire to do justice to Ireland. This faith in Britain cut no ice with Davis, who in his reply recurred to the progress of Ireland in the years 1782–1800, in contrast to its position since, provincialized and impoverished under the Union, neglecting, as O'Connell always did, the wider economic factors which would explain so much of the difference. Davis concluded:

I cannot close . . . without expressing the delight I feel . . . that we have at length found it possible and pleasant to differ without violence, and to carry on a political controversy without forgetting the courtesies of private life.[16]

O'Brien's second general report, issued in November 1844, is interesting from a number of viewpoints. He spoke especially of Davis, "to whose untiring energy, and singular ability the Repealers of Ireland are so much indebted."[17] The report, however, suggested the long-range thinking of both men. They did not talk about agitation, but about information. They were going to dis-

---

14. Ibid.   15. Ibid., 355–56.
16. Ibid.; Davis's concluding remarks to Lord Wicklow.
17. Ibid., 263, 391 (Davis).

tribute their political research to both Irish and British MPs. They were fully aware that what they were doing might not be attended by immediate results.[18] As best they could, they would keep the cause alive during O'Connell's absence and beyond. The work of the Repeal Committee would demonstrate to all who cared to notice that there were in Ireland men of talent and education who were seriously attentive to public business and who would in the future be probable members of a restored Irish parliament. They were an Irish intelligentsia.[19]

What did these reports say about the form of a reconstituted Irish parliament? We have earlier called attention to the interest some Repealers had in the policies which the British government was pursuing in Canada. In O'Brien's report there is no mention of Canada, but there is a significant reference to responsible government. O'Brien concluded:

Many . . . the most intelligent of our fellow countrymen who have hitherto stood aloof from us are watching . . . the movements of the Repeal Association in order that they may conjecture . . . what will be the spirit in which the affairs of Ireland would be administered under the agency of *an Irish executive amenable to the control of an Irish parliament.* Shall we not prove to them that the spirit of Irish patriotism is elevated in its aims—comprehensive in its objects— tolerant and enlightened—wise in deliberation—just and beneficial in action?

Let this conviction firmly establish itself in the minds of all classes of Irishmen, and the functions of the Parliamentary Committee of the Re-

18. Their studies and reports would have an effect over time, they hoped.

19. See Jacqueline Hill, "The Intelligentsia and Irish Nationalism in the 1840s," *Studia Hibernica* 20 (1980): 73–109. This valuable article examines the levels of education for the members of the various political action societies in the 1840s. Those holding third-level university education played disproportionate parts in these groups—as members and leaders. Both Catholics and Protestants had legal educations and were in general young, beginning or recently entering their profession. The increasing centralization coming from England, and the appointment to Irish offices of Englishmen and Scotsmen, was a threat to the career prospects of young, well-educated Irishmen. "To possess and rule their native country," to use a phrase of Gavan Duffy's, was one of the drives behind Repeal. Dr. Hill examines all aspects of this situation and contributes greatly to our understanding of Repeal politics.

peal Association will soon devolve upon the Queen, Lords, and Commons of Ireland.[20]

O'Brien and Davis are here thinking of the internal form of a future Irish parliament. Its external relation to Great Britain would have to be part of some arrangement whereby the link with the imperial power would be defined. This matter would emerge in the controversy over federalism which developed in the autumn of 1844, after O'Connell's acquittal and release from prison. To federalism we shall return.[21]

The second volume of Repeal Association reports contains Davis's analysis of the general financial estimates for 1844–45, five reports on the army, and one on the navy. There is a long report by T. M. Ray, the secretary of the Repeal Association, on Repeal Reading Rooms, and three separate reports on the land question signed by O'Connell himself.[22] Davis's name is missing from these reports on the land. There is evidence to suggest, however, that Davis had worked on the land question with O'Connell, and worked cordially. As so often, the direct evidence comes from letters to London to John Pigot. Early in March 1845, Davis wrote that he and O'Connell were on better terms than they had been for a long time.[23] On March 22, Davis wrote again to London: "The Land Question is now everything and O'Connell and I very cordial on it and most things. So far so good. Our power is getting genuine at last."[24] On April 15, the day after the first land report was presented to the Association, Davis wrote again to Pigot:

20. *Repeal Reports*, vol. 1, 396. These reports would lay a basis for future legislation. "To convince is our aim."

21. In his biography of Davis, Duffy speaks of the interest in federalism. Duffy, *Davis*, 256.

22. *Repeal Reports*, vol. 2, 295, 317, 319.

23. Davis to Pigot, 5 March 1845. The Davis-Pigot correspondence is to be found in *Irish Monthly* 16, nos. 179 and 180 (1888), part I, 261–70; part II, 335–48; this letter, 340. The Davis-Pigot letters are cited hereafter as *Irish Monthly* 16, with dates of letters. See infra for other Pigot letters *(Irish Monthly)*.

24. Ibid., Davis to Pigot, 22 March 1845.

We have spent an awful time on the Land Question. O'Connell, O'Brien and I prepared sets of plans; mine were most extensive. Our first report was brought up yesterday. . . .[25]

Detailed proposals for land reform were presented in the third report read to the Repeal Association on May 12, 1845. It is these proposals to which Professor Joseph Lee alluded when he wrote his essay on O'Connell's social and economic ideas, calling the report the most "radical land reform program proposed by any public figure at that date."[26] The report recommended the legalization of Ulster Tenant Right, compensation for improvements, an absentee tax, compulsory conacre[27] on pasture holdings over 200 acres, reclamation of waste land, the division of crown estates into small lots, county agriculture schools, the development of public works, and the modification of present ejectment legislation giving more favorable terms for the tenant.[28] Peasant proprietorship, which Davis had advocated earlier in his *Citizen* essay "Udalism and Feudalism," was not a feature of this report.[29] But one must ask, in view of the letter to Pigot, how much did these proposals owe to the collaboration or the influence of Davis?

Some mention must be made of Davis's reports on the British army. They are marked by orderly detail, by comparisons with the armies of various European states, with military and historical backgrounds filled in. Nor was criticism missing, for we find adverse remarks about the purchase of commissions, and the ad-

25. Ibid., Davis to Pigot, 15 April 1845.

26. J. J. Lee, "The Social and Economic Ideas of O'Connell," in *Daniel O'Connell: Portrait of a Radical,* ed. Kevin B. Nowlan and Maurice O'Connell (Belfast: Appletree Press, 1984), 70–86.

27. A cottier's labor for a cabin and a piece of rented land. Land was rented for farming of a single crop, most commonly potatoes.

28. Lee, "Social and Economic Ideas of O'Connell," 71.

29. See *Voice of the Nation,* 192: "We seek prospective laws which shall tend, by a natural and easy change to reduce the great estates, and create a body of small properties in fee throughout every part of Ireland. But we are not ready to jump into a servile war for this purpose." In the essay on the *Nation's* first year.

vocacy of a policy of promotion from within the ranks.[30] The essays and statistical tables cover 150 pages. The report on the navy, also thorough, is shorter. One wonders here whether Davis talked with his brother, an army medical doctor, about military affairs. In any case these reports surely required an appreciable amount of time and meticulous research. The working of the military establishment is examined, and once again one is left with a deep respect for the breadth of Davis's talents. Considering his intensive responsibilities for the *Nation,* the amount and variety of his correspondence, and his various literary projects, his own and those of others, one does wonder whether he was working beyond his strength. Of the versatility of his talents one can be left in no doubt.

We cannot here review all the remaining reports of the Repeal Committee, but to one we must give special attention, namely the report of T. M. Ray, the secretary of the Association, on Repeal Reading Rooms. We do this because the subject was one of Davis's most dedicated interests: the education of the people. "The enlightenment of the people, by the diffusion of useful information," the report begins, "has ever been an object of deep solicitude with the Repeal Association."[31] O'Neill Daunt credits Ray as the originator of the reading room idea, but Davis was his close partner in all that concerned them.[32] Ray had reorganized the Reading Rooms, sent out to all of them a questionnaire, and had drawn up rules for the guidance of local committees. We do not have information from his reports on the kinds of location chosen, except that no Reading Room could be located in a public house. All the returns agree that the Reading Rooms had been productive of good effects, bringing people together, creating pa-

---

30. *Repeal Reports,* vol. 2, 43–170.
31. Ibid., 329–66.
32. See his essay "Repeal Reading Rooms," in D. J. O'Donoghue, ed., *Essays Literary and Historical by Thomas Davis* (Dundalk: Dundalgan Press, 1914), 220–24.

triotic spirit, promoting temperance, and drawing young men
away from harmful amusements. General popular improvement
in all directions was the theme. Ray's report read:

It is impossible to exaggerate the benefits that may arise from these institutions; under cautious management they will withdraw the people
from vice and idleness, and familiarize them with habits of virtue, patriotism, and industry. The artisan can resort to them as a delightful recreation in his leisure hours, while the illiterate can become acquainted
with the passing events of the day by hearing the public journals read
aloud. . . .[33]

In a *Nation* essay on August 17, 1844, Davis had written a warm
endorsement of all the Reading Rooms were doing and might do
in the future. Addressing his newspaper audience he wrote:

Your oppressor [sic] has millions, cunning in all arts and manufactures,
for your thousands. Her literature is famous among men—yours still to
be created. Her organization embraces everything, from the machinery
for moving an empire to that of governing a parish. You, too, must learn
arts and literature and self-government, if you would repel and surpass
her.[34]

Among Davis's recommendations was that a thousand pounds
be spent for the purchase for the Reading Rooms of full sets of
the books of the National Board of Education. "These books," he
wrote, "include mathematics, arithmetic, grammar, and an immense variety of instruction for the intellect and imagination in
the reading selections."[35]

The sentencing of O'Connell on May 30, 1844, to a year's imprisonment prompted a letter from Davis to the Duke of
Wellington. It is worth quoting as another affirmation of the high
regard in which Davis held O'Connell.

33. *Repeal Reports,* vol. 2, 335.
34. Reprinted in O'Donoghue, *Davis Essays,* 220–24.
35. Ibid.

You have got O'Connell at last into gaol. But does your grace really believe *that* will stop the agitation? Don't you know that all the Roman Catholics, Repealers or not, look upon him as their Liberator? Indeed, my lord, I think they underrate the services done by Grattan, Wolfe Tone, Plunket and your Grace in bringing about emancipation. But this, you see, is an error that makes his imprisonment more unpopular.

Then, O'Connell is a great man—has stood in the foreground of Irish history for near thirty years. Much as we may sneer at it, he, in some sort, represents Ireland, and every Irishman feels this. The imprisonment of such a man is, after all, a national insult. I doubt its being forgiven for a long time. . . .

Recollect, the populace idolize him. . . . There is hardly a man, woman, or child from Newry to Tralee, but has looked on his manly figure and his winning manner, and heard his wonderful voice, and tender eloquence. . . . They prefer him to priest or neighbor or angel. He is their hero. . . . If you had doubled the tithes, or restored the hearth and window tax, or put an excise on potatoes, you could not have so deeply and lastingly irritated the people. I think better of the people for such devotion; but whether better or worse, the fact is material, and you seem to have forgotten it. The repute of having carried emancipation, reduced the tithes, obtained corporations, praised and defended the people were his. . . .[36]

Davis's views on O'Connell's imprisonment had support not only in Ireland, but in England as well. Macaulay, in the House of Commons, disavowing any sympathy for the views O'Connell was pursuing, could still say:

I wish to speak with the respect which is due to eminence and misfortune; but with the respect that is due to truth. I must say, too, that the respect which Mr. O'Connell holds in the eyes of his fellow-countrymen, is a position such as no popular leader—ever occupied.[37]

We turn now, during these months of O'Connell's trial and imprisonment to Davis's personal life, to his reflections and feel-

36. The address to the Duke is printed in Duffy, *Davis*, 228–29.
37. House of Commons, 19 February 1844.

ings on the public life he was leading. The evidence for all this comes largely from his letters to John Pigot, still in London working on his legal studies. These letters were given to Matthew Russell, presumably by some member of Pigot's family, and were published by him in his *Irish Monthly,* the journal he edited so long and so successfully from 1873 to 1912.[38] We gain from these letters insight into Davis's affection for and devotion to his family, especially to his sister Charlotte, whose long and tender care of their aunt Mrs. Ridley had put her own health in jeopardy. Her health continued to worry Davis all through 1844, and in May of 1845 he reports that he is going with his family to Dundrum "for my sister's health. She has never been out since last summer."[39] His friend's health was something of a preoccupation as well, nor did he fail to report his own. He worries about Pigot's friend Miss Prendergast (later Pigot's wife) and about Dr. Phelan, her stepfather. In May of 1844 he mentions his own attack of scarlatina, and two weeks later his relaxed throat and the debility which followed.[40] Later, in December 1844, he reports himself deaf and breathless with a heavy cold.[41] Despite these continuing evidences of periodic illness, Davis now and again uses the word "iron" to describe his own good health. But in June 1844 he advises Pigot: "Believe me, who have tried it, that it is folly to be reckless about health as you are prone to be. Do, dear John, take care of yourself. . . . Your have much to do for your country."[42]

During 1844, Davis reported his activities regarding Wolfe Tone's grave. Matilda Tone, living in the United States, in Georgetown, outside of Washington, D.C., had written to John Gray of

38. Father Matthew Russell's *Irish Monthly,* founded in 1873, is a source for the letters and memoirs of many Irish public figures, poets, statesmen, lawyers, and clergymen, including the Davis-Pigot correspondence.

39. *Irish Monthly* 16, Davis to Pigot, 28 May 1845.

40. Ibid., Davis to Pigot, 8 May 1844. Also 28 May 1844.

41. Ibid., Davis to Pigot, 31 December 1844.

42. Ibid., Davis to Pigot, 9 June 1844.

the *Freeman's Journal* asking that he do something about mark-
ing the site of her husband's grave in Bodenstown, County Kildare. She had hoped to come to Ireland to see to this herself but
at seventy-six she was, she felt, too old and too feeble to make
such a journey.[43] Gray consulted Davis and they arranged for the
stone and the inscription. Davis, engaged on his biography of
Tone, was the natural person for Dr. Gray to choose to join him
in this patriotic task. On April 17, 1844, Davis wrote to Pigot:

Enclosed is a sprig of ivy from over the grave at Bodenstown. Gray and I
were there to-day, and the first Irish monument to him will be put on
his tomb Sunday next at half past eleven. The monument . . . is a plain
black marble slab, very massive, on it are to be the words—

THEOBALD WOLFE TONE

Born 20th June, 1763

Died 19th November, 1798

FOR IRELAND

I like the inscription, though 'tis mine. It says enough for his and
perchance for all time. The reason of its being put down now is that
Mrs. Tone wrote to say she wished it. Her letter is plain and heroic; better than ever a woman of Sparta wrote-[44]

A delay occurred, however, in the ceremony of setting up the
stone. Some of the counsel defending O'Connell and his conspirators objected to its being held "just then." The ceremony would
be postponed until the end of June.[45]

It is regrettable that these Pigot letters, as well as those in the
Davis papers in the National Library and of course the missing
ones found only in Duffy's biography, are not readily available.

---

43. Some of the correspondence regarding Tone is in the Davis Papers, MS 1791,
National Library of Ireland.

44. *Irish Monthly* 16, Davis to Pigot, 17 April 1844. Years later, Gray wrote an account of his journey to Bodenstown with Davis; published in *Freeman's Journal*, 16
September 1873. I am indebted to Dr. Christopher Woods for this information and
the text of Gray's account.

45. *Irish Monthly* 16, Davis to Pigot, 23 May 1844.

One has only to refer to the wonderful gift to Irish historical studies which the publication of O'Connell's correspondence has recently made.[46] In it we see O'Connell's daily life, his friendships and family, his enormous energy, his faults, his doubts, his certainties and uncertainties, his contradictions, his resilience. Davis's short life and his fewer letters give us nothing comparable, but slender in bulk they do tell us something about the kind of human being he was and illuminate the regard in which he was held. Summarizing and analyzing his newspaper essays does not tell us all we would like to know about a complex young man trying to live his life and to understand and serve his country. Nor was he always sure of his way.

He reported regularly on the ups and downs of his relations with O'Connell; he hoped to visit London in the summer of 1844 and talk with Pigot, but feared they would get little work done. Music, words and tunes, is a frequent subject, and was of course a link with Pigot, and with Hudson, who was sending Davis tunes from Wales. The letters revealed clearly that Davis had no illusions about any quick answer on Repeal. On 28 May 1844, while reporting on his illness, he wrote:

If Wyse and his federalists would work as we're working all might end quietly in our favour in two or three years; but the chances are in favour of a more remote and sterner ending. I hope the former.[47]

He asks Pigot to buy him books, among them a translation of Lessing's *Laocoon*, and Winklemann in English. He is sending a box of books to the Mallow Repeal Reading Room. He is enthusiastic about Taylor's play *Philip Van Artevelde*—calling it a better study than any other work since Shakespeare.[48] In Dublin he had met Helen Faucit, the famous English actress, at a party at Dr. Stokes's but had "only dreamt of her once since ... when she

---

46. In eight volumes, published 1972–80.
47. *Irish Monthly* 16, Davis to Pigot, 28 May 1844.
48. Ibid., Davis to Pigot, 5 March 1845; 22 March 1845.

seemed strangely combined with a Repeal Essay. Burton has been picturing her, and a body of 'us academicians' addressing her."[49] As for the Repeal Essay contest, Davis and his two fellow judges had to read forty-seven entries, finally awarding the first prize to Michael Joseph Barry.[50] Of these essays we shall take later notice.

One of the last letters in this Pigot collection, though undated, is probably from 1845. In it, among Repeal reports, notes on music, and news of John Dillon's activities, Davis includes a paragraph about his own direction and ambitions.

I am equally glad of your health and your hard reading. Vigorous habits, power equal to your need and position, and something over for adornment and benevolence are the conditions of happiness. *I, sometimes, when I see fine spirits, like rudderless ships drifting to ruin, think to be a preacher and to guide individual minds,* but end by returning to my public mission. Ever toil at your sober duties. If great opportunities, lightening inspirations come, be the man of the hour and act and create, but never *toil* for these things. Emerson's best critical thought is that nature does not endure a spy. Again I congratulate you at having got into masculine work, and am as ever yours.   T.D.[51]

We return now to public events. Davis had been busy during the period of O'Connell's imprisonment with Duffy and the other "conspirators." He went regularly to visit Richmond jail, where the prisoners, comfortably housed, had been able to carry on their work and study. Duffy wrote his regular editorials, although Davis was his necessary link with the *Nation* office. Writing to Pigot regarding the events surrounding the news of O'Connell's acquittal and release, Davis suggests something of his mood at this unexpected event.

You may guess our wonder when in Committee to-day (Repeal Association) the news came in that judgement was reversed; it literally rang through Dublin, strangers stopping each other to tell it. 'Tis a great and

49. Ibid., Davis to Pigot, 22 March 1845.
50. Ibid. Davis gave the essay high praise.
51. Ibid., Davis to Pigot, n.d.

useful triumph; would it had not come from a triumvirate of English Whigs![52]

We have arranged a procession for Saturday to bring our friends from prison, and carry them by the Four Courts, Castle, Parliament House, with bands and banners, and a *review* of the trades at Richmond; but don't suppose we're off our legs. O'Brien and I have just parted after grave speculations as to the future, and I, as usual, after success, am in low spirits.

I trust your mother, David [53] and all of you are getting as strong as the waves of Kilkee.—[54]

If Davis was, as he wrote to his friend Pigot, gloomy and depressed despite the victory of O'Connell's release, he would soon have disturbing religious and political conflicts to give him real worries. For the moment, however, in this late 1844 summer, everyone was in holiday mood. Davis himself, after his heavy and confining work on the *Nation* during Duffy's weeks in Richmond prison, probably needed a vacation. It was Duffy, however, urged by Davis, who took the holiday, leaving with Denis McCarthy and John O'Hagan for a tour of Leinster, Munster, and Kerry. Each tourist kept a daily journal of activities and impressions, but only O'Hagan's has been published.[55] His journal is worth noting here, even though peripheral to our Davis story, for it illustrates so well the kinds of things in which Young Ireland was interested.

Duffy and O'Hagan had an eye out for the character of the people they either met or observed, thinking always of their qualifications to be citizens of a future independent Ireland. They especially noted the upstanding free spirit of the Kilkenny people, for whose city they had special praise, enjoying there the hospi-

52. The Whig judges on the High Court (House of Lords) which had exonerated O'Connell.

53. *Irish Monthly* 16, Davis to Pigot, n.d., but certainly September 1844. Davis had become familiar with Pigot's family. David was his brother.

54. Kilkee, the Pigots' summer retreat.

55. John O'Hagan, "Leinster and Munster in the Summer of 1844," *Irish Monthly* 40 (1912): part I, 434–70; part II, 517–28; part III, 580–90. Cited hereafter as O'Hagan, "Leinster and Munster."

tality of Dr. Robert Cane, a well-known physician who was soon to become a correspondent of Davis. They visited the portrait gallery in the castle of the Dukes of Ormond, Duffy being most interested in the picture of the famous and controversial Earl of Strafford. They noted that the *Kilkenny Journal* had published a review of their *Spirit of the Nation,* Young Ireland's recently published anthology of the *Nation's* poetry. In Cork they spent some time and shared some meals with Father Mathew, the good and hospitable temperance reformer, noting the simplicity and austerity of his life. O'Hagan reported his saying how much had to be done for his people, and how little they seemed to initiate for themselves. They visited Sir Walter Raleigh's house in Youghal. Everywhere the natural beauties of the countryside brought up reflections on Sir Walter Scott and Thomas Moore. And at the end of each day, at the parlour fire of some hostelry or other, they read poetry. And we find in O'Hagan's diary such journal entries as "tea and Wordsworth."[56]

One morning in Cork O'Hagan, waiting for Michael Barry to join him, recollected his seeing a beautiful estate, Woodstock, and wrote:

Would you really like to see a purely democratic country with the land split up into *small* pro-prietaries and no demesnes of this kind where wealth might be employed in producing all that beauty and art which has so humanizing an influence on the mind?

Later at New Ross O'Hagan wrote:

I observe in the case of old Martin Doyle, as I before observed in several others, that those who were actors or witnesses in the scenes of '98 have the strongest horror of any appeal to arms at present and are the strongest supporters of O'Connell's peaceful policy. Duffy's experience agrees with mine in this respect. Ought not we in our ignorance to learn from those who know what civil war is?

Then, also at Cork:

56. O'Hagan, "Leinster and Munster," I, 456.

It is utter folly to say that Young Ireland, as a party distinct from O'Connell has any hold on the minds of the people. The *Nation* has immense circulation as the ablest Repeal organ; but it is O'Connell and the priests who are the bone and marrow of the movement. The "Thibetism," as Davis calls it, of the people to O'Connell is beyond anything I could have conceived. I saw one woman prostrate herself before Duffy, "the gentlemen who was in prison with Mr. O'Connell."[57]

The picturesque scenery in Kerry is thoroughly described as well as monuments, ruins, and churches. The journey ended at Derrynane, O'Connell's famous home. "Felt as we approached," wrote O'Hagan, "as if we . . . were coming into the territory of some old chieftain." The three tourists were received most cordially by O'Connell's son John; O'Connell himself was taking a bath! John Pigot and his brother David were already there, the end point of a journey of their own. A morning walk next day prompted reflection on scenery and mood: "The situation of Derrynane is one of the most magnificent I can conceive, just the place to fill one with great thoughts and unbounded love of freedom."[58]

At dinner there was much good talk. O'Connell did not remember Shelley's visit to Dublin in 1812, but he did speak in praise of Goethe's *Faust*. The young men's notions of O'Connell were somewhat shaken as they discerned the old leader's familiarity with books and literary matters. After tea there was dancing, the music furnished by two harps. In the morning there was eight o'clock mass. Later there were more recollections from O'Connell going back to his boyhood in late-eighteenth-century Kerry. At the end O'Hagan notes that John O'Connell was "kindly, good humoured, hospitable and playful: His father also was as kind to us as he could possibly be."[59] It is perhaps of interest to have this happy picture of O'Connell and Young Ireland before

57. Ibid., I, 468.   58. Ibid., III, 587–88.
59. Ibid., III, 589.

us as we return to the political story about to be played out in Dublin.[60]

After O'Connell's release from prison, the central question was what he would now do. For to him it was clear that agitation could not continue as it had existed before the proclamation of the Clontarf meeting in 1843. At first, O'Connell considered dissolving the Repeal Association, restructuring it on different lines. To this the young men of the *Nation,* as well as others, strenuously objected; O'Connell yielded. But what policies were now possible? Davis and his companions fell back on their program of political education for the Irish people, to be carried forward by the *Nation,* by the Association's activities, and by the further growth of Repeal Reading Rooms. But for Davis, there was his future. Was he to continue as an agitator for a cause unlikely to be won except in the far future?[61] There was, of course, his projected *History of Ireland,* and perhaps the literary work he often talked about, but for serious concentrated writing he would probably have to forgo involvement in both journalism and public affairs. For the present, in the autumn months of 1844, both he and O'Connell took up briefly the cause of federalism which others, not Repealers, had been discussing off and on since the earlier 1830s. The man who had been most prominently associated with federalism was the Ulsterman William Sharman Crawford.[62]

Federalism, a term widely used to describe a constitutional arrangement which would give Ireland some kind of subordinate assembly for its domestic affairs was a subject of considerable murkiness. At one point Crawford wanted not only a local Irish parliament, but the continued presence of Irishmen in the impe-

---

60. As to what life to pursue after O'Connell's acquittal and vindication. Whither?

61. It was quite clear to everyone that the momentum of 1843 had been lost.

62. On Crawford see B. A. Kennedy, "Sharman Crawford's Federal Scheme for Ireland," in *Essays in British and Irish History,* ed. H. A. Cronne, T. W. Moody, and D. B. Quinn (London: F. Muller, 1949), 235–54.

rial Parliament. Above all, whatever the arrangement, the connection with Britain must not be broken. O'Connell had never rejected that connection, but Davis, who was more absolute in his views, would have been ambivalent on the subject, judging from all he had written. None the less in mid October Davis went to Belfast to talk with leading federalists, accompanied by Robert Hutton of Dublin, who a short time later nearly became a relative of Davis's.[63] Here we must ponder motives. Was Davis, despite his later words on "unbounded nationality" showing statesmanlike qualities, taking the long view, aware of the necessity for compromise at least in the short run? To include Ulstermen in any national demand separate from the Repeal Association would possibly impress the British government. Or were his affections engaged in his decision? Annie Hutton, Robert's niece, was already Davis's cherished friend and, despite obstacles, would become his fiancée a year later.[64] Thomas Hutton, Robert's brother and a firm Unionist, was none the less interested in federalism as a solution to the problems of Irish government. Was some unspoken loyalty to a family of different, anti-nationalist political views part of Davis's decision, conscious or unconscious, to go north with Robert Hutton? At a meeting at the Royal Hotel, Belfast on October 26 the two men met with Sharman Crawford, Henry Caulfield, David Ross, Thomas O'Hagan, and perhaps others.[65] No public statement was issued from the meeting, so presumably whatever their conclusions and directions, the federalist group was still in an informal, unpublished state.[66]

Meantime, in residence at Derrynane, O'Connell was considering initiatives and alternatives, and while Davis was in Belfast composed a long letter to the Repeal Association which was a

63. See chap. 5 for Davis and the Huttons.
64. Ibid.
65. Duffy, *Davis*, 256.
66. Ibid.

tentative feeler toward federalism.[67] The letter to which we now turn reveals an O'Connell fully in command, giving no sign of the weakening mental powers which Gavan Duffy believed had begun to appear during the old leader's imprisonment.[68] Always the optimist, in public at least, O'Connell did not begin his message with his defeat at Clontarf but with his acquittal in the appeal to the House of Lords. The success of the appeal had been, he wrote, a triumph for the first principles of civil liberty, a vindication of the constitutional principle which sanctions "the right of free discussion to the inhabitants of these realms." The object he had sought to attain had always been a legal and constitutional one: the repeal of an act of Parliament. The packed jury which had convicted him was illegal, and the Law Lords had done a great service for British and Irish justice by overturning its verdict. Legally victorious, O'Connell was not, however, abandoning his public cause. But there was no need of more monster meetings. Those in 1843 had demonstrated beyond a shadow of a doubt that the Irish "people" had emphatically pronounced in favor of Repeal. As for the Protestants who held off, he devoted a considerable part of his long letter to assuring them that the Catholics desired "no civil or ecclesiastical ascendancy." Were any such attempted, Protestant Irishmen would always have a defender in England. Instead of Repeal meetings he looked forward to a revived national movement encompassing all parties and religions; O'Connell even talked of a national confederacy led not by himself but by others—and he named the Duke of Leinster, Grey Porter, Sharman Crawford, or Smith O'Brien as possible leaders.[69] The time was ripe, he suggested, for simple Repealers

---

67. O'Connell to the secretary of the Loyal National Repeal Association, 12 October 1844, in W. J. Fitzpatrick, ed., *Correspondence of Daniel O'Connell*, 2 vols. (London: John Murray, 1888), vol. 2, appendix, 433–48.

68. Duffy's writings on O'Connell's condition have been recently challenged by scholars.

69. Fitzpatrick, *Correspondence of Daniel O'Connell*, vol. 2, appendix.

and federalists to come together, and for the federalists to state more precisely their ideas on constitutional reconstruction, discussions which O'Connell hoped would be conducted in a "fair, impartial and amicable manner." For himself, he was coming to the conclusion that the federalists were asking "more" for Ireland than the simple Repealers; for the federalists, in addition to a domestic parliament would retain Irish members in the imperial Parliament and give Ireland weight and importance in matters of imperial concern. But as yet he had no formal document and so asked the federalists to produce one so that consultations might go forward. O'Connell wrote:

> For my own part, I will own, that since I have come to contemplate the specific differences such as they are between "simple Repeal", and Federalism, I do at present feel a preference for the Federative plan as tending more to the utility of Ireland, and to the maintenance of the connection with England than the mode of simple repeal. . . . But I must either deliberately propose or deliberately adopt from some other person a plan of a Federative union, before I bind myself to the opinion I now entertain.[70]

Before continuing with the wider repercussions of O'Connell's letter we should note some of Davis's thoughts and feelings on the subject of any renewed initiatives. In his Davis biography, Duffy reported finding among Davis's papers a memorandum suggesting his belief that there was wide support for a revision of the terms of the 1801 Act of Union. Indeed William Hudson, Davis's friend and earlier the supporter of the defunct *Citizen,* had compiled a list of supporters real or tentative who might endorse such a move. The list included peers, gentry, and members of the middle classes in all four provinces. The list for Ulster was the briefest.

Already in his letter to the Duke of Wellington, Davis, arguing in the guise of a federalist, had written:

70. Ibid., 446.

I do not ask a raw repeal of the Act of Union. I want to retain the Imperial Parliament with its imperial responsibilities. I ask you only to disencumber it of these cares which exhaust its patience and embarrass its attention: I ask you to give to Ireland a senate of some sort selected by the people, in part or in whole; levying their customs and excise, and other taxes; making their roads, harbours, railways, canals and bridges; encouraging their manufactures, commerce, agriculture, and fisheries; settling their poor laws, their tithes, tenures and grand juries, and franchises; giving vent to ambition, an opportunity for knowledge, restoring the absentees, securing work and diminishing poverty, crime, ignorance, and discontent. . . .

A local parliament granted soon and in a kindly candid spirit would be fairly worked, and would conciliate that large and varied body, which, from wisdom or want of patriotism, or ambition are intolerant of having their local laws made and their local offices filled, by Englishmen. Allow them to try their hands and heads at self-government; it will consume their passions, and unless they are blockheads will diminish their sufferings. . . . Believe me, my lord, if you and half a dozen men of business were to sit down in earnest to devise a plan for satisfying the wants and calls of Ireland for self-government while you guaranteed the integrity of the empire, you would accomplish your object without much difficulty, and disappoint the foreign foes of that empire who justly regard Ireland as an ally.[71]

In the event nothing was to come of these federalist moves. As well, Peel and his Tory government were adamantly opposed to repeal or revision of the Act of Union. What Peel was not opposed to, as we shall see, was the better government of Ireland. But, none the less, Davis's actions, and above all the above remarks to Wellington, deserve some comment. First of all they reveal a *moderate* Thomas Davis who sees a small degree of self-government as a step to something more extensive. A local legislature would involve Irishmen in their own affairs and create a healthy public spirit. To be sure, Davis is writing in the guise of a federalist, but his listing of the subjects which should concern a local parliament

71. Duffy, *Davis,* 257–58.

come, surely, from his own sense of what a home government should attend to. His list is in no way nostalgic for any earlier Ireland. He talks of roads, bridges, manufactures, and railroads—a thoroughly modern agenda.[72] Furthermore, freedom needs practice, and in a domestic legislature, Irishmen might learn that one school of liberty is liberty itself. The position taken is the opposite of that which we have already examined on the part of Count Cavour,[73] who feared that the historical animosities of Irishmen would make it impossible for them to reform, peacefully and by themselves, their own country. The task had best be left to an imperial parliament. The two views are central to all discussion of nineteenth-century Ireland and are discussed by Irish historians to the present day.[74]

Davis was less disturbed than Duffy by O'Connell's letter, calling it, in a letter to O'Brien, "very able of its kind"[75] but poor policy at the moment. For himself, he asserted that federalism could never be a final answer. Duffy, however, had felt that he, on his own, must protest. Davis was in Belfast talking to federalists; he must not be embarrassed. So Duffy wrote a letter under his own name and printed it in the *Nation,* asserting the priority of the full national claim.[76] It must have been disconcerting to Davis, who in the end had to back Duffy up. He did so, tactfully, writing in the *Nation:*

We shall rejoice at the program of the Federalists because they advocate national principles and local government . . . no anti-Irish organ shall stimulate us into a quarrel with any national party. . . . Let the Federal-

---

72. Ibid.   73. See chap. 2.

74. See Liam Kennedy and David S. Johnson, "The Union of Ireland and Britain, 1801–1921," in *The Making of Modern Irish History,* ed. D. G. Boyce and Alan O'Day (London: Routledge, 1996), 34–70.

75. Duffy, *Young Ireland,* 589. Duffy quoting from Davis's letter to O'Brien: "I believe," Davis wrote, "that there would be no limit to our nationality in twenty years whether we pass through Federalism or not."

76. *Nation,* 19 October 1844.

ists be an independent and respected party; the Repealers an unbroken league—our stand is with the latter.[77]

During these same autumn months, while Federalist initiatives were developing, controversies arose over a famous book published during 1843–44 by Davis's friend Daniel Owen Maddyn: *Ireland and Its Rulers Since 1829.* Reading it today one can enjoy its frankness, its sharp, sometimes harsh observations, its vivid portraits of leading personalities in Irish public life. It is, of course, a journalist's, not a scholar's, book. Despite their total difference on the Repeal question, Davis and Maddyn were agreed on many things, and one can see from Maddyn's book why they were sympathetic friends. But in 1844, from the viewpoint of any ardent Catholic nationalist, Maddyn was "politically incorrect." He was both fair and unfair to O'Connell. Some might call his judgments impartial. Others might rather say scurrilous. In his third volume there were two chapters on Young Ireland, including a sympathetic sketch of Davis, described under the name of Dormer.

A chapter on the Irish Catholic priesthood, comparing it to various priesthoods in continental Europe, gave great offense. Picturing the Irish priests as mostly peasant in origin, with a narrow educational and cultural background, Maddyn none the less gave them credit for piety, devotion to duty, and sympathetic dedication to their mostly poor parishioners. Asked by Maddyn to take some notice of his book in the *Nation,* Davis could hardly refuse. His review appeared on September 14, 1844.[78]

Davis judged Maddyn's third volume as the best, praising especially the portraits of Michael O'Loghlen, Thomas Drummond, and Lord Plunkett.[79] He noted Maddyn's zeal for education, for uplifting the Irish people, and for healing old political and religious prejudices—all part of Davis's own program. In-

77. *Nation,* 2 November 1844.   78. *Nation,* 14 September 1844.
79. Ibid.

stead of criticizing Maddyn's asperities, Davis saw them as stimulants to honest political debate. No book like Maddyn's had ever appeared. In conclusion, however, Davis delivered a mild rebuke, saying that "the author might have avoided many a sneer, qualified many a censure, and omitted many an unjust charge that are the thorns of this fair book."[80] Davis had managed to bring off a diplomatic review.

During September another notice of Maddyn's work appeared in the *Dublin Review*, written by the Reverend Patrick Murray, a professor of theology at Maynooth, but published anonymously.[81] It was a rambling review, giving little attention to the work itself, but instead presenting a long defense of Daniel O'Connell against Maddyn's charges. Writing under the assumption that Maddyn was a Protestant, Murray later learned that he had been a Catholic but had converted to Protestantism. This discovery led Murray to write a sarcastic footnote: "Of course the opinion of such a writer against the Catholic priests and the Catholic religion are entitled to great respect!"[82]

Davis reacted angrily to Murray's review. Perhaps he would have been wiser to ignore the professor's remarks about Maddyn's conversion, but it must be remembered that his and the *Nation*'s public mission had been dedicated to removing religious altercation from public life, to supporting true freedom of conscience. So in replying to the *Dublin Review*, he called Maddyn's book "that brilliant work."[83] Recalling an earlier occasion when O'Connell and the Repeal Association had censored some men in Cork for hissing a convert to Protestantism, Davis wrote:

If this be a threat all we can say is that it shall be met. . . . neither O'Connell nor any of our party will stand tamely by and see any man

80. Ibid.
81. *Dublin Review* 17 (September 1844): 1–34.
82. Ibid.
83. *Nation*, 12 October 1844.

threatened or struck either by hand or mouth for holding or changing his creed.[84]

A week later, on October 19, a letter written by Dr. Murray but signed "An Irish Priest" appeared in the *Dublin Weekly Register,* one of Michael Staunton's newspapers. It read in part:

... the un-Catholic and infidel spirit which has been exhibited in the *Nation* from time to time ... has been ... a source of pain and alarm to many pious and patriotic clergymen in several parts of Ireland and to some of our bishops. ... Every Catholic priest ... has a right ... every Catholic layman has a right to protest against such un-Catholic sneers and sarcasm put forth in such an organ.[85]

We need not follow here all the further details of this story. But as provincial papers and private talk spread the story of an infidel *Nation,* Davis grew alarmed and urged O'Connell to put a stop to these aspersions; he expressed as well his fears to Smith O'Brien, urging him to speak to O'Connell on the subject. From Belfast he wrote:

I wrote that a man has as good a right to change from Catholicity to Protestantism as from Protestantism to Catholicity. ... I shall do so again. ... I will not strive to beat down political, in order to set up religious ascendancy. ... The Federalist leaders here go entirely with me, and in fact, now or never, we Protestants must ascertain whether we are to have religious liberty.[86]

O'Brien replied that he had written to O'Connell requesting he intervene to put a stop to the dissensions arising among the national party. But he also reminded Davis that "you and I should remember that we are Protestants and the bulk of the Irish are Catholics."[87]

To Staunton, whom he knew well from his earlier days on the *Morning Register,* Davis also wrote:

---

84. Ibid. See also Duffy, *Davis,* 270.   85. Duffy, *Davis,* 271–75.
86. Ibid., 272.   87. Ibid.

You are a patriot and not a bigot . . . and I am at a loss to account for your having published an anonymous letter full of illiberal principles and malicious hints. Nothing would have tempted me to do so towards you. . . . If his opinions [on the Irish priest] be patronized by the Irish Catholics, the Irish Protestants must feel that religious liberty is in danger and will take measures to preserve it. Such, I assure you is the feeling amongst the members of my church, strongly so among the Repealers, and still more among the Federalists.[88]

The irony in this story is, of course, that Davis, whose whole intent was against these sectarian exchanges, had inadvertently fallen into a religious controversy. Davis wanted O'Connell to intervene with newspapers that seemed to be attacking religious liberty.[89] Catholics, like Dr. Murray, wanted to censor the *Nation* for defending what it saw as religious liberty. It all illustrates, surely, that Davis had probably underestimated the difficulties in bringing about greater civility in public discourse. He received some advice on his reactions to these disputes from Dr. Robert Cane of Kilkenny, a Repealer and a friend, as we have noted, of the Young Irelanders. Dr. Cane essentially advised Davis to behave like a true statesman, not to dash blindly against these bigotries, but slowly, steadily, and cautiously to work against them. In essence he was saying to Davis that realizing his ideals was going to be slow work, given the state of public discourse in Ireland.[90]

MacNevin, in a long letter to the *Vindicator* reprinted in the *Nation*,[91] wrote a stirring defense of Davis and his friends, repudiating the accusation that Young Ireland was a separate party opposed to O'Connell. He pointed out that the majority of the party

88. Ibid., 273–74. For a detailed account of these exchanges that is critical of Davis, see Maurice R. O'Connell, "Young Ireland and the Catholic Clergy in 1844: Contemporary Deceit and Historical Falsehood," *Catholic Historical Review* 74 (1988): 199–225.

89. Duffy, *Davis*, 272, quoting Davis to Smith O'Brien.

90. Ibid., 277. Dr. Cane had heard rumors that these religious disputes might drive Davis and others from the Repeal movement. Dr. Cane was reminding Davis of some of the inevitable troubles of political life.

91. *Nation*, 2 November 1844.

was Catholic, resolving to do in literature, the arts, and society what O'Connell was doing in the public forum. Of Davis he wrote:

It is true that Mr. Davis is a Protestant; and woe, woe to a country wherein could be found a single tongue to slander so pure, so upright, so earnest a man—one whose ceaseless energy, whose indomitable labour, whose wonderful information, and whose glorious enthusiasm are devoted, . . . to the elevation of Ireland, to the arduous task . . . of "raising our country." . . . That I have done my utmost to assist in that work of national conciliation, which *must precede* national independence, you will easily perceive.[92]

MacNevin's letter covered many aspects of Young Ireland's activities, but keeping to the point of religious liberty he concluded:

I hope I have convinced all who have read this letter that we are as incapable of betraying or deserting the cause of Religion and Morality, as we are of dictating to the consciences of our fellow countrymen, or laying profane hands on the ark of Religious Liberty.[93]

The conclusion of this altercation is an anticlimax: Dr. Murray ultimately admitted the error of his judgments on Young Ireland and indeed became a friend of Duffy's. As for Davis and the sketch of himself which appeared in Maddyn's book, he wrote to his friend:

It would be folly to say that I do not see you meant to describe me in one of its chapters. I am warmly grateful for the affection which misled you into it. I am but one of many, resolved as a river is to descend, to lift the English rule off Ireland and give our country a career of action and thought. . . . Our work is only beginning . . . I have thought it better, considering the bitterness of your attacks on O'Connell, not to write an analysis of your third part. Do you mean to write a fourth part? I advise you not. Indeed, I go further and recommend you to avoid touching your Irish political contemporaries for years to come.[94]

---

92. Ibid.   93. Ibid.
94. Duffy, *Davis,* 248–49. For Maddyn's sketch of Davis under the name of Dormer, see his *Ireland and Its Rulers Since 1829,* 3 vols. (London: Newby, 1843–1844).

These words to Maddyn—"to lift English rule from Ireland and give our country a career of action and thought"—can be taken as a definitive theme in Davis's thinking. Beyond absolute Repeal, beyond constitutional history and theory, there was Ireland, inhabited by a body of people, who, whatever their differences of class, religion, or circumstance, had more in common than they all had with England and Englishmen. Self-government, however limited, would in itself have therapeutic effects. Individual issues might drive Irishmen apart, but working toward solutions might be the best way of bringing them together. One must respect a faith while remembering the obstacles which Davis of course knew and was working to transcend.

Meantime, both after O'Connell's acquittal and earlier, the British Prime Minister, Sir Robert Peel, had been thinking about Irish reform. He had been present at the Commons debate in July 1843 when O'Brien, after his long prefatory speech, had moved that the House become a committee of the whole to examine the condition of Ireland. And later, in February 1844, there had been a further long debate at the instigation of Lord John Russell. More directly, Peel had been dealing with Irish problems which had arisen because of differences between the Lord Lieutenant, Lord de Grey, and the Chief Secretary, Lord Eliot, on questions of Irish patronage. On the one hand, Peel, having once been Irish Chief Secretary himself (1812–18), saw the administrative difficulties; on the other, he was aware of the longer-range consequences of the Catholic emancipation he had been finally forced to endorse in 1829. Eligible Irish Catholics, he saw, could no longer be disregarded in the making of government appointments.[95] In October 1843, a few days after O'Connell's arrest, writing to his

95. For an analysis of all Peel's Irish policies and their motivations, see Norman Gash, *Sir Robert Peel: The Life of Sir Robert Peel After 1830* (Totowa, N.J.: Rowman and Littlefield, 1972), chap. 12, passim. Peel saw the matter of patronage as clearly as O'Connell. Catholic emancipation was not an end, but a beginning.

Home Secretary, Sir James Graham, Peel had observed that "mere force, however necessary in the application of it will do nothing as a permanent remedy for the evils of Ireland."[96] Earlier, he had written to Graham that there might come a time when to a Britain at war stability in Ireland might be a matter of national importance. These observations to Graham were the background to the legislative and administrative program which Peel would endorse and carry through during 1844–45.[97]

There would be the appointment of a Land Commission chaired by Lord Devon; a Charitable Bequests Act; an enlarged grant, to be made permanent, to the Catholic theological seminary at Maynooth, with a grant as well for an additional building; provision for collegiate education at three locations in the south, west, and north of Ireland: certainly at Cork, at Limerick or Galway, and at Belfast.

The story of the fate of these enlightened policies has been thoroughly explored in several learned works, most recently and critically by Donal Kerr in his *Peel, Priests, and Politics* (1982). I shall discuss the reforms which are most relevant to Davis's public life and opinions: the Maynooth grant and the Colleges Bill. Davis is remembered by many people today for the sentence so often associated with him: "Educate that you may be free." But he was not alone in his campaign for increased educational opportunities for both Catholics and Protestants. Thomas Wyse and Smith O'Brien had been active in the education cause from the 1830s on; no history of education in Ireland can be studied without attention to the work of Thomas Wyse and the Report of the Education Commission in 1838.[98] It was directly after this report

96. Ibid., 411.
97. Ibid., chap. 12. Also K. B. Nowlan, *The Politics of Repeal: A Study in the Relations Between Great Britain and Ireland, 1841–1850* (London: Routledge and Kegan Paul, 1965), 1–92.
98. For background on the education question, see T. W. Moody and J. C. Beckett, *Queen's, Belfast, 1845–1949*, 2 vols. (London: Faber and Faber, 1959), i, lxi–lxii.

174 Public and Private Life, 1843–1845

that the campaign began in Cork for higher educational facilities in which Wyse took a leading part. All this was the background, but not the only cause, of Peel's projected Irish educational reforms.

Among the scanty remains of Davis's papers in the Royal Irish Academy there is a draft of an essay on Peel's Irish policies and their reception in the British Parliament from which we quote. Davis began:

Whatever good the British Parliament does it magnifies our desires for self-government—yes—the British Parliament has done some good and we hasten to acknowledge it. A debt to an enemy is a heavy burden. It passed the Maynooth Bill and thus gave to the instructors of the coming generation of Irish catholic clergy the means and all the motives of pride and piety to make their church as eminent in literature and social accomplishments as it has ever been for godliness and patriotism.[99]

Davis went on to say that the Maynooth Bill during its passage faced the opposition of a million British people, including the best of the Dissenters who petitioned against it.[100] This, despite the fact that the old pre-1800 Protestant parliament had originally established Maynooth in 1795. Peel, in forcing the bill through, had lost many of his followers. British public opinion, Davis argued, would always obstruct justice for anything Irish. He continued: "It has done another service. It has voted 100,000 pounds to build colleges in Ireland and guaranteed an income for the professors in them. . . ."[101] But his gratitude soon yielded to animosity. The mode of introducing the bill without consultation in Ireland was criticized. Then there followed a long list of measures that Parliament had still to enact for Ireland. Concluding more hopefully, Davis wrote:

99. Gavan Duffy Papers (Davis materials), P.12 and 15, Royal Irish Academy.
100. Ibid.
101. Ibid.

Still a great event has happened. The most ripe of English statesmen, the most powerful and long the most stern to Ireland has . . . practically abandoned the attempt to govern Ireland by force. The policy of bayoneting opinion and riding down discontent has been declared obsolete. . . . If England determines to resume her war policy it will be with lessened and distrustful powers against a larger and more confident enemy.[102]

When Peel delivered his speech on his resignation in June of 1846, Davis had been nearly a year dead. But he would have been justified in his prophecy of 1845. We quote Peel:

. . . there ought to be established a complete equality of municipal, civil, and political rights . . . the favour of the Crown ought to be bestowed and the confidence of the Crown reposed, without reference to religious distinctions . . . the present social conditions of the people in respect to the tenure of land and to the relation between landlord and tenant . . . deserves our immediate though most cautious consideration.[103]

In the two years before his resignation as Prime Minister in 1846, Peel had carried through significant legislation for Great Britain as a whole, and for Ireland in particular. He had repealed the Corn Laws and carried a bill for higher education in Ireland which resulted in the foundation of three Irish colleges at Cork, Galway, and Belfast, which have all recently celebrated their 150th anniversaries. With his Maynooth Bill Peel had faced, as Davis's memoir had noted, immense opposition from Anglicans and Dissenters in England who feared and suspected any legislation for Ireland that seemed pro-Catholic, limiting what any English minister could safely propose with any prospect of getting the votes he required. For among all religious groups in both England and Ireland there was, throughout the nineteenth century, a rigidity about the importance of religious teaching, and the re-

102. Ibid.
103. Donal Kerr, *Peel, Priests and Politics* (Oxford: Clarendon Press, 1982), 350, quoting Peel's speech on his resignation.

ligious atmosphere which should surround education at every level. For many this meant that each religious group must have its own schools. In carrying the Maynooth Bill, which turned out to be widely popular in Ireland,[104] Peel lost numerous votes in his own party and depended on Whig votes to pass the endowment for Maynooth.

Peel's Colleges Bill was to face serious difficulties in Ireland. It provided that the three projected colleges should be non-residential and open to all religious denominations, and should offer no religious instruction. Graham, the Home Secretary, emphasized in presenting the bill that there would be no interference with any student's religion. All students were to be educated together; provisions, however, might be made, by private gift, for faculties of theology. All these provisions had been developed without consultation with Catholic or Presbyterian clerical leaders in Ireland. One of Peel's own Tory party, Sir Robert Inglis, called the measure a "gigantic scheme of godless education," a phrase soon taken up by Irish Catholic opponents of the measure. Initially, appointments to the professional staffs were to be made by the government.[105]

A week after Graham had presented the Colleges Bill for a first reading, Davis in the *Nation* wrote a strong editorial in favor of the bill but with some reservations. He argued:

The objections to separate education are immense; the reasons for it are reasons for separate life, for mutual animosity, for penal laws, for religious wars. 'Tis said that communication between students of different creeds will taint their faith and endanger their souls. They who say so should prohibit the students from associating *out* of the colleges even more than *in* them. In the colleges they will be joined in studying mathematics, natural philosophy, engineering, chemistry, the principles of

104. Ibid., 286. Heytesbury (Lord Lieutenant) told Graham (Home Secretary) that the satisfaction among all classes "exceeded my most sanguine expectations."
105. Ibid., 300.

reasoning, the constitution of man. Surely union in these studies would less peril their faith than free communication out of doors. . . .[106]

Davis's reservations were several. He would have preferred a residential system—students living within the college walls rather than finding housing outside. Also he objected to the dangers of patronage in the government appointment of professors. Finally he regretted that Peel's bill left Trinity College untouched. Since 1793, Catholics attending Trinity had had no access to its scholarships, fellowships, and prizes, a situation which Davis wished to correct. Not to do so was a continuing affront to Catholics. Concluding his *Nation* article, he foresaw that there would be questions about every part of Peel's bill, but he wrote hopefully: "However these questions be decided we trust in God they will be decided without acrimony or recrimination . . . and will not lead to disunions which will prostrate our country".[107] He was to be disappointed.

The lengthy disputes which took place in Ireland between May and the final passage of the Colleges Bill in July can only be briefly noticed.[108] There were arguments among both Presbyterians and Catholics; O'Connell followed the most obstinate of the Catholic bishops, MacHale of Tuam, in opposing the bill. O'Connell's position is hard to understand, for earlier in his career he had seemed to support mixed education. Possibly he was feeling an obligation to MacHale, who had supported his Emancipation and Repeal campaigns; he was also motivated by a desire to make such trouble for the ministry that they might propose in the next session a better bill. The ministry, however, was to prove adamant, except for the slightest of concessions. The Irish bishops were also divided. Juxtaposed to MacHale were Archbishops

106. *Nation,* May 17 1845. Reprinted in T. W. Rolleston, ed., *Prose Writings of Thomas Davis* (London: Walter Scott, 1890), 273–79.
107. Ibid., 279.
108. For the detailed story, see Kerr, *Peel,* 300.

Crolly and Murray, who were disposed to work with the government despite their own objections to aspects of the bill.

In examining the harsh and dramatic exchanges which took place at the Repeal Association meeting on May 26, it is important to keep in mind many things which were not mentioned, older memories and prejudices on all sides. There had been after 1800 a considerable amount of missionary proselytism on the part of Protestants—sometimes called the "New Reformation"—which put many Catholics, especially the hierarchy, on the defensive.[109] During 1844, as we have seen, the *Nation* had been attacked for the "infidelity" of its views, which had led Davis to write so many letters to Smith O'Brien about his concerns. He was not, he kept insisting, working against an older Protestant political "ascendancy" to replace it with a Catholic religious one, something O'Connell himself always publicly averred he was against.[110] The May 26th debate was to be another sharp reminder to Davis that his dream of a secular unifying patriotism would not necessarily cover or soften earlier animosities.

Prior to May 26, the Irish bishops had made public a series of objections to Peel's bill. Taken together they might seem to say "we reject the bill utterly," as O'Connell would do, calling it "execrable" and saying "a more nefarious attempt at profligacy and corruption never disgraced any minister."[111] (It hardly seems necessary to note the unfairness to Peel.) As for the bishops, their proposals were these: (1) that a fair proportion of professors in the new colleges be Roman Catholics; (2) that all office bearers

109. See Desmond Bowen, *The Protestant Crusade in Ireland, 1800–1870* (Dublin: Gill and MacMillan, 1978). For background on attitudes, see Emmet Larkin, "The Quarrel Among the Roman Catholic Hierarchy over the National System of Education in Ireland, 1838–41," in *The Celtic Cross*, ed. Ray B. Browne, W. J. Roscelli, and Richard Loftus (Purdue, Ind.: Purdue University Studies, 1964).

110. O'Connell to Davis, 30 October 1844. O'Connell, *Correspondence*, vol. 7, letter 3109.

111. Denis Gwynn, *O'Connell, Davis and the Colleges Bill* (Cork: Cork University Press, 1948), 62.

should be appointed by a Board of Trustees of which the Roman Catholic prelates of the provinces where the colleges shall be erected shall be members; (3) that Roman Catholic pupils could not attend lectures on history, logic, metaphysics, moral philosophy, geology, or anatomy without danger to their faith and morals unless a Roman Catholic professor be appointed for each of these studies (the corollary would seem to require *two* professors in each of these subjects); (4) that if any president, vice-president, professor, or other office bearer should attempt and be convicted of undermining the faith and morals of a student, he should be removed from office by the Board of Trustees.

It is quite apparent to us today, and surely was to the bishops then, that the Peel government would not and could not get through a bill containing all these provisions. The question was rather, did this set of provisos constitute a total condemnation, a statement of non-cooperation, or a preliminary to possible negotiation? The bishops' opening sentence said that they were disposed to cooperate on "fair and reasonable terms" with the government. But what could "fair and reasonable" turn out to mean?

But to return to the Conciliation Hall debate. O'Brien made a plea for peace, and while praising the bishops' concerns for faith and morals saw no reason why provisions for religious education could not be made. O'Connell again, speaking after O'Brien, condemned the bill utterly, but said that all were ready to accept a bill based on just and tolerant principles. In other words, a new and better bill. The Young Irelander Michael Barry from Cork spoke next and claimed to be "utterly indifferent" by what name the measure was called; but while endorsing the bishops' views on religious education, he supported the plan for educating Protestants and Catholics together. Michael Conway, a Catholic who had been educated at Trinity, spoke next. Without entering into Conway's character, as Gavan Duffy was later to do in a derogatory sense, one can hardly be patient with the twisted way Conway

talked. He picked up Barry's word "indifferent" and used it to infer that Barry was a lapsed Catholic. Turning for help to St.
Patrick, Conway said the saint was no friend of masked infidelity,
of mixed education! One does wonder how O'Connell could
have so conspicuously and loudly cheered this twisted speech.

Davis spoke next, and clearly must be criticized for the way he
began by calling Conway's speech "useful, judicious and spirited,"
then saying "my old college friend, my Catholic, my very Catholic
friend, Mr. Conway." Even at this distance the words come across
as sarcastic, however Davis may have meant them. O'Connell in-
terjected: "It is no crime to be a Catholic, I hope." Surprised,
Davis answered, "No . . . my truest friends are Catholics," ending
with a plea for good will among all sects. Davis went on to approve the bishops' four conditions, which we have outlined
above. Despite endorsing the bishops' demands, Davis insisted
that none of their proposals destroyed his own goal of "mixed education." Others, including O'Connell, had a different interpretation, namely that the four demands in essence killed off "mixed
education."[112]

O'Connell's interpretation was that the principle of the bill,
named "mixed education," had the "unequivocal and unanimous
condemnation of the bishops."[113] He moved on to an attack on
the *Nation* and Young Ireland, "anxious to rule the destinies of
this country. . . . There is no such party as that styled Young Ireland. . . . I am for Old Ireland . . . and I have some slight notion
that old Ireland will stand by me."[114]

Consternation and embarrassment reigned. Smith O'Brien
and Henry Grattan, sitting near O'Connell, talked to him and he
quickly rose to withdraw the nickname Young Ireland, as he understood it was disclaimed by those to whom it was applied.
Davis replied agreeably that he was glad to be rid of the assump-

112. Ibid., 64.   113. Ibid.
114. Ibid., 68.

tion that there were two parties in the Repeal Association, ending with his own strong affection for Daniel O'Connell, "a feeling which he had habitually expressed in his correspondence with his dear and closest friends."[115] Emotion took over and Davis burst into tears. O'Connell, no less emotional than Davis, came forward with expressions of good will. The two men shook hands.

Resuming his speech, Davis concluded with a plea for unity and a prayer "that the Irish people and their leaders might continue united in the pursuit of liberty in which they were so often defeated before . . . and with a supplication to God that they might not be defeated again."

No one comes off in this encounter with great credit, but the break was not so severe as was subsequently believed. Four days later there was a celebration in the Dublin Rotunda to commemorate the anniversary of O'Connell's imprisonment on May 30, 1844. It had been organized by Davis and Sir Colman O'Loghlen on behalf of the Repeal Association. O'Brien was chosen to administer a pledge that there would be no shrinking in the demand for Repeal. Davis, as so often, wrote off to Maddyn:

. . . If I had to deal only with O'Connell we would never fall out, but he is surrounded by sycophants who lie away against every man whose honesty they fear. However, we are good friends now. . . .[116]

The bill went through with only minor changes, one for the provision of halls as centers for religious instruction. The Roman church, however, was finally to condemn the colleges at the Synod of Thurles in 1850, and the question of proper provision for Catholic university education was to continue as a leading political issue until its settlement in 1908 by the Irish Universities Act. It might be pertinent at this point to note that none of the issues surrounding the Colleges Bill were ever entirely polarized simply

115. Ibid., 69.
116. Duffy, *Davis*, 310.

between Old and Young Ireland. John O'Hagan, whose generous appreciation of Davis we have noted in our Introduction, sided with the bishops and later was to write an interesting article on the subject.[117] Himself a Catholic and a graduate of Trinity, he argued that however excellent the intellectual training at Trinity, the atmosphere was overwhelmingly Protestant. It was that kind of intangible that also concerned the bishops when they stood firm for colleges more Catholic in spirit. The most detailed study of this whole question is by Denis Gwynn, *O'Connell, Davis and the Colleges Bill* (1948), which (in my view) passes unduly harsh judgment on Davis. A more complete, judicious, and impressive work, which we have already mentioned and which covers Peel's policies toward Ireland, is Donal Kerr's *Peel, Priests, and Politics* (1982). No student of Davis and the political and religious milieu in which he moved should fail to study this excellent book.

The aftermath of the Davis-O'Connell altercation was the subject of much newspaper comment, and the account in the *Pilot* Davis sent off to Denny Lane in Cork. Lane replied in a long letter with a frankness which suggests the confident friendship which existed between the two young men. Admitting that the whole episode was a heavy blow to Young Ireland, Lane went on with a series of "lessons" he had drawn from the encounter. He wrote:

The first is that O'Connell is the most popular man that ever lived and will be implicitly obeyed by a great body of the people whatever be the orders he gives them. Next he is so used to implicit obedience and has so often been able to get on after having cast off those who mutinied against him that he will think nothing of doing the same again. . . . next the man is so thoroughly Irish and hearty, and so devoted to the religion to which the people are devoted, that he is, without exaggeration loved by them as a father. Next, the Catholics are bound to him by their grati-

117. *Irish Monthly* 26 (March 1898), 113–22. Reprint of the essay published by John O'Hagan in the *Dublin Review,* September 1847. O'Hagan was then twenty-five years old.

tude for . . . Emancipation, and nine tenths of the priests throughout Ireland are his servants and the peoples' masters. . . . Well what does all this come to? To this, that his power is irresistible . . . next he does not bear control; you can give him no more than a hint of differing in opinion from him . . . if it becomes absolutely necessary to differ from O'Connell you must get O'Brien, who is a sensible man, and who will do so only in an extreme case, to express in the most temperate manner, your dissent. O'Connell would never have dared to treat him as he treated you. . . . I have heard people remark, what *I never observed myself* that there is often in your manner something very dictatorial. . . .

Lane continued:

. . . it frequently makes enemies and always deters those who would otherwise become converts. Try and see yourself as others see you and mend the fault. You must, in the first place, feign the modesty which I believe you possess, and do not irritate a man like O'Connell; consider your own position relatively to his, and wear that deference of manner to him which you know he loves. You will then make yourself as useful to the country as you possibly can under the present circumstances. . . . I have more to say to you, but I am afraid you are tired already. . . .[118]

Davis generously accepted Lane's criticisms and replied:

. . . What you say of my general manner (in the General Committee of the Association) is, I fear, quite true. I lose patience with the lying, ignorant, and lazy clan that surround O'Connell. Indeed, I have to maintain a perpetual struggle to prevent myself from quitting politics in absolute scorn; but my heart melts when I think it possible for a union of brave, patient men to lift up the country in more ways than politics. But till the "scene" in Conciliation Hall, O'Connell and I were always courteous in manner to each other, though frequently opposed in opinion.[119]

From Limerick came a letter from William Griffin, brother of the novelist Gerald Griffin, congratulating Davis on the "noble stand you made in favor of the principle of mixed education. . . ."

118. Duffy, *Davis,* 300–301, Lane to Davis, from Cork, 11 June 1845.
119. Duffy, *Davis,* 302.

Griffin continued:

... as a Catholic and a serious advocate for Repeal of the Union I am most anxious to tell you how truly I deprecate his conduct [Conway's] and how every thinking and intelligent Catholic here differs from him. Nothing could betray the utter hypocrisy of his pretension to patriotism ... more than the recklessness with which he cast the seeds of disorder among members of the Association. The audacity with which he attacked a party who have done more to create a feeling of nationality and self-respect in Irishmen than even the oppression of the centuries ...[120]

Earlier, a few months before the dissension over the Colleges Bill, Dr. Cane of Kilkenny, of whom we have earlier spoken, was giving some thought to Davis's role in the country, indeed to his whole future. On 14 March 1845 Cane wrote to him:

You but half serve your country while your services are confined to the press only. You have the capabilities if you had the courage of serving her as a speaker! Why not do it? Your usefulness and influence would be tenfold increased once you took up that position. Why not do it? Why not be as powerful in the public assembly and in debate as you are in the Committee Room and at the press. Davis, you must work and begin the work soon in one more department or someone else may soon occupy the place that should be yours ... ground which he may occupy for mischief to the cause—as effectively as you would have done it for the public good. You must not take offense at this letter ... its purpose is to awake you to the destiny of a country we both love and would die for. ...

Ponder, act as becomes the man, the time, the circumstances.[121]

In the spring of 1845 some of Davis's younger friends, believing him to have the talents which would make a great lawyer, urged him "to go circuit" and establish relations with the profession for which he had prepared. Dillon was against the idea, be-

120. Griffin to Davis, 2 June 1845. Davis Papers, MS 2644, National Library of Ireland.

121. Dr. Cane to Davis, 14 March 1845. Davis Papers, MS 2644, National Library of Ireland.

lieving such a move would lead to the accusation that Davis had been driven out of politics. Instead he urged that Duffy and Davis found another penny magazine . . . to pull Davis deeper into journalism. Quite other advice came from the practical Denny Lane:

I am glad to hear that you are coming down to the Assizes. The going circuit, I think, . . . can make a man acquainted with the provincial mind of Ireland, which is of much greater proportionate power than the ex-metropolitan mind of any other country. In fact we have no metropolis . . . neither the court or claret-colored coats nor that of wigs and gowns is enough to make Dublin anything but a country town. We have no theater, no periodical literature, no gathering of artists, no great merchants, above all, no legislative assembly collecting into focus every ray of intellect and enterprise in the country. In fact we have nothing of what makes Paris or other capitals the governor of the Great Engine of a Nation.[122]

It is not surprising, after the clash with O'Connell, and the evidence that Repeal was probably something in the distant future, that Davis's friends should have been concerned about his future political career and his course in general. The Repeal Association was becoming a shadow of its vigorous 1843 self; and the strain over the Colleges Bill, however muted, continued. O'Connell, increasingly absent at Derrynane, was leaving the direction of the Repeal Association to his son John, who, as the Young Irelanders saw things, was giving more and more a Catholic bias to the Association, endangering whatever future support might still come from Protestants.[123] The Colleges Bill which finally passed in July 1845 contained none of the provisions which the bishops and O'Connell had advocated. None the less there would be three colleges, and for Davis and his friends this educational advance was a positive gain.

122. Denny Lane to Davis, 16 June 1845. Davis Papers, MS 2644, National Library of Ireland.
123. Duffy, *Davis*, 313–17.

Davis in these stressful weeks was both depressed and angry, but coaxing himself into hopefulness. His letters tell some of the story. To Denny Lane he wrote:

If anything could change my mixed feelings of admiration and censure of O'Connell into genuine hostility it would be the vicious adulation and lying incentives proffered to him by the little, stupid, mercenary devils about him, and his patronage of the vilest and weakest of them. They are trying to drive O'Brien, myself and others to secession,—but they shall be disappointed and beaten.[124]

To O'Brien, who was in London for the final debate on the Colleges Bill, Davis wrote:

O'Connell goes over to London to-night and so much the better—It is desirable that he should be removed for a while from the persons who suggest suspicions, alarm his Catholic feelings and stimulate his large but vehement soul. 'Tis marvelous what evil influence such little creatures can exercise over so great a mind. . . .[125]

In this same letter to O'Brien, Davis, deploring the current dissensions in the Association, reemphasized that its sole business was Repeal, and the introduction of extraneous topics would destroy it. But, anticipating the worst, he wrote that if a break should occur, the longer it could be postponed the better.[126]

On July 26, 1845, in another long letter to O'Brien, Davis wrote that the doctrines put out by the O'Connellites on the Colleges Bill had lost Repeal some of its best friends and that those friends would not be regained if the agitation continued on its present course. But hopeful again, he continued:

—Still we have a sincere and numerous people, a rising literature, an increasing staff of young, honest, trained men, Peel's splitting policy, the chance of war, the chance of the Orangemen, and a great, though now misused organization; and perhaps next autumn a rally may be

124. Ibid., 304.   125. Ibid., 305.
126. Ibid.

made. . . . At this moment, the attempt would utterly fail; but parties may be brought down to reason by the next four months. . . . A dogged temper and a point of honour induce me to remain in the Association at every sacrifice and will keep me there while there is a chance, even a remote one, of doing good in it. . . .[127]

From late July 1845 until the end of August, Davis's chief responsibility was the *Nation*, for Duffy, with several friends, was off for a walking holiday in northern Ireland.[128] Davis, as we shall see in our next chapter, had compelling personal reasons for remaining in Dublin and was quite agreeable to taking over the *Nation*'s editorship for a month or so. And so it happened that a large part of the paper for August 1845 was written by him, or by occasional contributors whose articles he had earlier arranged for. We shall conclude this account of Davis's public life with a look at what he was thinking and writing during what, tragically, would be the last month of his life.

These August issues of the 1845 *Nation* reflected all of Davis's interests: the growth of an Irish literature in English; the hoped-for conversion of northern Orangemen to nationality; the condition of poorer people both in Ireland and in England; the recently concluded contest for Repeal prize essays on a future constitution for Ireland; the uses of the imperial Parliament; agricultural improvement; projects for the education of the people. Finally, in early September there was a plea for a new emphasis on the teaching of Gaelic in the schools of the western counties, where work for the preservation of the Irish language would likely be most successful. This essay was probably the last Davis wrote before his September illness.

Let us look at a few of these August essays, unsigned as usual,

127. Gwynn, *Colleges Bill*, 86–87.
128. Duffy, *Davis*, 355. For an account of this journey see John O'Hagan, "Ulster in the Summer of 1845," *Irish Monthly* 41 (1913), 38–42, 487–88.

but identifiable by their subject and style, with the additional proof that Davis was working alone in the editorial office.[129]

On 23 August there appeared "Repeal Registries," which opened with an exhortation to eligible voters to register so that they might be ready to make their choices when an election came. Out of the 105 Irish members of Parliament, only twenty-five at the most were Repealers. These numbers, Davis argued, would have to change before parliamentary action could get anywhere with serious Irish reform. Then there was the curious observation that the Irish cause could not win respect and attention from the people of England until there were about seventy-four Irish Repeal members representing "the wealth, the intelligence and the spirit of the country."[130] One cannot avoid some surprise that Davis, who in the previous three years had been castigating the English, was now stressing the need for winning their respect. Going beyond mere parliamentary numbers, he pleaded for seriousness, attention to business, and cooperative action among the Irish MPs. Taking counsel together, acting and voting together when need might be, would make for attention and success in the imperial Parliament. These observations anticipated Irish parliamentary history in a future which would only be realized in the 1870s and 1880s under Parnell. Davis, however, did not link his opinions with a discussion of the extension of the suffrage, which of course would affect the kinds of members elected.

Actually this emphasis on the uses to which the imperial Parliament could be put was an earlier interest of Davis's, and indeed of Duffy's. A year before, on 11 May 1844, Davis had written an essay on Irish members for which Maddyn had congratulated him, calling it "the finest thing you have done."[131] Davis's standards for

---

129. Ibid.
130. *Nation,* 23 August 1845.
131. Maddyn to Davis, May (no further date). Davis Papers, MS 2644, National Library of Ireland. Maddyn's point was that seriousness and sound argument would always get attention from the Westminster Parliament.

parliamentary representatives were high. He called for a serious knowledge of agriculture, trade, and commerce, and a familiarity with Ireland's history. As well, a member should be aware of the history and struggles of smaller countries resembling Ireland in their experience of subjection and provincial status. As an example of members whom he admired, Davis cited among others Thomas Wyse, who, though not a Repealer, brought dignity and respect for Ireland by his calm, laborious work at Westminster, and his constant assiduous campaign on behalf of educational reform.[132]

On 2 August Davis called attention to the recently published *Repeal Prize Essays,* especially the winning essay written by Michael Joseph Barry. The judges had been Davis, John O'Connell, and Smith O'Brien.[133] Essentially, Barry's essay asked for complete responsible government for Ireland, for an executive bound by the opinion and votes of a popular assembly. As well, any future settlement must guarantee the inviolability of such responsible government, once it had been granted.[134] Earlier, as we have seen, O'Brien, in the Repeal Association's parliamentary committee, had endorsed such a solution. With some retrospective observations, and omitting crucial developments and tensions in Irish history between 1782 and 1830, Davis concluded that had true responsible government been effected in 1782, the two countries would have moved to harmony and balance in their relationships. It is an improbable and curious assertion. Leaving out judgment on what could or could not have happened in 1782 and beyond, we merely note here that Davis and Barry were only asking in 1845 for the responsible government which Canada was gradually going to achieve within the next decade.[135]

132. *Nation,* 11 May 1844.
133. *Repeal Prize Essays* (Dublin: James Duffy, 1845). All four essays were published in a single volume.
134. *Repeal Prize Essays,* 77.
135. We might note here that one of the beneficiaries of the responsible govern-

On 16 August, in an essay called "First Principles," Davis called attention to the ills of the lower classes both in England and in Ireland. In speaking of England, he may have drawn on what he had seen in London during his law student days. Referring to the fact of England's great wealth as a nation, he deplored the plight of her lower classes, many of whom lived without any idea of God or of "man's moral responsibilities," imprisoned as they were in "the sordid life of barbarous poverty."[136] As for Ireland's poor, and the physical evils which they suffered, Davis saw "none of that brutal ignorance of religion which prevailed in the neighboring country."[137] These reflections on poverty and injustice led him to Edmund Burke and the French Revolution. He wrote:

His [Burke's] grand but angry genius could only see the crimes of the revolution; he was blind to the vast benefits which were to spring from that bold recurrence to first principles.[138]

These August *Nations* continued as before with regular essays on literary and cultural matters. On 23 August there was a long review of John O'Donovan's *Irish Grammar*. O'Donovan had worked since 1828 with the Irish Ordnance Survey on Irish place names, as well as editing the publications of the Irish Archeological Society. Davis saw O'Donovan's labors as contributing to the rescue of the Irish language, and gave his *Grammar* an enthusiastic notice, calling it a "profound and discursive treatise on the pronunciation, inflection, structure and prosody of the most perfect of the Celtic tongues."[139] It was a work, Davis believed, for which European philologists would be grateful. He commented on O'Donovan's wide reading, and on his rich use of illustrative materials chosen from the hymns of the early saints on down to the Jacobite ballads and beyond. One could not open the gram-

---

ment which went from Canada to the Australian colonies was Gavan Duffy, who emigrated to Victoria, Australia, in 1855. He ultimately became Prime Minister in Victoria.

136. *Nation*, 16 August 1845.   137. Ibid.
138. Ibid.   139. *Nation*, 23 August 1845.

mar, Davis wrote, without finding some revelation of the history and customs of the Irish countryside. As for the chapter on prepositions, it would be interesting even to a person ignorant of Irish. Davis went on to discuss dialects, noting that regional speech was found in the languages of every country. He concluded by seeing the work of O'Donovan and O'Curry as continuing to produce such standards as to make "this age the founding time or the epoch of restoration for the Gaelic language."[140] The essay illustrates as well as any which Davis had ever written his gift for making complicated subjects clear and interesting. He had unquestionably the gifts of the born teacher.

Duffy's famous book *The Ballad Poetry of Ireland* had appeared in 1845 and was widely noticed in various newspapers. Davis reprinted these favorable reviews in the *Nation* and gave some attention of his own to Duffy's work, quoting and endorsing the observations which Duffy had written in his preface. The ballads would purify and invigorate public taste, combining as they did "literary excellence with native character." He hoped that in time the *Ballad Poetry* would be found in every farmhouse and would furnish the young inmates of Irish cottages "with early ideas of beauty." But with Duffy's observation that the English language must be the highroad by which the ideas of Ireland would pass forth to the outside world he did not quarrel. We might note here that by 1866 the *Ballad Poetry* was to reach its fortieth edition.

Without summarizing all of these August issues we can surely emphasize Davis's versatility. To the very end he was writing about the government of Ireland, about political tactics, about art and literature, about the Irish language, and about the necessity for popular education, especially on subjects which the national schools would not touch. As for the great movement he had joined in 1841, he looked forward to strengthening and reviving it in the late autumn of 1845.

140. Ibid.

Bust of Annie Hutton by Christopher Moore.

National Gallery of Ireland.

Chapter 5

The Last Summer: Annie Hutton

ꗡ

For most of August 1845 Davis, as we have seen, was alone in the management of the *Nation*. Duffy, with John O'Hagan, John Mitchel, and John Martin, Mitchel's schoolfellow and long-time friend, was on a holiday walking expedition in northern Ireland. Davis wrote to his friend Maddyn on 31 July 1845 suggesting a later autumn reunion in Dublin.

As Duffy, and indeed everyone who at all contributed to the *Nation* (save myself) will be out of town for five or six weeks, your sending me the *Burke*, and if possible, one or two other papers, would be a great—a very great—convenience to me. I would not ordinarily mind having the entire of the paper thrown on me; but I have been for sometime—in a state of feverish anxiety on a subject purely personal, and which I hope I may yet be able to talk of to you. There is hardly anyone I shall so rejoice . . . to see in October or November; now I am too much troubled in mind to be worth your society. Won't you come in the autumn? We will have delightful projects, and gossips, and expeditions, and I trust some good to our common principles and country may follow too. . . .[1]

Maddyn promptly replied:

I am the more sorry for whatever is troubling you, as I cannot be of any assistance, but I hope that, whatever it is, it will soon be over, and that you will not be disappointed. . . . be calmly ready to bear the worst, and

---

1. Duffy, *Davis,* 355.

if it comes, indifference will be a shield—if the best, you will have so much the more cause for joy.[2]

Maddyn had no inkling of the cause, but Pigot, John O'Hagan, and probably the artist Frederick Burton knew. Davis was in love with Annie Hutton, from whom he had been separated for many months by the decision of her family. But now, in this late summer, he had been readmitted to her family's home, and an engagement to marriage was being arranged. During some part of these intervening months, Annie had been in Rome with her mother, avoiding the Irish winter.

Davis and Annie Hutton had first met on 22 December 1843, when her father, Thomas Hutton, brought him for dinner to Elm Park, where the family lived in Drumcondra, now a suburb of Dublin but then more open country. In a later letter to Davis's sister Charlotte, Annie remembered that in the six months before she had learned of and read Davis's writings, prose and poetry, and had wanted to meet him. She had six brothers and perhaps had heard more of Davis through them. But this is speculation. There was an immediate and strong attraction on the part of both, and soon Davis was visiting her, talking to her about Irish music, brightening up her invalid state, for Annie had not been well. Never, she was to write later, did she dream of such happiness as that Davis should care for her.[3] The Huttons, descended from settlers who had come to Ireland in the seventeenth century, were wealthy coach builders. One ancestor, Henry Hutton, in 1804 had been a Lord Mayor of Dublin. We learn from an anonymous traveler that the coach manufactory, located at Summerhill outside Dublin, was the best managed of any of its kind in the

2. Maddyn to Davis, 4 August 1845. Davis Papers, MS 2644, National Library of Ireland.

3. Some of the Davis-Annie Hutton story is in Duffy, *Davis*, 355–62. The more detailed account is found in Joseph Hone's introduction to the volume he edited, *The Love Story of Thomas Davis, Told in the Letters of Annie Hutton* (Dublin: Cuala Press, 1945). Cited hereafter as Hone, *Annie Hutton*.

British Isles. Attached to a park of fifty Irish acres, the family home soon became a welcoming place which Davis dearly loved to visit. Annie's mother, Margaret, was also a Hutton by birth, but from a different northern Ireland family. The mother of nine children, six sons and three daughters, Mrs. Hutton, despite heavy family responsibilities, found time for artistic and intellectual pursuits. She had family connections with Archibald Hamilton Rowan of United Irish fame, and was also remotely connected to the Dufferin Blackwoods. For all that, she did not accept invitations to social events at Dublin Castle, taking the stand that as the wife of a coach builder it was not in order for her to go! Lady Ferguson, the wife of Sir Samuel, in her *Memoir* of her husband, recalls the Hutton household:

. . . their home was a delightful social center. Mrs. Hutton was an accomplished artist. She had herself decorated her charming home at Elm Park . . . with elegant designs from Pompei. There and elsewhere, she diffused around her an atmosphere of goodness and refinement. Even in her old age . . . she promoted the artistic culture of her sex by a series of readings on Italian art which she gave to the young lady students of Alexandra College. . . . Mrs. Hutton was very noble and dignified in appearance as well as in character. She was the mother of the beautiful and accomplished girl . . . the betrothed of Thomas Davis. . . .[4]

If only a small inner circle knew something of Davis and Annie Hutton, it was with the publication of Duffy's biography in 1890 that their story became more widely known to a later generation. Duffy seems never to have known all the details, but did know that at some point in the courtship the Hutton parents intervened. The couple were parted, forbidden to write, and Davis's visits to Elm Park were over.[5] Was it fears for Annie's delicate health, or hesitation because of her youth? She was eighteen and Davis twenty-nine when they met. Her mother had already taken

4. Lady Mary Ferguson, *Sir Samuel Ferguson in the Ireland of His Day,* 2 vols. (Edinburgh: William Blackwood, 1896), vol. 1, 180.
5. Hone, *Annie Hutton,* viii–ix.

her more than once to Rome for the warmer, drier climate. Or was it the family's disagreement with Davis's political views? Mrs. Hutton had recorded in no uncertain terms her disapproval of O'Connell. In 1844, however, Annie's uncle, Robert Hutton, had worked with Davis in exploring the possibility of a federalist approach to the Irish constitutional problem. Knowing Davis better, did the parents rethink the family's stand against marriage? All these questions give us no answers. In the end, could it have been the tenacity of Annie's affections which carried the day and brought Davis back?

While preparing his life of Davis, Duffy was in touch with Davis's sister Charlotte, who gave him information and also at least one letter from Annie to Davis from which we quote.

How shall I tell you how happy I was to get your dear, dear letter, for which I love you twenty times better than before, for now you are treating me with confidence, not like a child. . . . Do you know that was (but it is nearly gone) the one fear I had that you would think of me as a plaything, more than as a friend, but I don't think you will since last night. . . .[6]

This letter sheds interesting light on the seriousness of Annie's character and also on Davis's appreciation of her feelings, and probably his respect for her views in general. An undated letter from her mother is also included in Duffy's book, a letter to which we have already referred and which opens up many questions about the political difficulties which might have loomed for Davis when he became the son-in-law in a Unionist family:

. . . Don't believe I love my country less because, with all true and deep acknowledgement of Mr. O'Connell's early services, I abhor his late and present courses, and fervently wish such minds and souls as yours and a few others were exorcised of this evil-spirit and its influence.[7]

We now have more letters, Annie's not Davis's, which were published in 1945.[8] Sometime before that anniversary year of

6. Duffy, *Davis*, 359–60.   7. Ibid., 361.
8. Hone, *Annie Hutton*.

Davis's death, a great-grandniece of Thomas Davis, a descendant of his brother James, found, while examining a packet of newspaper cuttings relating to the Young Ireland period, a small collection of seven letters written by Annie. Six were to Davis; the seventh was addressed to his sister Charlotte and written several months after his death. They were put into the hands of Joseph Hone, who years earlier had written a brief study of Davis for the Noted Irish Lives series (1934). The letters were issued by the Cuala Press, in a beautifully printed, limited and numbered edition. The present writer was fortunate to find number 123 in a Dublin bookstore. Some of our information, especially on the Hutton family, has been taken from Hone's introduction to these letters.[9] One could wish for Davis's side of the correspondence, but if it exists it has never come to light. One does not easily write about love letters, but only hopes that those interested in Davis's life will find their way to the moving letters contained in this slender book.

That Annie was loving, devoted, and also intelligent they leave no doubt. The letters reveal her grief at her earlier separation from Davis; her inability—self-confessed—to say all she thinks and feels; her excitement as she awaits Davis's coming, and her difficulty in settling down after he has gone. She is going to play Irish airs, and wishes she could sing them. Just looking forward to his coming is a pleasure in itself. She talks of another journey to Rome and the joy of returning again to Ireland and to Davis. She hopes for a longer time together so that she may hear the whole history of his life. Apparently he had told her of his loneliness, and she had written:

. . . and were you so very lonely, ah! how sad not to have anyone to tell your feelings to, and they did not understand you! How hard and cold that would have made many people, but not you, but you will never feel that loneliness again, will you, oh it will be all my fault if you do, in the midst of all my happiness a terrible fear sometimes comes across my

9. Ibid., i–xiv.

mind, suppose when you know me better, you do not find me all you thought, and you are disappointed! That would be dreadful, and the more I love you, the more the fear grows, the more I know you, the more I see what I ought to be and am not. We must talk about that on Thursday and you will tell me all. Yes, dearest, I will take care, and be so well and strong when I come home, that perhaps you won't know me! . . . Enclosed is the note on Wolfe Tone.[10]

On September 10, Annie had learned of Davis's illness. She wrote that she had thought of twenty things that had prevented his writing, but never of illness until Dr. Stokes had sent word the evening before to tell the family of Davis's sickness. She urges him to think of himself, not to try to write to her unless Dr. Stokes gives his permission. Nor should he attempt to go out. "I wonder how you caught cold," she wrote, and quoted Dr. Stokes on "the sad sore throat that is so much going about."[11]

If these autumn weeks with Annie had been worrisome they had also been a time of the deepest happiness for her and Davis, and John O'Hagan remembered of Davis that "his eyes got a new fire . . . and the look of proud purpose sat on him."[12]

During the first week of September Duffy returned to Dublin, finding Davis in apparently excellent health and exuberant spirits, "except when the talk fell on the calamities at Conciliation Hall."[13] Davis had been coming nearly every day to the *Nation* office, but on the ninth day of September there was a note to Duffy which read:

My dear D.,

I have had an attack of some sort of cholera, and perhaps have slight scarlatina. I cannot see any one, and am in bed. Don't be alarmed about me; but don't rely on my being able to write. . . .[14]

10. Ibid., Annie to Davis, August 1845. (I have retained Annie's punctuation.)
11. Ibid., Annie to Davis, 10 September 1845.
12. Duffy, *Davis*, 361.   13. Ibid., 362.
14. Ibid., 363.

Two days later Duffy received another note emphasizing the scarlatina and a horrid sore throat. It is curious that before a week had gone by, Davis had insisted on going out for an hour. Would Dr. Stokes have permitted this? Did Davis act so rashly on his own? He had always had vigorous notions about the values of fresh air. Also he had told Pigot in 1844 over a year before this attack that he had scarlatina. Had it lingered in his body, having been improperly treated during the first attack? Several years later, Stokes, exhausted and in low spirits from his labors during the famine, wrote a sad letter to his wife in which he mentioned Davis:

. . . My profession on the whole is not a depressing one. . . . But when a death of importance happens, and that . . . busy devil within you whispers that had you done something else, the result would have been different, and when such an idea, from your own weakness becomes fixed then there is misery produced which corrodes one's very vitals. The deaths of George Greene, of Curran, of Davis and of McCullagh struck me down heavily, for in my treatment of all these cases, I feel something to regret. In many such instances the feeling is a mistaken one, for we fret for not having done that which we had no knowledge we ought to have done. And if we do our best why should we be dissatisfied?[15]

A relapse followed Davis's going out, and his condition grew worse. On 15 September, Duffy was summoned to 67 Baggot Street to find Davis dead. It fell to Duffy to get in touch with Davis's many friends, whose tributes and grief he has recorded in his *Life of Davis*. With the consent of the Davis family, a public funeral was arranged, and there was a long procession through Dublin on the way to Mount St. Jerome cemetery where Davis was buried, and where the family monument, erected later,

---

15. William Stokes, *William Stokes: His Life and Work, 1804–1875* (London: T. Fisher Unwin, 1898), 114–16. The Stokes family was distinguished for several generations, producing physicians, a United Irishman (Whitley 1763–1845), and Gaelic scholars. The Dr. Stokes who attended Davis wrote a work, *Diseases of the Heart and Aorta* (Dublin: Hodges and Smith, 1854), which gave him a medical reputation outside Ireland. The cited biography is by his son.

stands. The funeral procession included members of the Eighty Two Club, the Corporation of Dublin, the Committee of the Repeal Association, members of the Royal Irish Academy,[16] the Councils of the Archeological and Celtic Societies, the artists of the Royal Hibernian Academy, the committee of the Dublin City Library. Among the chief mourners were Davis's brother James, Duffy, Robert Webb, his old school fellow, and John Pigot, who had returned a week earlier from London.[17] The procession attested to the affection and regard which Davis had won among those who represented the cultural and civic life of Dublin.

Annie's father, but not Annie, was present at the funeral. Several months later, after her return from Rome, she wrote the letter, the last of those included in the Hone collection, to Charlotte, Davis's sister. Dated March 27, 1846, the letter tells of her reading and her reflections on life and death, and reveals both her grief and her courage:

Oh, Charlotte dear is it not enough to make us love mankind to think that such a spirit as we loved was on earth even for so short a time: is it not enough to make us love God to think that he lent the world such a mind to show us what our nature is capable of?[18]

Annie Hutton died on June 7, 1853, in her twenty-eighth year. After Davis's death she had set to work on a project which he, knowing her facility in Italian, had suggested to her. It was a translation of a book published in Florence in 1844 which concerned Archbishop Rinuccini, the papal envoy to Ireland during the years of the confederated Catholics, 1645–49.[19] Some of the

16. Duffy, *Davis*, 367. Also the *Nation* for 20 September 1845. Davis had been elected a member of the Royal Irish Academy in January 1845.

17. For details of the funeral procession see Duffy, *Davis*, 367. Also again the *Nation*, 20 September 1845. There are accounts in the *Freeman's Journal* and *The Warder*.

18. Hone, *Annie Hutton*, 13–18.

19. G. Aiazzi, ed., *Nunziatura in Irlanda di Monsignor G. B. Rinuccini, Archbishop of Fermo, in the years 1645–1649* (Dublin: A Thom, 1873). For a short critical account of this period in Irish history, see J. C. Beckett, "The Confederation of Kilkenny Reviewed," in his *Confrontations: Studies in Irish History* (London: Faber, 1972), 47–66.

work may have been done in Rome, some in Ireland. In any case Annie, who worked on during her illness, did not leave a finished work before her death. Her mother completed it, and the translation was published in 1873. Presumably the subscribers furnished financial assistance. Their names, included in the volume, bring to mind much Irish and British history: Princess Louise, Bartholomew Lloyd, the young Professor Mahaffy, John O'Hagan, members of the Hutton family, including R. H. Hutton, the editor of the *Spectator*. Gladstone was among the subscribers, as was Froude, the historian, and Harriet Martineau. The lovely sculpture of Annie by Christopher Moore can be seen today in the National Gallery of Ireland. It expresses repose and serenity. The brother who remembered her best suggested, however, that it did not reveal her "spirited vivacity."[20]

We return now to Davis and the friends and acquaintances who walked in the long funeral procession to Mount St. Jerome cemetery. A month later, on 17 October 1845, many of them gathered at the book shop of Hodges Smith on Grafton Street to discuss a proper memorial for the man who had won for himself so prominent a place in the civic and literary life of Dublin. Surgeon William Wilde proposed a resolution seconded by Richard O'Gorman:

Resolved: That the death of our distinguished countryman, Thomas Davis calls for a testimony of our affectionate respect for his personal worth and pure honesty of purpose, for his love of country and for his faithful and untiring diligence and zeal in the promotion of its arts and literature: That these qualities and services surrounded him while living with friends of every political opinion; and that this union of sentiment so cherished by our departed friend constitutes the basis on which we now assemble.[21]

20. Hone, *Annie Hutton*, 12.
21. Davis Commemoration Proceedings, MS 3225, National Library of Ireland. Sir William Wilde (born 1815) was a close contemporary of Davis and also prominent in the intellectual and cultural life of Dublin. An eye and ear specialist, he was a founder of St. Mark's Hospital, edited *The Dublin Journal of Medical Science*, and

It was then proposed that a subscription list be opened for the purpose of erecting a suitable testimonial to Davis's memory. Several meetings followed. At some of these Annie Hutton's father took the chair. The memorial was to be a statue, and the commission was to be given to John Hogan, whose statue of O'Connell had prompted Davis's well-remembered poem on the great agitator's life.

The statue when completed went through various vicissitudes of location. Displayed at the Irish Exposition in 1853, it was afterwards for a time at the Royal Dublin Society and later at Mount St. Jerome cemetery. It stands today in the foyer of the Dublin City Hall, along with Hogan's statue of Daniel O'Connell.[22]

There were also outside of Dublin those who mourned Davis. It will be remembered that Davis's poems in the *Nation* had been written under the pseudonym of *The Celt*. As well, his editorials, essays, and book reviews had been anonymous. In the *Nation*'s commemorative issue of 20 September 1845, Davis's identity was revealed, and an account of his life told Irishmen something of the ideals of the man whose work they had admired. In his biography of the Fenian Charles Kickham, Dr. Vincent Comerford tells of his family's devotion to the *Nation* and their reading aloud of the paper's significant essays, poems, and editorials. The Kickham family was full of grief when they learned who the anonymous Celt really was. Kickham himself, shortly before his own death in 1882, remembered his mother's tears for the untimely death of a man she had never known.[23] O'Connell, away at his country home in County Kerry, wrote a famous and often-

---

wrote travel books and learned reports, such as the one on the census of 1851. Knighted 1864. Father of Oscar Wilde. His wife was the former Francesca Elgee, who had written for the *Nation*. The Commemoration Proceedings are based on the notes of its two secretaries, Samuel Ferguson and John Pigot.

22. There is also in the City Hall foyer a statue of Charles Lucas, the eighteenth-century patriot.

23. R. V. Comerford, *Charles Kickham: A Study in Irish Nationalism and Literature* (Dublin: Wolfhound Press, 1979), 18–19.

reprinted letter at the time of Davis's death which may come as a surprise to readers who have followed our account of O'Connell's quarrel with Davis in the earlier spring of 1845. I quote a portion of this public letter to the Repeal Association, directed to its secretary, T. M. Ray:

I do not know what to write. My mind is bewildered and my heart afflicted. The loss of . . . my noble minded friend is the source of the deepest sorrow to my mind. What a blow—what a cruel blow to the cause of Irish nationality: He was a creature of transcendent qualities of mind and heart; his learning was universal, his knowledge was minute as it was general. And then he was a being of such incessant energy and continuous exertion. . . . His loss is irreparable. What an example he was to the Protestant youths of Ireland: What a noble emulation of his virtues ought to be instilled in the Catholic young men of Ireland.[24]

Some have seen in this letter an insincere effusiveness, but I think O'Connell meant it all. He had every evidence over several years of Davis's admiration for him, and he had worked closely with him in the Repeal Association. One old, one young, they were both strikingly intelligent and perceptive men, each able to see the worth of the other despite their differences.

Another famous tribute came belatedly from Samuel Ferguson, who had been ill and abroad in Europe at the time of Davis's death. Four years older than Davis, a firm Unionist and a leading spirit on the anti-nationalist *Dublin University Magazine,* Ferguson was none the less Davis's friend, though not an intimate one. At one time, unable to complete a piece of writing because of illness in his family, Ferguson asked Davis to do it for him. Making his request and explaining why he felt free to ask such a favor he wrote: "There is something in our feeling about this country that makes us brothers."[25]

Ferguson's tribute appeared in the form of an article and a

24. O'Connell, *Correspondence,* vol. 7, letter 3169.

25. Ferguson to Davis, 8 April 1845. Davis Papers, MS 2644, National Library of Ireland.

poem, published in the *Dublin University Magazine* in February 1847.[26] He recalled how the Unionist editors and contributors of the *University Magazine*, despite their pro-Union views, had come to admire Davis, who is described by Ferguson as "a gentleman of the most unaffected charming deportment, a poet, a judge and lover of art and elegant literature, exceedingly well read, and of a character and temper the most genial and humane," who "speedily became the friend and favorite of the elite of the intellectual world of Dublin."[27]

After measured criticism of Davis's prose and poetry, Ferguson paid tribute to his services for Irish art, Irish national history, and Irish antiquities, paying attention to all these matters in the *Nation*. But finally Ferguson's emphasis was on a broader aspect of Davis's contribution to Irish political life. He wrote:

But the great essential service which Mr. Davis personally effected among the better classes of his countrymen, was, the diffusion of amicable feelings among those who differed in politics and religion. Wherever he went he was surrounded by an atmosphere of good will which hostile politicians could not enter without mutually conceding "the right to differ" and agreeing to do something together for the common good . . . and so reasonable and candid was he that it was a pleasure even to differ from him.[28]

A poem of nine verses came at the conclusion of Ferguson's eulogy. We quote his last stanza.

> *Oh brave young men, my love, my pride and promise*
> *Tis on you my hopes are set,*
> *In manliness, in kindliness and justice*
> *To make Erin a nation yet:*
> *Self-respecting, self-relying, self-advancing*
> *In union or in severance free and strong*
> *And if God grant this, then under God to Thomas Davis*
> *Let the greater praise belong!*

26. "Our Portrait Gallery," *Dublin University Magazine* 29 (February 1847): 190–99.

27. Ibid., 190.   28. Ibid., 197.

Chapter 6

Davis and the Writing of History

茶沒茶

Historical writing in Ireland from the Act of Union to Catholic emancipation was heavily polemical. Narrative history was tied to passionate views on the rebellion of 1641, on the Treaty of Limerick, and on the passage of the Act of Union. Nor were these histories grounded on what we would define as serious historical research. How much of this generally intemperate writing Davis had read we do not know; but from his own evidence he had certainly read some of it and considered no one work to be what he would finally envisage as an ideal history of the country.[1]

This post-Union historical writing was perceptively analyzed several years ago by Donal McCartney in an essay in *Irish Historical Studies*.[2] Whatever their bias, McCartney concluded that these historians popularized historical ideas "which acted as a germinating force on Irish politics. For had the historical notions been other than they were, the history of Ireland in the nineteenth century must have been other than it was—so inseparable are historical myths and political reality."[3] More recently, in an

1. O'Donoghue, *Davis Essays*, 301–7.
2. "The Writing of History in Ireland, 1800–1830," *Irish Historical Studies* 10, no. 40 (September 1957): 347–62.
3. Ibid., 362.

essay in his *States of Mind*,[4] Oliver MacDonagh noted that in early-nineteenth-century Irish historical writing there was in general an absence of a "developmental or sequential view of past events." Circumstances of whatever mitigating character were left out; instead, the historical incident or proceeding was viewed as either excusable or necessary or illegitimate, depending on an author's political views. All students of nineteenth-century Irish history are familiar, of course, with the later nationalist argument that the Union of 1801 was a nullity, that it should not have taken place at all. This, in face of the fact that the Irish people by 1900 had lived under it and had been molded by it for a century.[5] All events, indeed, were subject to similar moral judgments and all became, in the eyes of the protagonists, North or South, "an arsenal of weapons" to defend their deep-seated prejudices about the Irish past. Very different, MacDonagh points out, was the *History of England* which Macaulay was publishing in the 1840s, in which the past was seen in its own terms, with allowance for behavior which, to be sure, would not pass muster in the more enlightened nineteenth century.[6] It was a view which if taken seriously would make the past less of a millstone around a country's neck, not something one had to go on avenging. But in popular Irish opinion, insofar as it was affected by historical knowledge, it was not the developmental view which, over the century, prevailed.

Our question now is: where do we find Thomas Davis in this historiographical story? As we have noted earlier, Davis had been eager to try his hand at writing a history of Ireland; as we have also seen, he had tried to persuade Duffy to agree to his leaving the *Nation* for a year or so in order to carry out plans for historical research and travel to European archives. In the event, Davis

4. Oliver MacDonagh, *States of Mind: A Study of Anglo-Irish Conflict, 1780–1980* (London: Allen and Unwin, 1983), 1–14.
    5. "Ireland Under the Union," in J. C. Beckett, *Confrontations: Studies in Irish History* (London: Faber, 1972), 142–51.
    6. MacDonagh, *States of Mind*, 10–11.

gave up the idea, believing that he had as a journalist taken on obligations to the Repeal cause which he could not lightly abandon.
But to ask what kind of history he would have written takes us beyond the prose and poetry he had written for the *Nation* to other
writings which are for the most part unknown or forgotten. I refer here to a fragment of a lecture on the seventeenth century; to
the series of essays on the 1689 parliament of James II; to a dozen
articles published in the *Dublin Monthly Magazine* on the activities of the English East India Company and the eventual conquest
of India; to a biographical sketch of John Philpot Curran, published as a preface to an edition of his speeches; to various short
biographical and historical pieces printed in the *Nation*. Our purpose is to look more deeply into Davis's way of seeing history, to
examine the larger perspective he brought to his understanding
of men and events, and to present evidence, beyond what we have
already given, that he was more than a patriotic journalist and
poet.

I begin with a fragment of manuscript in the National Library
of Ireland. It is incomplete, and starts out to be the first in a succession of lectures for Dublin law students who belonged to what
Davis defined as an Institute for Historical Study, possibly an off-
shoot of the Trinity College Historical Society.[7] Planned to cover
the period from Strafford to Castlereagh, the manuscript which
remains to us only reaches the year 1641, stopping before the famous uprising of October 23 of that year. A great part of these
fragmentary pages are devoted to the Tudor background, so that
the law students might properly understand the reigns of James
and Charles as well as the work of Strafford. Before beginning,
however, Davis made a plea for history as a humane study, a necessity for every educated person. We quote his introductory
words: "If you would influence the future, you must know the

---

7. T. S. C. Dagg, *College Historical Society: A History (1770–1920)* (Cork: Privately
printed, 1969), 137–76.

past . . . philosophy may be the compass, but history is the chart of the politician. Feeling and ambition urge us to study our native history. We have a land which produced famous men; we have a land in which great battles of mind and body have been fought . . . patriotism and piety have left their hallowing footprints. Nor are the vices and follies of our sires (for they were men) less restrictive though they are less attractive. The opinions of our predecessors are woven into our social state; their acts have determined our condition as surely as our thoughts and doings will influence the condition of our posterity. Shall we breathe the native air of the preceding races, . . . walk over their graves, and survey the monuments of their power, own the same blood, boast the same country, yet know not themselves?"[8]

This introductory passage reflects many things that recur in all Davis's writings: a romantic imagination about the past, the philosophical value of history, and the importance of biography. A knowledge of the past could guide men wisely, not by telling them what to do in their own time, but endowing them with examples of error, of valor and wisdom, of the consequences of any given course of action.

He went on to tell his young lawyer audience that there was among some Irish people, presumably among their contemporaries old and young, a fear of history, of its capacity, given the nature of the Irish past, to excite angry feeling. To this Davis answered that a real study of history, an immersion in complicated reality would abate "unqualified and unscrupulous zeal." "History tells us," he continued, "that we are limited in our powers and should therefore be moderate in our opinions. . . ." He pleads for "the great principle of free discussion"—and urges its extension to Ireland's history. He spoke, at the conclusion of these introductory remarks, of those who derive their opinions and inspiration from newspapers, not histories, as most dangerous. Real study

8. Davis Papers, MS 3199, National Library of Ireland.

would dilute vehemence and fury, and opinion would become more discriminatory. Interestingly, Davis made clear that his lectures would not come down to the present day, for on very late— that is, presumably, current—history his views could not be impartial.

Probably thinking of the mindset of his largely Protestant audience, he urged them to think of those who fought for "home and country" as well as for those "who fought for conquest and supremacy." His sympathies for the native Irish and old English are clearly evident, but he did note as a surrounding circumstance, when he spoke of the Elizabethan wars, that the Catholic powers of Europe were seeking every means of injuring Elizabeth. None the less, viewing the whole time span on which he was lecturing, he remarked on the "unscrupulous appetite for power and plunder which in every age marked the conduct of the Norman and Saxon race living east of the Severn and south of the Tweed, and calling themselves English. . . ." Further passages attack England, English officials, and English writers for putting a good face on reprehensible acts. Nor did he show any sympathy with English arguments for "civility," the giving to Ireland what the English saw as their superior law and order. Neither James nor Charles nor Strafford came off with any credit from this narrative; as for Strafford, "the most accomplished schemer of Italy might be apprentice to Black Tom Wentworth." As he approached 1641, Davis listed the sufferings of the Irish: "forfeitures, disenfranchisements, fines, imprisonment, exile, death." There was not, however, in these fragmentary pages any discussion of the 1641 rising, except to say he would talk about it later—but for this subject there are "other more accomplished guides than I can pretend to be."

The whole question of the 1641 rising and its relation to Davis's nationalist political stance should perhaps be mentioned here. The discovery of the famous Catholic plot against the English occurred on October 23, 1641. The date later became part of the Church of Ireland liturgy, a service of thanksgiving that the plot against the Protestants had been discovered. Discovery did not prevent, however, the massacres and countermassacres during which both Protestants and Catholics were murdered or subjected to cruelty and abuse. As a Protestant, Davis would have had to be fully aware of the collective neurosis of his people: that what the Catholics had attempted once, they might in other ways attempt again. To be sure, Protestant fears had quieted during the eighteenth century, but the Catholic resurgence from 1778, culminating in the rebellion of 1798 and emancipation in 1829, had reawakened old insecurities. And for Davis it might have been an irony that his own birthday, October 24, should be so close to the anniversary date of October 23. Here, of course, we are not dealing with fact alone, but suggesting the kind of trauma Davis may have undergone in breaking with the Protestant history of his family and close relations. He was engaged in an exercise of remembering and forgetting: remembering a history that needed to be clarified; forgetting, by arguing for a combination of all Irishmen of whatever stock to make Ireland a nation. Both aims were to prove more difficult than he had imagined.[9]

By 1843, Davis's studies in Irish seventeenth-century history had crystallized into more systematic form with the publication of a series of articles in the *Dublin Monthly Magazine* on the parliament summoned by King James II in the spring of 1689. These essays were called originally *Irish State Papers, No. 1, Statutes of 1689.* Later, in 1893, they were reprinted as *The Patriot Parliament of 1689,* with an introduction by Gavan Duffy, who, as a member of the recently founded Irish Literary Society, had urged their publication.[10] Not surprisingly the work had a tepid reception.

9. For the significance of 1641 in the Protestant consciousness, see T. C. Barnard, "The Uses of 23 October 1641 and Irish Protestant Celebrations," *English Historical Review* 106 (1991), 889–920. On conflicting dates for Davis's birthday, see chap. 1.

10. Thomas Davis, *The Patriot Parliament of 1689, With its Debates, Votes, and Proceedings,* ed. Charles Gavan Duffy (London: T. Fisher Unwin, 1893). Cited hereafter

Yeats called it "dry but informing," fit only for the proceedings of a learned society.[11] It was quite otherwise with the historian Lecky, who, as we have seen, had earlier praised the scholarship and care which had gone into Davis's essays. Our perspective here is a different one from either poet or historian; rather it is to see what the *Patriot Parliament* reveals about the temper of Davis's mind, the quality of his historical judgments. But first, a few words on the political setting in 1689, on the milieu within which this famous parliament had to act.

The years 1688 and 1689 had a far different significance for England and for Ireland. For England these were the years of the Glorious Revolution, the defeat of a Catholic king and the threat of a Catholic dynasty, the foundation of lasting constitutional government. For Ireland, they marked a Protestant victory, the confirmation of the Cromwellian conquest and land settlement, the prelude to an eighteenth-century Protestant domination supported by penal laws against the Catholics. Fleeing to France after the arrival of William in England, James, encouraged by Louis XIV, returned to Ireland in March 1689, determined to make a last stand. The way for him had been prepared by his viceroy, Richard Talbot, Earl of Tyrconnell, and in May 1689 James summoned an Irish parliament to meet in Dublin. He wanted, of course, a grant of money, which the parliament duly made. On its agenda, however, were other matters, some rooted in events earlier in the century, and others which looked forward to Ireland's future, particularly to its relations with England. In examining its sessions Davis delivered praise and blame, but in both cases he attempted rational arguments for his views. None the less, his work is a mixture of the feelings of an early-nineteenth-century Repealer and the judgments of a serious historian.

---

as *Patriot Parliament.* For a scholarly commentary on this parliament, see Brian Farrell, "The Patriot Parliament of 1689," in *The Irish Parliamentary Tradition,* ed. Brian Farrell (Dublin: Gill and MacMillan; New York: Barnes and Noble, 1973), 116–27.

11. W. B. Yeats, *Autobiography* (New York: Macmillan, 1953), 138.

Introducing his main text in a short preface, he defended the parliament from later critics who had seen it as an example of what an independent Irish government would be: "unruly, rash, rapacious, and bloody."[12] Attached to a displaced king as it was, the Irish parliament's first act nevertheless was for Ireland, declaring that the English Parliament had no right, and never had had any right, to legislate for Ireland, and that none save the king and parliament of Ireland could make laws to bind Ireland. Davis saw this as a continuation of the Confederation of Kilkenny; as a prelude to Molyneux's famous *Case of Ireland*, published in 1698; as a forerunner to the ideas and eighteenth-century claims of Swift, Lucas, Flood, Grattan, and the Volunteers. "Thus, then," he wrote, "the idea of 1782 is to be found full grown in 1689. The pedigree of our freedom is a century older than we thought and Ireland has another parliament to be proud of."[13] Davis praised its attempts to repeal Poynings Law (foiled by King James); to found an Irish Inns of Court; to grant liberty of conscience; to have tithes given to both Catholic and Protestant clergy; to provide relief for poor debtors; to forbid the importation of foreign coal; to provide for a navy and for shipping and navigation; to support schools for technical education.[14]

The two acts on which Davis spent most time have to do with the 1689 parliament's handling of the Cromwellian land confiscations, and the subsequent acts of Charles II at his restoration: the Acts of Settlement and Explanation, which essentially had left the Cromwellians in possession of most of their lands.[15] In dealing with this question Davis had a sensitive awareness of the complexity of the issues. The repeal of the Restoration-era Acts seemed natural, "seeing how great and how recent was the injury they had inflicted." None the less, many persons had come into possession of lands in Ireland under the Restoration laws, and

---

12. *Patriot Parliament*, xcii.   13. Ibid., xciii.
14. Ibid., 137–53.   15. Ibid., chap. 5.

these properties had been sold, leased, subdivided, improved, and encumbered, and here Davis shows his moderation, arguing that many owners under Charles II's Acts had found justification for the Cromwellian conquest in the conduct of the Irish, "as the well sustained falsehoods of the English describe it."[16] He seemed to be saying that to some questions there are no simple answers, and what people believe is true may not be so at all. He concluded by recalling all the confiscations in Ireland from the Tudor period forward and wrote that critics of the parliament should remember this dark history, and "be at least moderate in censuring the Parliament of 1689"[17] Coming finally to the Attainder Act against the persons and properties of Protestants who had fled to England in 1688 and 1689, he wrote: "We heartily censure this Attainder Act. It was the mistake of the Irish parliament. It bound up the hearts and interests of those who were named in it, and of their children, in William's success. It could not be terrible until victory sanctioned it, and then it would be needless and cruel to execute."[18]

War, in the end, decided everything. William won and James lost. The parliament was condemned as illegal and its records destroyed.[19] The Boyne, Londonderry, Aughrim, and Limerick would erase the acts of the "Patriot Parliament." Partisan, representing the Catholic and old English landed interest, the parliament of 1689 became a legend, its faults magnified, its good intentions misunderstood, its constructive acts for religious toleration and economic development forgotten.

The history and misfortunes of this parliament were the text for Thomas Davis's debut as a serious historian. He saw the parliament's good points; he tried to understand both the mentality

16. Ibid., 70.   17. Ibid., 73.
18. Ibid., 141.
19. For the historiography of this parliament, see Brian Farrell's essay and accompanying bibliographical note in Farrell, *Parliamentary Tradition*, 271–73.

of the men who voted, against King James's wishes, to overturn the Cromwellian settlement and to understand as well King Charles II's compromises. He censored its extreme measures but tried to put himself inside the heads, the emotions, even the selfish interests of the parliamentary members.

> We are conscious of many defects in our information and way of treating the subject: . . . trying to come to some clear understanding on a most important part of it . . . in hopes that some of our countrymen would take up the same study . . . and possibly that one of those accomplished historians of which Ireland now has a few would take the helm from us, and guide the ship himself . . . we cling to the belief that owing to us some few persons will . . . be found, who will not allow the calumnies against our noble old parliament of 1689, to pass uncontradicted.[20]

For the *Patriot Parliament* Davis can certainly be given good marks for fairness, for attempting to understand an historical milieu, for accuracy and scholarly responsibility. Without being guilty of attacking Davis for not doing something he never intended to do, we can, however, make one observation. In dealing with 1688–91, he might have noticed the background of religious war in seventeenth-century Europe, and noted also the fears of the Protestants as they contemplated the revocation of the Edict of Nantes in 1685 in France. As French Hugenots poured into England and Ireland, so in 1691 would Catholic refugees leave for the continent.

Earlier, before his parliamentary history, Davis had busied himself with a very different kind of historical subject, one which by its nature was unlikely to invite his impartiality. This was a series of studies called "India, Her Own and Anothers," published in installments in the *Citizen/Dublin Monthly Magazine* between 1839 and 1841. As usual these essays were unsigned, but Gavan Duffy, passing lightly over their existence, tells us that they were written by Davis.[21]

---

20. *Patriot Parliament,* 152–53.   21. Duffy, *Young Ireland,* 57.

Beginning with the first appearance of the Europeans in India after the famous voyage of Vasco da Gama in 1498, Davis proceeded to the arrival of the English East India Company (founded in 1601), continued through the careers of Clive and Hastings, and concluded with the second Mahratta war in the early nineteenth century. His intention was that these essays were to be part of a larger work which he hoped eventually to publish.[22]

Although James Mill's *History of India* was his main source, Davis had done wide reading in both secondary and primary sources, as his footnotes indicate.[23] Some of the participants in the Anglo-Indian story, the writers of letters, memoirs, and narrative histories, would have been surprised at Davis's sharp perception of what they unconsciously reveal. Recognizing the probable inevitability of some European involvement with the successor states of the old Moghul empire, Davis nevertheless presented a powerful personal thesis: that the British conquest of India in the form it took should never have happened. Like Burke before him, he pleaded for the native people, deploring their sufferings during wars and usurpations. Nor did he fail to point out the virtues of some of the native rulers, mentioning particularly the Princess Ahalya of Malua.[24] We cannot reproduce here the history which Davis has written with much detail, scholarly reference, and clear point of view. Doubtless his way of seeing things, his historical perspective, derives from his reading of Thierry, from his strong interest in the history of conquests, from his thoughts and emotions about his own Irish history. It all added up to a powerful aversion for English imperial conquests past and present.

Whatever the viewpoint, the conquest of India did take place,

22. "India, Her Own and Anothers," in thirteen parts published in the *Citizen,* later the *Dublin Monthly Magazine,* 1839–41.

23. These essays are carefully documented. English participants, their later histories, correspondences, and memoirs, and an Indian chronicler of the invasion are all noted.

24. "India," chap. 2, *Citizen* 1 (1839–40): 260–61.

and it has been the part of scholarship to examine and explain the various forces and accidents which drove the East India Company and later the British government forward. Davis had no doubts about the company's motives, and in his first essay he wrote:

Thus at the beginning of the eighteenth century, they had under the disguise of maintaining a monopoly of trade with the countries of the East, formed and commenced the working out of a deliberate plan of conquest, which for rapacity, wantonness, and cruelty, stands without likeness or example in the history of man.[25]

Noting that the faltering emperor, Aurungzebe, after whose death in 1707 the process of Indian imperial decay would proceed rapidly, had readmitted the East India Company to Surat after first forcing it out, Davis called this decision a fatal day for India. In one sense this could be true, but in saying it Davis was losing sight of the dynamic forces at work: the reappearance of local power structures after the death of Aurungzebe as well as the powerful commercial impulses that involved both East and West. To say this in no way belittles Davis's indignation at the chicaneries, deceits, and cruelties which followed.

But India itself had once been conquered by those who "professed the faith of Islam." This fact had to be faced, but in doing so Davis believed that over time the two races had begun to blend their sympathies, and unless fanaticism or "the craft of those hired by the common enemy kindled old jealousies the Hindu and the Mahometan lived happily together."[26]

Questions about the validity of this assertion presented Davis with questions with which he could not, certainly, fail to see analogies in Irish experience. At what point does a conquest, while remaining a conquest, become something else as well? History is full of conquests. But what in each case is the longer history of conquered and conqueror: in institutional, social, and eco-

25. Ibid., chap. 1, 258.   26. Ibid., chap. 2, 259.

nomic life, in manners and customs, in language and religion? We have here a compelling historical subject. Davis was not unaware of the ramifications of conquest history. He would have had to deal with it head on had he lived to write his projected history of Ireland.[27]

As for the Indian states now coming into their own as the empire of Aurungzebe weakened, they were, for the most part, irresponsible despotisms, with no coordinate restraining authority. But Davis notes European despotisms, not, however, making a precise comparison; it is here that he mentions the wise rule of Ahalya. What he is also doing is attacking European notions that all the inhabitants of India could be described as barbarians. Davis saw in Indian local institutions, in villages and municipalities, defenses against absolutism.[28] This attention to the local and customary was to be one of his long-sustained interests when he discussed the history of Europe itself and when he argued for nationality in the *Nation*.

As he began his detailed political history of the intrusion of the East India Company into the affairs of the native Indian states, Davis made clear that he was not going to be guilty of chilly impartiality. "Reprobation of what is wrong," he wrote, "is one of the unpopular duties which the historian is not at liberty to shun." It is his business, too, to disentangle the knotted wiles of guilt and hold up to view the behavior of cunning and designing power. "If this were not his privilege, or were it abdicated long, the spoiler would repose secure."[29]

His sketches of Alivardi Khan, of Suraja Dowla, of Tipoo Sahib show, for a young man, considerable maturity of judgment about character, about the patience and forbearance it takes to make a wise ruler. Davis's eyes were open to character, to the chains of events where one good or one evil leads to another. In one pas-

---

27. See O'Donoghue, *Davis Essays*, 301–7.
28. "India," chap. 2, 262–63.   29. Ibid., chap. 3, 419.

sage he grieved that the doings of the East India Company betrayed the best in Europe and betrayed as well those higher
achievements in which it could take just pride, presenting instead
an evil and cruel Western face.

Finally two questions remained. How, and why in the long
run, was this usurpation submitted to? How did the Indian national soul die out? (Davis's use of the word "national" as descrip-
tive of India in the eighteenth century raises critical historical
questions.) Secondly, who would eventually write the more valid
history, the conqueror or the conquered? This question arises
from Davis's account of Tipoo Sahib. His answer was that the los-
ers in history rarely control their later reputation.

The unfortunate are always worthless; the conquerors are always the
glorious and the valiant . . . but where are the annals of the conquered?
Who shall bring garlands to the nameless grave?

Of Tipoo Sahib we may not err widely if we content ourselves with
saying . . . that he was neither a much worse nor a much better man
than those who have been placed in similar situations elsewhere.[30]

From the essays on the parliament of 1689 and on the incur-
sions of Europeans into India, one can see in Davis opinions that
were not always in harmony: an honest intent toward fairness
and objectivity, a passionate feeling about injustice of any kind, a
strong bent toward seeing history in terms of conquerors and
conquered. This last would come naturally from his knowledge
of Irish history, but was reinforced by his study of the historical
work of Augustin Thierry, of which we have earlier made mention. In the two essays in the *Nation* late in 1842 (26 November
and 3 December), Davis, in appraising Thierry's work, had included his own nationalist philosophy, which would in due time,
he hoped, transcend the historical facts of conquest. In the sim-

---

30. "India," chap. 10, *Citizen* 2 (1840): 325. For perspectives on Davis's views on In-
dia, see Percival Griffiths, *The British Impact on India* (London: MacDonald, 1952).
Also C. H. Philips, ed., *Historians of India, Pakistan and Ceylon* (London: Oxford
University Press, 1961).

plest terms, all Irishmen of whatever origin must now join in a confederacy to make Ireland a nation. But let us look more closely at what Davis had to say about Thierry's life and work. Giving special notice to Thierry's *History of the Conquest of England by the Normans* (1825), and to his collection of shorter pieces, *Dix Ans d'Etudes Historiques* (1834), Davis noted the French historian's hatred of military despotism, his sympathy for lost causes, his belief that the medieval towns of Italy and France had been the guardians of European liberties. All Thierry's studies, Davis observed, brought him to a preference for governments with the greatest possible number of independent guarantees for men's freedom. He commented:

This is the creed of a Conservative Republican-a creed having among its professers many of the greatest men of opposite parties all through Europe. It seeks to guard against tyranny *over* the majority or *by* the majority; and for these great ends it sacrifices some wealth, some uniformity, some vigor in states; and it appeals to history-from Athens to Florence-from Switzerland to Norway-for its justification against the aristocrat, the free trader, and the demagogue.[31]

It was Thierry's reference to Ireland and its history, however, which especially arrested Davis's attention, and in his *Nation* articles he noted Thierry's famous observation that Irish history had cleared up for him the problem of conquests in the Middle Ages and their social results—here, of course, Thierry was thinking of the illumination which Ireland's history and present position in the early nineteenth century were giving to his investigations of conquest and settlement in Roman and Frankish Gaul. Davis quoted the French historian's famous analogy:

. . . conquest is marked on every page of the Irish annals. The consequence of this primitive fact, so hard to recognize and follow in other histories present themselves in it with an exactness and relief which at once catch the eye. There we see, in authentic features and with palpable

31. *Nation,* 26 November 1842.

forms, what we can only infer elsewhere-the long residence of two hostile nations on the same soil, and the diversity of political, social and religious quarrels which arise as from an unfathomed gulf from this hostile origin-the antipathy of races surviving all the revolutions of laws, manners, language: perpetuating itself through centuries-sometimes smoldering oftener blazing; yielding now and then to the sympathies arising from a common home and the instinctive love of country, then suddenly waking up and dividing men anew into enemy camps. This great and woeful spectacle, exhibited by Ireland for seven centuries, called up before me, . . . what I saw confusedly at the bottom of the European monarchies.[32]

If Thierry's hypotheses tell us something of the processes underlying the political formation of European states, they by no means are an all-sufficient explanation, as historical research has long since demonstrated.[33] Davis himself, we should re-emphasize, without presenting any deep or extensive historical criticism, pointed to one serious flaw in Thierry, "a too exclusive notice of the distinctions arising from race, and occasionally attributing to alienage in blood differences arising from legal or personal incidents."[34]

In both of his *Nation* articles on Thierry, Davis had much to notice and praise beyond the main theme of conquest: Thierry's interest in Irish music and its role in keeping alive patriotic sentiment; his praise of Thomas Moore, on whom Davis would write his own essay; his admiration for Sir Walter Scott, and most particularly for *Ivanhoe*, a novelist's gift to the historian. For Thierry, Sir Walter Scott possessed the poetic gift of insight and was a master of historical divination.[35] Recounting Thierry's work as an historian of France, and describing his zeal in research, Davis conveyed his admiration for the historical vocation and for the disinterested search for truth despite all obsta-

32. Ibid.
33. On Thierry, see G. P. Gooch, *History and Historians in the Nineteenth Century* (London: Longman's Green, 1928), 169–85.
34. *Nation*, 26 November 1842.   35. *Nation*, 3 December 1842.

cles.[36] It should be noted that these *Nation* essays on Thierry are written in an engaging style, presenting a serious subject with directness and simplicity, capturing the interest even of readers who might not originally know much about the subject.

During his three years as a journalist, Davis was working on a life of Wolfe Tone, originally scheduled for publication late in 1846. It was never completed, and all we have is an outline and some brief pages on Tone's family and earliest youth. Among the papers is a dedication to Tone's wife Matilda, dated January 1846.[37] Davis had an enormous admiration for Tone, and one must speculate as to why the book was never finished, indeed, hardly begun. Was it the pressure and the demands of weekly journalism? Or was the subject of a complexity which Davis had underestimated? Or was he, as his own involvements with national politics developed, revising his original pure enthusiasm for Tone? That enthusiasm had been expressed in a *Nation* article in 1843 from which we quote:

A better ruler for Ireland than THEOBOLD WOLFE TONE never lived. He was a man of unaffected, deep plain patriotism-possessed of the highest political sagacity, of exact and comprehensive judgment; a man of quiet courage-perfectly conscious of, and confident in, his own power-yet conciliating in manner, laborious in business, and gay and warm in heart. Such was that man: one of the greatest Ireland ever produced. . . .

Peace to his spirit! and oh, may the longings of that pure and patriot soul be fulfilled. May Ireland be a nation! May she win her independence by a free concession of her rights! For *this*, too was the wish of his heart, though fate compelled him to forego it, and seek freedom with an armed hand.[38]

36. Ibid. Thierry was widely read in Europe. One Irish reader should be noted: John Patrick Prendergast, author of *The Cromwellian Settlement of Ireland* (London, 1865). For Prendergast's early enthusiasm for Thierry, and his subsequent change of attitude, see Donal McCartney, *Democracy and Its Nineteenth Century Critics*, O'Donnell Lecture (Dublin: National University of Ireland, 1979).

37. Davis Papers, MS 1791, National Library of Ireland.

38. *The Voice of the Nation*, 126. For recent appraisals of Wolfe Tone, see Marianne Elliott, *Wolfe Tone* (New Haven: Yale University Press, 1989), and Tom Dunne, *Theobold Wolfe Tone: Colonial Outsider* (Cork: Tower Books, 1982).

One piece of historical work Davis did finish, however, just before his death: an edition of the speeches which John Philpot Curran had made as a lawyer or as a member of the old Irish parliament, prefaced by a biographical memoir.[39] For each speech Davis wrote a short explanatory note, putting Curran's remarks in their historical setting, a work requiring considerable study of Irish eighteenth-century history. The memoir itself covers Curran's childhood, his education, his legal studies in London, his efforts to improve his speaking voice, his marriage. Brief though it was, the memoir is a kind of cameo-like "life and times," and is not a mere catalogue of an official legal career. We see Curran's daily life at Holly Park, which he called the Priory, near Marlay outside Dublin, the former residence of the La Touche banking family; his long meditative walks, his playing of the violin; his hospitality; his sorrow over his wife's desertion. Never is the human story forgotten, and if told briefly, it is done with sympathy. Recounting Curran's visit to Scotland, Davis makes a striking comparison between Robert Burns and Curran, their control of language, their love of country, their seeking relief from intense melancholy in "undue social excitement." Good use is made of Curran's letters and we see vividly his post-Union life in Ireland, England, and France. There is a recognition of faults and virtues, but as well a sure understanding of a significant human life.

Local history was also an interest of Davis which had appeared in his pleas for those smaller states or regions of Europe that disappeared as entities through conquest or absorption by centralizing monarchies. But he was also drawn to the humbler local history of the towns and regions of Ireland, distrusting, as he said, the errors of historical generalizers. Writing in the *Nation* in March 1843, he turned his attention to a history of Carrickfergus published in 1811 and written by a native of that town, Samuel

39. *The Speeches of the Right Honorable John Philpot Curran,* ed. Thomas Davis, with a Memoir by Davis (Dublin: James Duffy, 1845).

McSkimmin, a notice of whose death Davis had recently read.[40]
McSkimmin had kept a grocery and provision shop in Carrickfergus and it is clear from the sketch that Davis had been in
Carrickfergus, had visited the humble quarters of this local historian, had talked with him, and had been impressed by McSkimmin's versatile talents and interests. He had taught himself to
write, subscribed to and wrote for some of the best magazines of
the day. Irish history and antiquities and zoological studies were
his major interests. He hated the United Irishmen and thought
them all rogues and villains. Noting McSkimmin's prejudices,
Davis none the less gave credit where it was deserved and praised
the way McSkimmin had gone about gathering materials for an
essay on the Peninsular War, taking down, for one thing, the reminiscences of an old blind pensioner who had served in that conflict.

Appearing in 1811, the *History of Carrickfergus* contained 140
pages on the history, topography, and antiquities of the town and
its neighborhood, with seventeen appendices of documents. Mc-
Skimmin had used Anglo-Irish histories for some of his work but
also manuscript records of the town "which seem to have been
carefully kept." Noting that McSkimmin did not know Irish,
Davis observed that this lack limited what he could say on "our
older history" and limited research in those areas to Anglo-Irish
authorities. It is not necessary here to discuss all Davis had to say
on the details of this Carrickfergus chronicle. We only observe his
admiration for the work of an untrained historian and the scholarly standards he applied in judging it. "It is to be hoped," Davis
concluded, "that the manuscripts of this patient, learned, and
original man will be taken care of and published."

We come now to Davis's announcement, in the *Nation* for 5
April 1845, of a prize sponsored by the Repeal Association for a

40. *Nation,* 4 March 1843. Reprinted in *Irish Book Lover* 6, no. 6 (January 1915):
85–87.

new history of Ireland.[41] He makes clear from the outset some of the qualities which should belong to such a history. In the first place, a new history must be written from the original authorities. Secondly, he wrote: "Let us . . . have . . . a graphic narrative of what was, not a set of moral disquisitions on what ought to have been"[42] Nor would a dry chronicle be acceptable. Any prize winner "must fathom the social condition of the peasantry, the townsmen, the middle-classes, the nobles, the clergy (Christian and pagan), in each period-how they dressed, armed, and housed themselves."

Davis goes on:

He must exhibit the nature of the government, the manners, the administration of law, the state of the useful and fine arts, of commerce, of foreign relations. He must let us see the decay and rise of great principles and conditions-till we look on a tottering sovereignty, a rising creed an incipient war as distinctly as, by turning to the highway we can see the old man, the vigorous youth or the infant child.[43]

But if history must be colorful, and if the historian should display some of the novelist's gifts, he must not invent—"the arms must shine with a genuine, not a romantic likeness."[44]

Citing Thierry and Michelet as examples of how these things should be done, he repeats, in the case of Thierry, a warning which he had made in his earlier *Nation* articles on the French historian:

The only danger to be avoided in dealing with so long a period in Thierry's way (as in the Norman Conquest) is the continuing to attach importance to a once great influence when it has sunk to an exceptive power.[45]

He attached other conditions. The prize-winning history must be free of any religious bigotry; it should be free as well of "glow-

41. O'Donoghue, *Davis Essays*, 301–7.   42. Ibid., 301, 304–5.
43. Ibid., 305.   44. Ibid., 305.
45. Ibid., 305–6.

ing oratory"; there should be no plundering of earlier writers, no pedantic style, but clear graphic prose. Finally, Davis affirmed his faith in the national good which might come from a wide popular understanding of vividly written, accurate, and impartial history. He concluded:

To give such a history to Ireland will be a proud and illustrious deed- Such a work would have no passing influence, though its first political effect would be enormous; it would be read by every class and side; for there is no readable book on the subject; it would people our streets, and glens, and castles, and abbeys, and coasts with a hundred generations besides our own; it would clear up the grounds of our quarrels, and prepare reconciliation; it would *un-consciously* make us recognize the causes of our weakness; it would give us great examples of men and events, and materially influence our destiny.[46]

Sometime in this same spring of 1845 Davis was writing to his friend Maddyn about the value of historical fiction, and the appeal to the imagination of characters caught up in great historical events; but the optimism of his essay on a prize history is missing, and his letter suggests uncertainties about what any wider understanding of Irish history might mean. He wrote: "The weight of that past is upon us now, and sanguine as I am that this country could be rescued, I often doubt if it will, for history casts shadows on my hopes."[47]

What did Davis mean by his "weight of the past"? Was he saying that history had created in Ireland such bitter animosities that they might not, after all, be transcended? All his efforts, in his own view, had been dedicated to bringing Irishmen together, to encouraging a patriotic public spirit which might liberate them from older memories and prejudices. But by 1845, after his unhappy encounter with O'Connell over the Colleges Bill, was he doubting the work he had done toward conciliation and good-

46. Ibid., 306–7.
47. Duffy, *Davis,* 329–30, Davis to Maddyn, n.d. Duffy includes this letter with materials on 1845.

will? Or were his gloomy words to Maddyn expressing a momentary pessimism and melancholy?

Actually, however, it could be argued that Davis himself was contributing to that "weight of the past" which worried him. For besides the clear evidence of his ability to write scholarly and reasonably impartial history, he never ceased being a patriot of an evangelical cast. In 1844, in a *Nation* essay called "A Ballad History of Ireland," he turned to what he called the "higher ends of history." He had written:

Exact dates, subtle plots, minute connexions and motives, rarely appear in Ballads . . . but these are not the highest ends of history. To hallow or accurse the scenes of glory and honour, or of shame and sorrow; to give the imagination the arms, and homes, and senates, and battles of other days; to rouse, and soften, and strengthen and enlarge us with the passions of great periods; to lead us into love of self-denial, of justice, of beauty, of valor, of generous life and proud death; and to set up in our souls the memory of great men, who shall then be as models and judges of our actions-these are the highest duties of history and these are best taught by a Ballad History.[48]

Envisaging historical ballads read over any one person's lifetime Davis saw them, memorized in childhood, becoming doubly dear in old age, a poetic treasure passed on to children and grandchildren as part of a cherished historical inheritance. In his own poetry Davis was contributing to this store of national memories. The language of many of his poems, however, was full of hostility toward England. It can be argued, given the long and bitter history between the two countries, that this was perfectly understandable. However, Davis and his fellow Repealers had two tasks: first to bring all the people of Ireland together, Protestant and Catholic, Anglo-Irish and Irish; secondly, short of separation, to create some kind of workable political arrangement which a self-governing Ireland might make with England. And to

---

48. *Nation*, 30 November 1844. Reprinted in O'Donoghue, *Davis Essays*, 240–48.

England the Protestant Anglo-Irish people had loyalties. In his own mind heroic poems and objective history need not necessarily collide. But how about the readers of his ballads for whom objective history was unknown country? Maddyn, writing about Young Ireland in his *Ireland and Its Rulers* put it harshly:

It [Young Ireland] professes principles which cannot be realized without resorting to a bloody civil war. Its songs, its vehement effusions, its ballads, may *disturb* society and ferment angry passions, but assuredly they can achieve nothing further than bestowing a literature on the popular passions of the Irish lower nation.[49]

Should any armed struggles arise, Maddyn argued, Young Ireland's "be tolerant" would not be heard.

These critical comments raise profound questions about the nature of the Repeal agitation, and Davis's share in it. How could his task of remembering and forgetting have been better handled? The question brings us back to Thomas Wallis, who had longed for the autobiographical information which Davis had never provided.[50]

Davis had the talent, the judgment, the imaginative sympathy, the capacity for research which the writing of history required. Would study and maturity have enabled him to write the history of which he dreamed? And would it, unlike so much popular Irish history, have been a force, as he hoped, for reconciliation? As with so much else in his life, we are left with unanswerable speculations.[51]

49. Daniel Owen Maddyn, *Ireland and Its Rulers Since 1829*, 3 vols. (London: Newby, 1843–44), vol. 3, 245.

50. See chap. 1 for Wallis on the autobiography Davis had never written.

51. D. G. Boyce has paid considerable attention to what the Irish did read later in the century. See his *Nationalism in Ireland*, 3rd ed. (London: Routledge, 1995). Also J. Pope Hennessy, "What Do the Irish Read," *Nineteenth Century* 15 (June 1884), 920–32. For a recent analysis of the study of Irish history, see R. F. Foster, "History and the Irish Question," *Transactions of the Royal Historical Society*, 5th ser., 33 (1983); reprinted in his *Paddy and Mr. Punch* (London: Allen Lane, The Penguin Press, 1993), 1–20.

Chapter 7

Further Reflections and Epilogue

🐾🐾

D avis's dedicated service to O'Connell's Repeal movement has tended to identify him as a political figure and led others to judge and evaluate him in a political context, not always to his advantage. His interests, however, went far beyond politics, for he was as concerned for his country's moral, cultural, economic, and literary life as he was for its political independence, whatever form that might temporarily have to take. Among his interests were education at every level; music and art; literature written by Irish poets and novelists; historical writing, civil and military; the care of antiquities, and the restoration and preservation of old but still useful buildings; the biographies of famous Irishmen, their failures as well as their achievements.[1] On all these subjects he wrote in the *Nation,* putting his scholarly knowledge in readable prose written to interest a broader public.

Davis and his *Nation* colleagues were not alone in these efforts, for Dublin in the two decades before the famine was intellectually a lively place, in spite of Denny Lane's calling it provin-

1. Among Davis's papers were lists of projects of a cultural nature to be undertaken either by government or by private endeavor. One of these was a dictionary of Irish biography. There have been short dictionaries, but only now does the Royal Irish Academy have in process a several-volume *Dictionary of Irish Biography* such as Davis envisaged.

cial. In other words Davis worked in a broad intellectual setting, and was in touch with people whose work had to do with Ireland, its history and present condition.[2]

Let us start with the Army Ordnance Survey, begun in the 1820s under the charge of Thomas Colby and Thomas Larcom, both of the Royal Engineers. Their task was to prepare accurate local maps, each accompanied by statistical and historical information. The one published volume, of the parish of Templemore in Londonderry, shows how extensive the project might have become. Questions arose in London about the expense and extent of the undertaking, and the historical department of the Survey was closed down.[3] But the labor carried on in the 1830s had brought into Irish affairs some remarkable men, of scholarship, talent, and dedicated interest in the country: George Petrie, John O'Donovan, Eugene O'Curry, and the man who was to become Under-Secretary in Melbourne's Whig government, Thomas Drummond. A crucial figure in this story was George Petrie (1789–1866), whose breadth of interests were parallel to those of Davis. A generation earlier than that of the Young Irelanders, Petrie came of a Scottish family only recently established in Ire-

2. The manifold activities going forward in Dublin in the two decades before the famine are as interesting as anything in the 1890s. There is still much to be written about the cultural life of this period, and the interrelationships of the people involved. A valuable volume is Jeanne Sheehy, *The Rediscovery of Ireland's Past, 1830–1930* (London: Thames and Hudson, 1980), 7–40. I am much indebted to the early chapters in this book. The Dublin doctors were much praised by Davis's friend Daniel Owen Maddyn for their cosmopolitan attitudes and freedom from local prejudice. He attributes this to their travels abroad as medical students, to Paris or to Edinburgh for instance. They entertained mixed religious company at their dinners and receptions. Also, their profession brought them into contact with all classes and conditions of people. Dr. Stokes and Dr. Corrigan were well-known hosts. It was at Stokes's home that Davis met Helen Faucit, the Shakespearean actress of whom he wrote to Pigot. See F. O. C. Meenan, "The Victorian Doctors of Dublin: A Social and Political Portrait," *Irish Journal of Medical Science* 7th ser., 1, no. 7 (July 1968), 311–20.

3. For the full story of the Ordnance Survey, see John H. Andrews, *A Paper Landscape: the Ordnance Survey in Nineteenth-Century Ireland* (Oxford: Clarendon Press, 1975).

land. His interest in Irish antiquity seems to have blossomed early. At eighteen he made a tour of County Wicklow, taking notes on its music and antiquities. Later he was to use his training as an artist in watercolors to contribute to illustrated guide books, enabling him to earn a living and pursue his scholarly interests. Already at thirty he was a member of the Royal Irish Academy and soon, as a member of its governing board, he took on a scientific reordering of its collections, besides adding new treasures, many of them now in the Irish National Museum. Actually, in intellectual journalism, as we have seen, he was ahead of the *Nation,* founding with Caesar Otway in 1832 the *Irish Penny Journal,* followed in 1841 by his own *Dublin Penny Journal,* which lasted only a year. Both these journals, with small circulations, were to stand for nonsectarianism and feature essays on Irish antiquities, language, history, poetry, and biography and the traditions of Irish localities. All his life a collector of Irish music, Petrie published only in 1855 his *Ancient Music of Ireland.* He was widely known in Dublin, was a friend of John Pigot and of Dr. William Stokes, who would eventually write his biography.[4]

The historical department of the Ordnance Survey needed Irish speakers, so Petrie and Larcom brought into the project John O'Donovan and Eugene O'Curry. Petrie's house in Great Charles Street was their office and a kind of center for scholars interested in Petrie's work and in Irish antiquities as well.

When the historical department of the Ordnance Survey was closed, O'Donovan, O'Curry, and Petrie went on with their own work, Petrie publishing in 1845 *The Ecclesiastical Architecture of Ireland* and including in it his already written *Essays on the Round Towers of Ireland.*[5] Earlier, there had been many fantastic theories

4. For Petrie on music, see Grace J. Calder, *George Petrie and the Ancient Music of Ireland* (Dublin: The Dolmen Press, 1968). Also William Stokes, *The Life and Labours in Art and Archeology of George Petrie* (London: Longmans, Green & Co., 1868).

5. *The Ecclesiastical Architecture of Ireland, Anterior to the Anglo-Norman Invasion,* Transactions of the Royal Irish Academy (Dublin: Hodges and Smith, 1845).

about these towers, but Petrie, in his carefully documented study, argued that they were ecclesiastical structures of Christian origin built as belfries, watchtowers, and storage places for monastic treasures.

In May 1845, Davis reviewed Petrie's *Ecclesiastical Architecture*, admitting that he had earlier formed opinions contrary to the arguments of the author. He confessed that Petrie had convinced him of his error, citing Petrie's long antiquarian studies, his familiarity with the country, and the aid he had received from the best Celtic scholarship during the progress of his work. Then Davis added: "The long time taken in preparation ensures maturity. . . ." He ended by thanking Petrie for having "the most learned, the most exact, and the most important work ever published on the antiquities of the ancient Irish nation."[6] Davis's language suggests his deep regard for scholarship though it was not his own.

It was not only the Ordnance workers like Petrie who were part of the Dublin intellectual scene in the 1840s. As we have noticed earlier, the *Dublin University Magazine*, founded in 1833 by a group of young Trinity graduates, Unionists to a man, was doing its work practically across the road from the *Nation* office. Among the editors and leading figures on the magazine were Isaac Butt; Charles Lever; John Anster, the translator of Goethe's *Faust;* and Samuel Ferguson, essayist and poet. Ferguson and Davis were to become good friends, and Ferguson's eulogy of Davis we have already noted. Some of its writers also contributed to the *Nation*. Among them were the novelist William Carleton, Petrie, O'Donovan, and Clarence Mangan, the poet. The *Nation* was very conscious of what the *University Magazine* was about, and some of its essays were noted in the *Nation*. Butt, one should notice, said that the *University Magazine* would be "a monthly advocate of the

6. *Nation*, 10 May 1845. Also in O'Donoghue, *Davis Essays*, 312–28.

Protestantism, the intelligence, and the respectability of Dublin."[7]
All the same, as Barbara Hayley observed, it spoke with an "Irish
voice," even though a non-nationalist one.

Davis, eager for the growth of art in Ireland, wrote regretfully
of the absence in England of the artists Daniel Maclise and
William Mulready, both Irishmen born. And then there was
Hogan, the sculptor, spending most of his creative life in Rome.
There was insufficient allowance in Davis's remarks for the simple fact that these gifted men could hardly make a living in Ireland. Nor was there the stimulus in Ireland that could be found
for any artist in great cities like Rome, Paris, Vienna, or London.
Nor was it only Irish artists who left home for wider possibilities
for their talents and careers. But of the power of visible works of
art Davis was fully aware. "To create a mass of great pictures, stat-
ues, buildings," he wrote, "is of the same sort of ennoblement to a
people as to create great poems or histories or make great codes
or win great battles."[8] Davis praised the work of Art Unions, doing what the government failed to do and working for prizes for
artists, some to be given by the Repeal Association as well. He argued for more art education and wrote on the casts taken from
Canova's molds, badly housed in the City of Cork.[9]

Despite his realization of the intangibles involved in artistic
creativity, Davis went ahead and drew up a list of Irish historical
events that could become subjects for paintings, trying to interest
his friend the artist Frederick Burton in the project.

Burton, who was a friend of Petrie and a collaborator in the
founding of an Irish Archeological Society, told Davis that free-
spirited art could never be forced.[10] Burton is an interesting man.

7. D. J. Hickey and J. E. Doherty, eds., *A Dictionary of Irish History Since 1800*
(Dublin: Gill and MacMillan; Totowa, N.J.: Barnes and Noble, 1980), 138.

8. *Nation*, 29 December 1843. Also in O'Donoghue, *Davis Essays*, 121.

9. *Nation*, 23 December 1843. Also in O'Donoghue, *Davis Essays*, 124–28.

10. See Duffy, *Young Ireland*, 153.

A friend of all the artists and writers in the various Dublin circles, he painted a number of Irish subjects such as *The Girl at the Holy Well* and *An Aran Fisherman's Dead Child.* Urged by Davis, he did the frontispiece for the *Spirit of the Nation.* Long years later, in the 1890s, as he was ending his career as Director of the National Gallery in London, he became a friend of Lady Gregory, who talked to him about his cover for the *Spirit of the Nation,* suggesting his inconsistency as a Unionist. Davis had persuaded him to do it, Burton told Lady Gregory. "He was such a dear fellow, I could refuse him nothing."[11] But if painters were absentees, there could still be a national gallery. This only came to pass in 1864, and one of the moving spirits in its creation was John Pigot, the long-cherished friend of Davis. It was a project which had been dear to the hearts of both young men.[12]

Two words sum up in part Davis's work and interests: improvement and preservation, and in this he was not unlike his English Victorian contemporaries. Looking constantly at ways the Irish could work together, he wrote, for instance, of all the work of preservation that the Catholic and Anglican clergy could do together in rescuing the ruins dotting the Irish countryside:

We cannot expect Government to do any thing . . . so liberal as to initiate the example of France, and pay men to describe and save these remains of the dead ages . . . but we do ask it of the clergy. Catholic, Protestant and Dissenter . . . we call upon the gentry, if they have any pride of blood, and on the people if they reverence old Ireland, to spare and guard every remnant of antiquity . . . we talk much of old Ireland

11. Lady Gregory, *Our Irish Theatre* (New York and London: G. P. Putnam's Sons, 1913), 52.

12. Catherine DeCourcy, *The Foundation of the National Gallery of Ireland* (Dublin: National Gallery of Ireland, 1985). Toward the end of 1853, John Pigot wrote a memorandum proposing a plan for founding a national gallery. The detail presented showed how much thought Pigot had given to the project. The first informal discussions were held at the home of Pigot's father, Lord Chief Baron, David Pigot. DeCourcy's book shows how extensive was the participation of the leading figures in the cultural and official life of Dublin, both Catholics and Protestants participating.

and plunder and ruin all that remains of it, we neglect its language, fiddle with its ruins, and spoil its monuments.[13]

He was equally vociferous in condemning some citizens of Meath who were planning a road which would go through what Davis called the Temple of Grange and we now know as New Grange. Tasteless blockheads, he called them, out of touch with the restoration work which was taking place in contemporary Europe, especially in France.[14]

Turning to more recent but still half-ruined buildings, he wrote:

Nor do we see why some of these hundreds of half spoiled buildings might not be used for civil purposes—as almshouses, schools, lecture rooms, town halls. It would always add another grace to an institution to have its home venerable with age and restored to beauty.[15]

Education, in its widest meaning, was also one of Davis's deepest concerns. We have already noticed his zeal for Repeal Reading Rooms, but his interests went far beyond, to the whole subject of how young people are educated. His essential moderation reveals itself in his attitude to the National Schools. He criticized them, as we have seen, for leaving Irish history out of their curricula, but praised them for making Ireland literate. He argued for better training and better wages for teachers, and for men and women who were dedicated to Ireland's welfare, not just doing a job. He called for schoolrooms with maps, globes, available reference libraries, situated and built so that the children would have around them gardens and small farming areas where they could learn something beyond what they saw at home, about efficient farming. Talking about books he urged young people who had the means to collect libraries, however small, but acknowledged that there were counties in Ireland without a single bookseller. He was

13. "Historical Monuments of Ireland," O'Donoghue, *Davis Essays,* 118.
14. "Irish Antiquities and Irish Savages," O'Donoghue, *Davis Essays,* 168.
15. Ibid., 172.

aware, always, that education went beyond the formal study of books, and wrote of the influences at work in children's lives; tolerance, curiosity, the setting of good examples were prominent in his thinking about educational influences.[16] His support for the plan for provincial colleges rested on a faith that educating young people together would have salutary effects on the future of Ireland, underestimating, probably, the pervasive religious animosities which would still be there when the young students came away from school back into general society.[17] Davis belongs outside of Irish political nationalism in a line of descent going back to the Royal Dublin Society (1731) and to the Royal Irish Academy (1785), and forward to the work of George Russell and Horace Plunkett.[18] In 1953, Radio Eireann began a series of lectures to make available to a wider public the findings of the newest scholarship, especially in history, literature, and language. A proposal was made and accepted that the series be called the Thomas Davis lectures. The lectures continue to this day, and exemplify exactly the kind of public education that Davis believed in. As a tribute and remembrance, the lectures are as fine as any Davis has ever received.[19]

Despite his advocacy of peasant proprietorship in his *Udalism and Feudalism*,[20] Davis left no further comprehensive economic treatise. As we have noted, he worked on the land question as a

16. See in O'Donoghue, *Davis Essays:* "Self-Education," "Popular Education," "Educate That You May Be Free," "Study," "The Library of Ireland." The Library of Ireland contained many volumes written by Young Irelanders, *The Volunteers* and *The American Revolution* among them. For a full list, see Francis MacManus, *Thomas Davis and Young Ireland* (Dublin: Government Publications, 1945), 109–13. Comments by P. S. O'Hegarty accompany the list.

17. *Nation,* 17 May 1845. Also in Rolleston, *Davis* (1890), 273–79.

18. The Royal Dublin Society (1731) was dedicated to Irish internal improvement. George Russell and Horace Plunkett were leaders in the Irish Agricultural Cooperative Movement at the end of the nineteenth century.

19. On the Thomas Davis lectures see T. W. Moody, "Thomas Davis and the Irish Nation," *Hermathena, A Dublin University Review* 103 (1966): 22.

20. See chap. 1.

committee member in the Repeal Association. In the *Nation* he wrote essays on self-help, on landlordism, and on the English industrial revolution as it might affect Ireland. Despite his fears of "dark satanic mills," he did not reject steam power and all that went with it. In a review of Robert Kane's *Industrial Resources of Ireland*,[21] he laments the loss of domestic manufacture. He wrote:

It may indeed be questioned whether the increased strength over matter then given to man compensates for the ill effects of forcing people to work in crowds, of lessening the distribution of wealth even by the very means which increase its production.

But if domestic manufacture is doomed, he argues, "we must make the best of our state, join our chief towns with railways, put quays to our harbours, mills on our rivers, turbines on our coasts and under restrictions and with guarantees set the steam engine to work on our flax, wool, and minerals."[22] Like Dr. Kane, he sees the need for industrial education. Nor does he note in this review the damage that English competition had already done to earlier Irish industries.

In another essay, "Commercial History of Ireland," he turns over to a prospective native parliament "this momentous subject," but advocates "protecting" duties in the first instance.[23]

Finally, we must say something further about Davis's attitude to England. Never did he underestimate its strength and fame, but always in his judgments condemned what he saw as its long oppression in Ireland. In the process he could sometimes write

21. A famous book. Kane, a chemist and lecturer at the Royal Dublin Society, was later president of Cork University. He felt strongly the need in Ireland for industrial education.

22. *Nation*, 25 June 1844. Also in O'Donoghue, *Davis, Essays*, 152–59.

23. "A Commercial History of Ireland," O'Donoghue, *Davis Essays*, 390. This essay is hardly profound when it talks of "creating vast manufactures." A constant lament in the Repeal Association was the disappearance of Irish industries in the face of British competition. See also "An Irish Steam Navy," in *Voice of the Nation*, 163–65. Davis brings up Norway's merchant navy and compares her connection with Sweden to that of Ireland's with England.

nonsense and make judgments unworthy of the historical sense he undoubtedly possessed. For instance, "France is an apostle of liberty—England the turnkey of the world."[24] One has only to look at the France of Louis Philippe and at the steadily reforming England of the 1830s and 1840s to see the unfairness of this comparison. Eventually, however, his attitude may have softened, and among his papers in the Royal Irish Academy there is a piece praising the British Parliament's grants to Maynooth and its enactment of the Colleges Bill. Furthermore Davis, like O'Connell, came to see that much might be gained by the dedicated work and services of the Irish members at Westminster. Peel's government, after his Irish reforms, could only go forward, presumably putting a new face on British-Irish relations. Also, as a judge with Smith O'Brien and John O'Connell of the Repeal Essay contest on a new constitution for Ireland, Davis and his two colleagues, in awarding a first prize to Michael Barry's essay, presumably endorsed his vision of a freely self-governing Ireland within the British Empire. It was a view which would evolve into the dominion status of a later time. One can surmise, possibly, that in these three years since the founding of the *Nation* Davis was reaching a more mature appreciation of the political relationship between the two countries.

Another aspect of Davis's evolving political thinking was his attitude to the Unionists, especially the Orangemen in Northeast Ulster and elsewhere. In his essay "Orange and Green,"[25] he picks up a theme from the *Evening Mail,* a strongly Protestant paper which had envisaged a truce among Irishmen with concessions on all sides. Davis looks forward to what he calls "more enlightened Orangemen," but also hopes that the other Ireland of Catholics will better understand "the apprehensions of the Or-

24. "Foreign Information," *Voice of the Nation,* 62.
25. Rolleston, *Davis* (1890), "Orange and Green," 270–72. See also in Rolleston the two essays "Moral Force," 250–52, and "Conciliation," 254–57.

angemen and allow for them in a more liberal spirit." There is not enough in this essay to draw any conclusions, but it does suggest that Davis might be realizing that his all-encompassing "nationality" might need some greater modification of attitude, some greater recognition of the pluralism of Irish society. What we write here is of course speculation, not fact.

We conclude with another piece from his private papers which has never appeared in any of the collections of his writings. It is a full explanation of what he understood nationality to be and indeed is a text for much of what he had written since 1842.

Nationality means the application of all the forces of a country to improve its physical comfort, enlarge its power, and enoble its soul. It means to a nation what prudence and great desires mean to an individual and can only be secured to the one as to the other by self-respect, self-rule, and self-reliance. A dependent mind is a false, an insecure, and a low mind. . . .

In seeking Nationality the Irish seek to get the whole means of Ireland at the disposal of those who know and love them best—their own chief spirits; and revolt against England because the English parliament has too little familiarity with us and too much elsewhere to regard, because it cannot feel for us with the . . . sympathy that Irishmen could, and because it has neither time nor a sufficiently powerful machinery for the wise government of Ireland.[26]

The immediate epilogue to our story, coming the same year as Thomas Davis's death, was the potato blight which brought on the famine and with it the terrible last years of the decade. Many commentators on Davis's life have speculated on what, had he lived, he would have done in the face of this national tragedy. We simply cannot know.

The larger epilogue is the whole history of Ireland in the years before 1900. During these years the British government so harshly castigated by Davis and Duffy turned its attention to serious

26. Gavan Duffy Papers, 12P15 (13), Royal Irish Academy.

Irish reforms, pushed, to be sure, by the Irish themselves. The franchise was extended both in England and in Ireland; the Ballot Act of 1872 took from the landlord control over his tenants' vote. The Anglican Church was disestablished in 1869. Various land acts, crowned by the Land Purchase Act of 1903, created the peasant proprietorship which Davis had advocated, changing the social texture of the country. The Local Government Act of 1898 as well took away the political power of the landlords in the countryside. Finally, the legislation of 1908 settled the long-standing claims of Catholics regarding university education. It had taken nearly a century but the prophecy of Count Cavour was fulfilled: that the British government would reform Ireland. In fact what had occurred was a revolution by constitutional means.[27] In the process the Protestant landed interest, though indemnified for its lands, was sacrificed, as was, ultimately, the wider Protestant influence in the greater part of the country. How Davis's own Protestant people would have fared under an Irish parliament, had one been brought into existence, can only be a matter for speculation. Both Davis and indeed Parnell had hoped for a serious Protestant role in the government of the country.[28]

As for Young Ireland, there are personal epilogues. Smith O'Brien and Dillon involved themselves in the ill-fated rising of 1848. For O'Brien it meant years of penal exile in Australia. For Dillon, escape to America was followed by a legal career in New York and a later return to Ireland. Death cut short the parliamentary career he had hoped to pursue. John O'Hagan was to have a successful legal career and to preside over the Land Court established after the Land Act of 1881. He remained as well a man with wide literary interests. Pigot had a less successful legal career, fi-

27. For the clearest brief statement of what happened, see J. C. Beckett, "Ireland Under the Union," in his *Confrontations: Studies in Irish History* (London: Faber, 1972), 142–51.
28. For Parnell and the Protestants, see the interesting thesis of Paul Bew, *C. S. Parnell* (Dublin: Gill and MacMillan, 1980), 142.

nally emigrating to India, where as a lawyer in Bombay he made something of a fortune. Returning to Ireland and perhaps again reentering public life, he died prematurely in 1871, at the age of forty-nine. Duffy outlived all the friends of his youth, dying in 1903 at the age of eighty-seven.

Duffy's career we have already noticed in our Introduction: his years as a colonial statesman in the Australian colony of Victoria, his voluminous writings on Young Ireland, his knighthood. Returning to Europe in 1879, he took no active public part in the controversies surrounding Irish Home Rule, but he did write some interesting articles on the subject. In 1887 he published in the *Contemporary Review* "A Fair Constitution for Ireland." Ireland, he wrote, was a heterogeneous not a homogeneous nation, and no constitutional settlement which did not content the Irish Protestants would be in the least lasting. The Catholics, despite their historical grievances, must not think of themselves as victors. Justice, not victory, would alone make a hopeful future for Ireland. Without abandoning Davis's and his own all-Ireland patriotism, he had nevertheless realized that it might have its limits. The entire essay reflects the experience of a man whose career had familiarized him with the realities of practical politics.[29]

As for Pigot, the deeper ideals of Davis remained his own. In a letter to Smith O'Brien in 1858 expressing his disapproval of the tone of the nationalist newspapers, he wrote:

To be national without exaggeration or boasting, to be separatist without seditious rhetoric, to be energetic without being ungentlemanly in violence, to be pure and free from mean personality was the boast of Davis's *Nation*.[30]

If one writes any final judgment on Thomas Davis, one must abandon the easy categories of success and failure. Looking at the

29. "A Fair Constitution for Ireland," *Contemporary Review* 52 (September 1887), 301–32.
30. Pigot to O'Brien, 17 December 1858. Smith O'Brien Papers, MS 446, letter 3077, National Library of Ireland.

state of his country in 1840 he saw how much needed to be done, and he moved to act in ways that he found open to him. But in joining with O'Connell for the repeal of the Union he never forgot his deeper aims, namely the regeneration and improvement of his country.

To be sure, he left a mixed legacy of ends and means, as we have suggested in examining some of the contradictions between his prose and poetry, and indeed in the larger body of his writings. In the end, however, he was like O'Connell, a constitutional reformer. It was a brief life nobly lived, dedicated to a better future for all his countrymen. It has been, outside political life, a moving memory which has never yet been forgotten.

Appendix
A Selection of the Poems of Thomas Davis

These poems of Thomas Davis have often been quoted and have lent emotional force to the themes and subject matter of his prose: Irish history, the cessation of old feuds, visions of a new Irish nation. As we have noted, there are contradictions between his prose and the poetry, which do not fully reveal all the complications of Davis's thinking.

Great poetry these were not, but they carried messages which had a place later on in nationalist thinking and feeling, beyond Davis's own views.

Celts and Saxons

I.

We hate the Saxon and the Dane,
*   We hate the Norman men—*
We cursed their greed for blood and gain,
*   We curse them now again.*
Yet start not, Irish born man!
*   If you're to Ireland true,*
We heed not blood, nor creed, nor clan—
*   We have no curse for you.*

II.

We have no curse for you or yours
*   But Friendship's ready grasp,*
And Faith to stand by you and yours
*   Unto our latest gasp—*
To stand by you against all foes,

Howe'er, or whence they come,
With traitor arts, or bribes, or blows,
From England, France, or Rome.

III.

What matter that at different shrines
We pray unto one God—
What matter that at different times
Our fathers won this sod—
In fortune and in name we're bound
By stronger links than steel;
And neither can be safe nor sound
But in the other's weal.

IV.

As Nubian rocks, and Ethiop sand
Long drifting down the Nile,
Built up old Egypt's fertile land
For many a hundred mile;
So Pagan clans to Ireland came,
And clans of Christendom,
Yet joined their wisdom and their fame
To build a nation from.

V.

Here came the brown Phoenician,
The man of trade and toil—
Here came the proud Milesian,
Ahungering for spoil;
And the Firbolg and the Cymry,
And the hard, enduring Dane,
And the iron Lords of Normandy,
With the Saxons in their train,

VI.

And oh!   it were a gallant deed
To show before mankind,

How every race and every creed
   Might be by love combined—
Might be combined, yet not forget
   The fountains whence they rose,
As, filled by many a rivulet,
   The stately Shannon flows.

VII.

Nor would we wreak our ancient feud
   On Belgian or on Dane,
Nor visit in a hostile mood
   The hearths of Gaul or Spain;
But long as on our country lies
   The Anglo-Norman yoke,
Their tyranny we'll signalize,
   And God's revenge invoke.

VIII.

We do not hate, we never cursed,
   Nor spoke a foeman's word
Against a man in Ireland nursed,
   Howe'er we thought he erred;
So start not, Irish born man,
   If you're to Ireland true,
We heed not race, nor creed, nor clan,
   We've hearts and hands for you.

Orange and Green Will Carry the Day

I.

Ireland! rejoice, and England! deplore—
Faction and feud are passing away.
'Twas a low voice, but 'tis a loud roar,
   "Orange and Green will carry the day."
      Orange! Orange!
      Green and Orange!

Pitted together in many a fray—
    Lions in fight!
    And linked in their might,
Orange and Green will carry the day.
    Orange! Orange!
    Green and Orange!
Wave together o'er mountain and bay.
    Orange and Green!
    Our King and our Queen!
    "Orange and Green will carry the day!"

II.

Rusty the swords our fathers unsheathed—
    William and James are turned to clay—
Long did we till the wrath they bequeathed;
    Red was the crop, and bitter the pay!
        Freedom fled us!
        Knaves misled us!
Under the feet of the foemen we lay—
        Riches and strength
        We'll win them at length,
For Orange and Green will carry the day!
        Landlords fooled us;
        England ruled us,
Hounding our passions to make us their prey
        But, in their spite,
        The Irish UNITE,
And Orange and Green will carry the day!

III.

Fruitful our soil where honest men starve;
    Empty the mart, and shipless the bay;
Out of our want the Oligarchs carve;
    Foreigners fatten on our decay!
        Disunited,
        Therefore blighted,
Ruined and rent by the Englishman's sway;
        Party and creed

For once have agreed—
Orange and Green will carry the day!
Boyne's old water,
Red with slaughter!
Now is as pure as an infant at play;
So, in our souls,
Its history rolls,
And Orange and Green will carry the day!

IV.

English deceit can rule us no more,
Bigots and knaves are scattered like spray—
Deep was the oath the Orangeman swore,
"Orange and Green must carry the day!"
Orange! Orange!
Bless the Orange!
Tories and Whigs grew pale with dismay,
When, from the North,
Burst the cry forth,
"Orange and Green will carry the day;"
No surrender!
No Pretender!
Never to falter and never betray—
With an Amen,
We swear it again,
ORANGE AND GREEN SHALL CARRY THE DAY.

The West's Asleep

I.

When all beside a vigil keep,
The West's asleep, the West's asleep—
Alas! and well may Erin weep,
When Connaught lies in slumber deep.
There lake and plain smile fair and free,

'Mid rocks—their guardian chivalry—
Sing oh! let man learn liberty
From crashing wind and lashing sea.

II.

That chainless wave and lovely land
Freedom and Nationhood demand—
Be sure, the great God never planned,
For slumbering slaves, a home so grand.
And, long, a brave and haughty race
Honoured and sentinelled the place—
Sing oh! not even their sons' disgrace
Can quite destroy their glory's trace.

III.

For often, in O'Connor's van,
To triumph dashed each Connaught clan—
And fleet as deer the Normans ran
Through Corlieu's Pass and Ardrahan.
And later times saw deeds as brave;
And glory guards Clanricarde's grave—
Sing oh! they died their land to save,
At Aughrim's slopes and Shannon's wave.

IV.

And if, when all a vigil keep,
The West's asleep, the West's asleep—
Alas! and well may Erin weep,
That Connaught lies in slumber deep.
But—hark!—some voice like thunder spake:
"The West's awake! the West's awake!"—
"Sing oh! hurra! let England quake,
We'll watch till death for Erin's sake!"

The Penal Days

I.

Oh! weep those days, the penal days,
When Ireland hopelessly complained.
Oh! weep those days, the penal days,
When godless persecution reigned;
When year by year,
For serf, and peer,
Fresh cruelties were made by law,
And, filled with hate,
Our senate sate
To weld anew each fetter's flaw;
Oh! weep those days, those penal days—
Their memory still on Ireland weighs.

II.

They bribed the flock, they bribed the son,
To sell the priest and rob the sire;
Their dogs were taught alike to run
Upon the scent of wolf and friar.
Among the poor,
Or on the moor,
Were hid the pious and the true—
While traitor knave,
And recreant slave,
Had riches, rank, and retinue:
And, exiled in those penal days,
Our banners over Europe blaze.

III.

A stranger held the land and tower
Of many a noble fugitive;
No Popish lord had lordly power,
The peasant scarce had leave to live
Above his head
A ruined shed,
No tenure but a tyrant's will—

Forbid to plead,
Forbid to read,
Disarmed, disfranchised, imbecile—
What wonder if our step betrays
The freedman, born in penal days?

IV.

They're gone, they're gone, those penal days!
All creeds are equal in our isle;
Then grant, O Lord, thy plenteous grace,
Our ancient feuds to reconcile.
Let all atone
For blood and groan
For dark revenge and open wrong,
Let all unite
For Ireland's right,
And drown our griefs in freedom's song;
Till time shall veil in twilight haze,
The memory of those penal days.

A Nation Once Again

I.

When boyhood's fire was in my blood
I read of ancient free men,
For Greece and Rome who bravely stood,
THREE HUNDRED MEN AND THREE MEN
And then I prayed I yet might see
Our fetters rent in twain,
And Ireland, long a province, be
A NATION ONCE AGAIN.

II.

And, from that time, through wildest woe,
That hope has shone, a far light;

Nor could love's brightest summer glow
Outshine that solemn starlight:
It seemed to watch above my head
In forum, field, and fane;
Its angel voice sang round my bed,
"A NATION ONCE AGAIN."

III.

It whispered, too, that "freedom's ark
And service high and holy,
Would be profaned by feelings dark
And passions vain or lowly:
For freedom comes from God's right hand
And needs a godly train;
And righteous men must make our land
A NATION ONCE AGAIN."

IV.

So, as I grew from boy to man,
I bent me to that bidding—
My spirit of each selfish plan
And cruel passion ridding;
For, thus I hoped some day to aid—
Oh! can such hope be vain?—
When my dear country shall be made
A NATION ONCE AGAIN.

Lament for the Death of Eoghan Ruadh O'Neill

I.

"Did they dare, did they dare, to slay Eoghan Ruadh O'Neill?"
"Yes, they slew with poison him, they feared to meet with steel."
May God wither up their hearts! May their blood cease to flow!
May they walk in living death, who poisoned Eoghan Ruadh!

II.

Though it break my heart to hear, say again the bitter words.
"From Derry, against Cromwell, he marched to measure swords;
But the weapon of the Sassanach met him on his way,
And he died at Cloch Uachtar, upon St. Leonard's day."

III.

Wail, wail ye for the Mighty One!   Wail, wail ye for the Dead;
Quench the hearth, and hold the breath—with ashes strew the head.
How tenderly we loved him!   How deeply we deplore!
Holy Saviour! but to think we shall never see him more.

IV.

Sagest in the council was he, kindest in the Hall!
Sure we never won a battle—'twas Eoghan won them all.
Had he lived—had he lived—our dear country had been free;
But he's dead, but he's dead, and 'tis slaves we'll ever be.

V.

O'Farrell and Clanrickarde, Preston and Red Hugh,
Audley, and MacMahon—ye are valiant, wise, and true;
But—what, what are ye all to our darling who is gone?
The Rudder of our Ship was he, our Castle's corner stone!

VI.

Wail, wail him through the Island!   Weep, weep for our pride!
Would that on the battle-field our gallant chief had died!
Weep the Victor of Beann-bhorbh—weep him, young man and old;
Weep for him, ye women—your Beautiful lies cold!

VII.

We thought you would not die—we were sure you would not go,
And leave us in our utmost need to Cromwell's cruel blow—
Sheep without a shepherd, when the snow shuts out the sky—
Oh! why did you leave us, Eoghan?   Why did you die?

VIII.

Soft as a woman's was your voice, O'Neill! bright was your eye,
Oh! why did you leave us, Eoghan?   Why did you die?
Your troubles are all over, you're at rest with God on high,
But we're slaves, and we're orphans, Eoghan!—why did you die?

Ireland [My Land]

I.

She is a rich and rare land;
Oh! she's a fresh and fair land;
She is a dear and rare land-
  This native land of mine.

II.

No men than hers are braver—
Her women's hearts ne'er waver;
I'd freely die to save her,
  And think my lot divine.

III.

She's not a dull or cold land;
No! she's a warm and bold land;
Oh! she's a true and old land—
  This native land of mine.

IV.

Could beauty ever guard her,
And virtue still reward her,
No foe would cross her border—
  No friend within it pine!

V.

Oh! she's a fresh and fair land;
Oh! she's a true and rare land;
Yes! she's a rare and fair land—
  This native land of mine.

Bibliography

Manuscript Sources

National Library of Ireland
　　Thomas Davis Papers
　　Charles Gavan Duffy Papers
　　William Smith O'Brien Papers
　　W. J. O'Neill Daunt Journal

Royal Irish Academy
　　Charles Gavan Duffy Papers (contain Davis materials)

Pearse Street Library

　　R. R. Madden Papers
　　Madden, the historian of the United Irishmen, was the author of a
　　History of the Irish Periodical Press, of which only two volumes were
　　published. Madden's notes for his projected third volume contain im-
　　portant interviews with Irish journalists. Duffy was among them and
　　talked to Madden about Davis and the *Nation.*

Trinity College, Dublin
　　John Blake Dillon Papers
　　W. E. H. Lecky Papers (correspondence with Duffy)

Parliamentary Debates
　　Hansard's Parliamentary Debates, Third Series, 1830–48
　　(especially 1842–45)

Parliamentary Papers
　　Report from Her Majesty's Commissioners of Inquiry Into the State
　　of the Law and Practice in Respect to the Occupation of Land in Ire-
　　land, *HC* 1845 (605), XiX, 1–56 (Devon Commission)

Newspapers and Periodicals

Citizen; later *The Dublin Monthly Magazine*
Dublin Review
Dublin University Magazine
Eire—Ireland
Freeman's Journal
History Ireland
Irish Book Lover
Irish Economic and Social History
Irish Historical Studies
Irish Monthly
Morning Register
Nation
New Ireland Review
Northern Whig
Studia Hibernica
Studies
Ulster Folklife
Vindicator
Warder

Writings by Thomas Davis

The Reform of the Lords; By a Graduate of the Dublin University. Dublin: Published for the author by M. Goodwin & Co. Printers, 1837. (Copy in Royal Irish Academy.)

An Address Read Before the College Historical Society, Dublin, 20 June 1840. Dublin: Printed for the Society by Webb and Chapman. (Copies in Trinity and National Library of Ireland.)

Articles in the *Morning Register,* Feb.–July 1841.

Essays in the *Citizen/Dublin Monthly Magazine,* 1839–43. Includes essays by Davis on India discussed in the present work, and also the well-known "Patriot Parliament of 1689." (Complete set of the *Citizen* in the Royal Irish Academy.)

Contributions to the *Nation,* 1842–45. Davis's bound copies, 1842–43 and 1843–44, are in the Royal Irish Academy. Only in Vol. 1 are the articles initialed. See K. M. MacGrath, "Writers in the *Nation,* 1842–45," *Irish Historical Studies* 6 (March 1949): 199–223, for identifications.

Contributions (poetry) to *Spirit of the Nation, or Ballads and Songs by the Writ-*

ers of the Nation. Part I, Dublin: The Nation office and James Duffy; Part II, Dublin: James Duffy, 1843.

Contributions to the quarto edition of the *Spirit* with music. Preface by Davis. Dublin: James Duffy, 1845.

Speeches of the Right Honorable John Philpot Curran. Edited by Thomas Davis, with a Memoir by Davis. Dublin: James Duffy, 1843. A new edition revised and corrected. Dublin: James Duffy, 1845.

Contributions to *The Voice of the Nation: A Manual of Nationality.* By the writers of the *Nation.* Dublin: James Duffy, 1844. (Articles all initialed.)

Contributions to *Reports of the Parliamentary Committee of the Loyal National Repeal Association of Ireland.* 3 vols. Dublin: J. Browne, 1844–46.

Work by Thomas Davis edited by others.
All published after 1845.

Press cuttings related to Davis, 1847–1922. National Library of Ireland MS 14056.

Davis, Thomas. *Literary and Historical Essays.* Edited by Charles Gavan Duffy. Dublin: James Duffy, 1846. (In American editions, poems and essays bound together.)

———. *The Poems of Thomas Davis: Now First Collected.* Edited by Thomas Wallis. Dublin: James Duffy, 1846.

———. *Letters of a Protestant on Repeal.* Edited by T. F. Meagher. Dublin: Printed by William Holden for the Irish Confederation, 1847. (These letters, written in the guise of an anonymous Protestant, were published in the *Nation,* 1842–43.)

Rolleston, T. W., ed. *Prose Writings of Thomas Davis.* London: Walter Scott, 1890.

Duffy, Charles Gavan, ed. *The Patriot Parliament of 1689 with its Debates, Votes, and Proceedings,* by Thomas Davis. London: T. Fisher Unwin; Dublin: Sealy, Bryers, and Walker; New York: P. J. Kenedy, 1893.

O'Donoghue, D. J., ed. *Essays Literary and Historical by Thomas Davis.* Preface by D. J. O'Donoghue and an essay by John Mitchel. Centenary edition. Dundalk, Ireland: W. Tempest, Dundalgan Press, 1914.

Rolleston, T. W., ed. *Thomas Davis, Selections From His Prose and Poetry.* London and Leipsic: T. Fisher Unwin, 1914.

Griffith, Arthur, ed. *Thomas Davis, The Thinker and Teacher: the Essence of His Writings in Prose and Poetry.* Dublin: Gill, 1914.

Davis, Thomas. *Essays and Poems, with a Centenary Memoir, 1845–1945.* Foreword by An Taoiseach, Eamon de Valera. Dublin: Gill, 1945. No editor indicated.

Contemporary Sources: Documents, Letters, Books, Articles.
Some written later but of contemporary significance.

Barry, Michael J. "Ireland As She Was, As She Is, and As She Shall Be." (First Prize Repeal Essay.) In *Repeal Prize Essays*. Dublin: James Duffy, 1845.

_____. *The Songs of Ireland*. Introduction by Thomas Davis. Dublin: James Duffy, 1845.

Burke, Bernard. *Burke's Genealogical and Heraldic History of the Landed Gentry of Ireland*. 4th ed. Edited by L. G. Pine. London: Burke's Peerage, 1958.

Calder, Grace J. *George Petrie and the Ancient Music of Ireland*. Dublin: Dolmen Press, 1968.

Dagg, T. S. C. *College Historical Society: A History (1770–1920)*. Cork: Privately printed, 1969.

Daunt, Alice O'Neill, ed. *A Life Spent for Ireland: Being Selections from the Journals of the late W. J. O'Neill Daunt*. London: T. Fisher Unwin, 1896.

DeBeaumont, Gustave. *L'Irlande, Sociale, Politique, et Religieuse*. 2 vols. Paris: Librarie de C. Gosselin, 1839.

Doheny, Michael. *The Felon's Track*. New York: Farrell & Sons, 1867.

Duffy, Charles Gavan, ed. *The Ballad Poetry of Ireland*. Dublin: J. Duffy, 1846.

_____. *Young Ireland: a Fragment of Irish History, 1840–1850*. London: Cassell, 1880.

_____. *Thomas Davis: the Memoirs of an Irish Patriot, 1840–1846*. London: Kegan Paul, 1890. (A source book as well as a biography.)

_____. *Short Life of Thomas Davis*. London: T. Fisher Unwin; Dublin: Sealy, Bryers and Walker, 1896.

_____. *My Life in Two Hemispheres*. 2 vols. (Vol. 1 to 1849). London: T. Fisher Unwin, 1898. Reprint 1969. Introduction by J. H. Whyte. Shannon: Irish University Press.

Ferguson, Samuel. "Thomas Davis." *Dublin University Magazine* 29 (1847): 190–99.

Ferguson, Lady Mary. *Sir Samuel Ferguson in the Ireland of His Day*. 2 vols. Edinburgh: William Blackwood, 1896.

Fitzpatrick, W. J., ed. *Correspondence of Daniel O'Connell*. 2 vols. London: John Murray, 1888.

Hayley, Barbara. *Carleton's Traits and Stories and the 19th-Century Anglo-Irish Tradition*. Gerrards Cross: Colin Smythe, 1983.

Hennessy, J. Pope. "What Do the Irish Read." *Nineteenth Century* 15 (June 1884): 920–32.

Hodgson, W. B., trans. *Count Cavour on Ireland: Thoughts on Ireland, Its Present and Future*. London: Trubner, 1868.

Hone, J. M., ed. *The Love Story of Thomas Davis, Told in the Letters of Annie Hutton.* Dublin: Cuala Press, 1945.

Hutton, Annie, trans. *The Embassy in Ireland of Monsignor G. B. Rinuccini, Archbishop of Férmo in the Years 1645–1649.* Dublin: A. Thom, 1873.

Kane, Robert. *The Industrial Resources of Ireland.* Dublin: Hodges and Smith, 1844.

Larkin, Emmet, ed. and trans. *Alexis de Tocqueville's Journey in Ireland, July–August, 1835.* Washington, D.C.: The Catholic University of America Press, 1990.

Levy, John, ed. *A Full and Revised Report of the Three Days Discussion in the Corporation of Dublin on the Repeal of the Union.* Dublin: J. Duffy, 1843.

Lewis, G. Cornewall. *Local Disturbances in Ireland and On the Irish Church Question.* London: B. Fellowes, 1836.

Locker-Lampson, G. T. L. *A Consideration of the State of Ireland in the Nineteenth Century.* London: Constable, 1907.

MacDermot, Brian. ed. *The Catholic Question in Ireland & England, 1798–1882: the Papers of Denys Scully.* Dublin: Irish Academic Press, 1988.

Madden, R. R. *The History of Irish Periodical Literature, From the End of the 17th to the Middle of the 19th Century: Its Origin, Progress, and Results: With Notices of Remarkable Persons Connected with the Press in Ireland During the Past Two Centuries.* 2 vols. London: Newby, 1867. (Notes for a projected third volume are in Pearse Street Library, Dublin.)

Maddyn, Daniel Owen. *Ireland and Its Rulers Since 1829.* 3 vols. London: Newby, 1843–1844. (Contained in vol. 3 is the famous portrait of Davis under the name Dormer.)

Mitchel, John. *The Last Conquest of Ireland (Perhaps).* Dublin: The Irishman, 1861.

O'Connell, Daniel. *Correspondence.* 8 vols. Edited by Maurice O'Connell. 1972–80. Vols. 1–3. Shannon, Ireland: Irish University Press. Vol. 4. Dublin: Stationery Office. Vols. 5–8. Dublin: Blackwater Press.

_____. *Daniel O'Connell: His Early Life and Journal, 1795–1802.* Edited by Arthur Houston. London: Pitman Press, 1906.

O'Connell, John, ed. *Life and Speeches of Daniel O'Connell.* Dublin: J. Duffy, 1846.

O'Hagan, John. "Diary: Leinster and Munster in the Summer of 1844." *Irish Monthly* 40 (1912): I, 454–70; II, 517–28; III, 580–90.

_____. "Irish Patriotism: Thomas Davis." *Contemporary Review* 58 (October 1890): 590–608.

O'Leary, John. *Recollections of Fenians and Fenianism.* 2 vols. Introduction by Marcus Bourke. New York: Barnes and Noble, 1969. First published in London, 1896.

Parker, Charles S. *Sir Robert Peel From His Private Papers.* 3 vols. London: John Murray, 1899.

Pigot, John E. "Letters from Davis to Pigot." *Irish Monthly* 16 (1888): 261–70, 335–48. (These letters were presumably given to Matthew Russell, editor of the *Irish Monthly.* by some member of Pigot's family. Pigot had died in 1871.)

Reports of the Parliamentary Committee of the Loyal National Repeal Association of Ireland. 3 vols. Dublin: J. Browne, 1844–46. (Davis wrote many of these reports.)

Russell, Matthew. "Contributions to Irish Biographies: John Edward Pigot." *Irish Monthly* 24 (May 1896): 225–37. (Contains excerpts from Pigot's *Journal* on the death of Davis and their plans for the future.)

Stokes, William. *The Life and Labours in Art and Archeology of George Petrie.* London: Longmans, Green & Co., 1868.

Stokes, William (son). *William Stokes: His Life and Work, 1804–1875.* London: T. Fisher Unwin, 1898.

Sullivan, A. M. *The Story of Ireland.* Dublin: A. M. Sullivan, 1867.

Thomson, David, and Moyra McGusty, eds. *The Irish Journals of Elizabeth Smith, 1840–1850.* Oxford: Clarendon Press, 1980.

Venedey, Jacob. *Ireland and the Irish During the Repeal Year.* Dublin: J. Duffy, 1844.

Wyse, Sir Thomas. *Historical Sketch of the Late Catholic Association of Ireland.* 2 vols. London: H. Colburn, 1829.

Zimmerman, Georges-Denis. *Songs of Irish Rebellion: Political Street Ballads and Rebel Songs, 1780–1900.* Dublin: Allen Figgis, 1967. First published as *Irish Political Street Ballads and Rebel Songs.* Geneva: Impr. la Sirene, 1966.

Selected Secondary Sources.

Akenson, Donald H. *The Irish Education Experiment: the National System of Education in the Nineteenth Century.* London: Routledge and Kegan Paul; Toronto: University of Toronto Press, 1970.

———. *Small Differences: Irish Catholics and Irish Protestants, 1815–1922.* Kingston, Canada: McGill-Queens University Press, 1988.

Andrews, John H. *A Paper Landscape: the Ordnance Survey in Nineteenth-Century Ireland.* Oxford: Clarendon Press, 1975.

Auchmuty, James J. *Sir Thomas Wyse, 1791–1862: the Life and Career of an Educator and Diplomat.* London: P. S. King & Sons, 1939.

Barrett, Cyril. "Irish Nationalism and Art." *Studies* 64 (winter 1975): 393–409.

Bartlett, Thomas. "The Catholic Question in the Eighteenth Century." *History Ireland* 1, no. 1 (1993).

_____. *The Fall and Rise of the Irish Nation: the Catholic Question 1690–1830*. Dublin: Gill and MacMillan, 1992.

Bartlett, Thomas, Chris Curran, Riana O'Dwyer, and M. A. G. O'Tuathaigh, eds. *Irish Studies: a General Introduction*. Dublin: Gill and MacMillan, 1988.

Beames, Michael. *Peasants and Power: The Whiteboy Movements and Their Control in Pre-Famine Ireland*. Brighton: Harvester, 1983.

Beckett, J. C. *The Anglo-Irish Tradition*. Ithaca, N.Y.: Cornell University Press, 1976.

_____. *Confrontations: Studies in Irish History*. London: Faber & Faber, 1972.

_____. "Ireland Under the Union." In *Confrontations: Studies in Irish History*, 142–51. London: Faber & Faber, 1972. Originally published in *Topic* 13 (1967): 34–44.

_____. *The Making of Modern Ireland, 1603–1923*. New York: Alfred A. Knopf, 1966.

_____. *The Study of Irish History: an Inaugural Lecture Delivered Before the Queen's University of Belfast on 13 March 1963*. Belfast: Queens University, 1963.

Bew, Paul. *C. S. Parnell*. Dublin: Gill and MacMillan, 1980.

Black, R. D. C. *Economic Thought and the Irish Question, 1817–1870*. Cambridge: Cambridge University Press, 1960.

Bolton, G. C. *The Passing of the Irish Act of Union*. London: Oxford University Press, 1966.

Bowen, Desmond. *The Protestant Crusade in Ireland 1800–1870*. Dublin: Gill and MacMillan, 1978.

Boyce, D. George. *Nationalism in Ireland*. 3rd ed. London: Routledge, 1995.

_____. *Nineteenth-Century Ireland: the Search for Stability*. Dublin: Gill and MacMillan, 1990.

Boylan, Henry. *A Dictionary of Irish Biography*. Dublin: Gill and MacMillan; New York: Barnes & Noble, 1978. 2nd ed., Dublin: Gill and MacMillan, 1988.

Boyne, Patricia. *John O'Donovan (1806–1861): A Biography*. Kilkenny: Boethius, 1987.

Bradshaw, Brendan. "Nationalism and Historical Scholarship in Modern Ireland." *Irish Historical Studies* 26, no. 104 (November 1989): 329–51.

Broderick, John F. *The Holy See and the Irish Movement for the Repeal of the Union with England, 1829–1847*. Rome: Gregorian University, 1951.

Broeker, Galen. *Rural Disorder and Police Reform in Ireland, 1812–36*. London: Routledge and Kegan Paul, 1970.

Brown, Terence, and Barbara Hayley, eds. *Samuel Ferguson: a Centenary Tribute*. Dublin: Royal Irish Academy, 1988.

Brown, T. N. "Nationalism and the Irish Peasant, 1800–1846." *Review of Politics* 15 (October 1953): 403–45.

Bryan, Dan. "Thomas Davis as a Military Influence." *An Cosantoir* 5 (1945): 551–58.

Cahalan, James M. "*Great Hatred, Little Room*": the Irish Historical Novel. Dublin: Gill and Macmillan, 1983.

Cahill, Gilbert. "Irish Catholicism and English Toryism." *Review of Politics* 19, no. 1 (January 1957): 62–76.

———. "The Protestant Association and the Anti-Maynooth Agitation of 1845." *Catholic Historical Review* 43, no. 3 (October 1957): 273–308.

Clark, G. S. Kitson. "The Romantic Element, 1830." In *Studies in Social History: A Tribute to G. M. Trevelyan,* edited by J. H. Plumb, 211–39. London, New York: Longmans Green, 1955.

Clark, Samuel, and James Donnelly, Jr., eds. *Irish Peasants: Violence and Political Unrest, 1780–1914.* Paperback edition. Dublin: Gill and MacMillan, 1983.

Clarke, Desmond. "The Contribution of the Royal Dublin Society to Science and Technology in Ireland." *Administration* 15 (1967): 25–34.

Clarke, Randall. "The Relations between O'Connell and the Young Irelanders." *Irish Historical Studies* 3, no. 9 (March 1942): 18–30.

Coldrey, Barry M. *Faith and Fatherland: The Christian Brothers and the Development of Irish Nationalism, 1838–1921.* Dublin: Gill and MacMillan, 1988.

Collins, Kevin. *The Cultural Conquest of Ireland.* Cork: Mercier, 1990.

Colum, Padraic. *Arthur Griffith.* Dublin: Browne & Nolan, 1959.

Comerford, R. V. *Charles Kickham: A Study in Irish Nationalism and Literature.* Dublin: Wolfhound Press, 1979.

———. "Nation, Nationalism, and the Irish Language." In *Perspectives on Irish Nationalism,* edited by Thomas E. Hachey and Lawrence J. McCaffrey, 20–41. Lexington, Ky.: University Press of Kentucky, 1989.

Connell, K. H. *The Population of Ireland, 1750–1845.* Oxford: Clarendon Press, 1950.

Connolly, S. J. *Priests and People in Pre-Famine Ireland, 1780–1845.* Dublin: Gill and MacMillan, 1982.

Corish, Patrick. *The Irish Catholic Experience: a Historical Survey.* Dublin: Gill and MacMillan, 1985.

Crone, J. S. *A Concise Dictionary of Irish Biography.* Dublin: Talbot Press, 1928.

Cronin, John. *The Anglo-Irish Novel.* Vol. 1, the Nineteenth Century; vol. 2, 1900–1940. Belfast: Appletree, 1980, 1990.

Crossman, Virginia. *Local Government in Nineteenth-Century Ireland.* Belfast: Institute of Irish Studies, 1994.

Crotty, Raymond D. *Irish Agricultural Production: Its Volume and Structure.* Cork: Cork University Press, 1966.

Cullen, L. M. "The Cultural Basis of Irish Nationalism." In *The Roots of Nationalism: Studies in Northern Europe,* edited by Rosalind Mitchison, 91–106. Edinburgh: Donald, 1980.

_____. *The Emergence of Modern Ireland.* New York: Holmes and Meier, 1981.

_____, ed. *The Formation of the Irish Economy.* Cork: Mercier Press, 1969.

Curtis, Edmund. "Irish History and Its Popular Versions." *The Irish Rosary* 29 (May 1925): 321–29.

Curtis, L. P., Jr. *Anglo-Saxons and Celts: a Study of Anti-Irish Prejudice in Victorian England.* Bridgeport, Conn.: Published by the Conference on British Studies at the University of Bridgeport, 1968.

_____. *Apes and Angels. The Irishman in Victorian Caricature.* Rev. ed. Washington, D. C., and London: Smithsonian Institution Press, 1997.

_____. "Moral and Physical Force: the Language of Violence in Irish Nationalism." *Journal of British Studies* 27, no. 1 (January 1988): 150–89.

Daly, Mary E. "The Development of the National Schools System." In *Studies in Irish History, Presented to R. Dudley Edwards,* edited by Art Cosgrove and Donal McCartney, 150–63. Dublin: University College Dublin, 1979.

_____. *Social and Economic History of Ireland Since 1800.* Dublin: Educational Co., 1981.

Daly, Mary, and David Dickson, eds. *The Origins of Popular Literacy in Ireland: Language Change and Educational Development.* Dublin: Department of Modern History (Trinity) and Department of Irish History (U.C.D.), 1990.

Davis, Richard. *The Young Ireland Movement.* Dublin: Gill and MacMillan, 1987; Totowa, N.J.: Barnes & Noble, 1988.

DeCourcy, Catherine. *The Foundation of the National Gallery of Ireland.* Dublin: National Gallery of Ireland, 1985.

De Freine, Sean. *The Great Silence.* Dublin: Foilseachain Naisiunta Teoranta, 1965.

Dillon, Myles. "George Petrie, 1789–1866." *Studies* 56 (1967): 266–76.

Donnelly, James S. *The Land and the People of Nineteenth-Century Cork: the Rural Economy and the Land Question.* London and Boston: Routledge and Kegan Paul, 1975.

_____. "The Land Question in Nationalist Politics." In *Perspectives on Irish Nationalism,* edited by Thomas E. Hachey and Lawrence J. McCaffrey, 79–98. Lexington, Ky.: University Press of Kentucky, 1989.

Dowling, P. J. *The Hedge Schools of Ireland.* London: Longman's, Green and Co., 1935.

Drudy, P. J., ed. *Irish Studies, II: Ireland, Land, Politics, People.* Cambridge: Cambridge University Press, 1982.

Dunne, Tom. "Haunted by History: Irish Romantic Writing, 1800–1850." In *Romanticism in National Context,* edited by Roy Porter and Mikulas Teich, 68–91. Cambridge: Cambridge University Press, 1988.

_____. *Theobald Wolfe Tone: Colonial Outsider.* Cork: Tower Books, 1982.

Durkacz, Victor E. *The Decline of the Celtic Languages: a Study of Linguistic and Cultural Conflict in Scotland, Wales and Ireland from the Reformation to the Twentieth Century.* Edinburgh: J. Donald, 1983.

Edwards, Owen Dudley. "Ireland." In *Celtic Nationalism,* by Owen Dudley Edwards, Gwynfor Evans, Ioan Rhys, and Hugh Mac Diarmuid, 1–209. London: Routledge and Kegan Paul, 1968.

Edwards, R. Dudley. "The Contribution of Young Ireland to the Development of the National Idea." In *Feilscribhinn Torna: Essays and Studies Presented to Tadg Ua Donnchadha,* edited by Seamus Pender, 115–33. Cork: Cork University Press, 1945.

_____. *Daniel O'Connell and His World.* London: Thames and Hudson, 1975.

Elliott, Marianne. *Wolfe Tone: Prophet of Irish Independence.* New Haven/London: Yale University Press, 1989.

Farrell, Brian, ed. *The Irish Parliamentary Tradition.* Dublin: Gill and MacMillan; New York: Barnes and Noble, 1973.

Fitzpatrick, David. "The Disappearance of the Irish Agricultural Labourer, 1841–1912." *Irish Economic and Social History* 7 (1980): 66–92.

Flanagan, Thomas. *The Irish Novelists.* New York: Columbia University Press, 1959.

_____. "Literature in English, 1801–91." In *A New History of Ireland* (5), edited by W. E. Vaughan, 482–522. Oxford: Clarendon Press, 1989.

Foster, R. F. "History and the Irish Question." *Transactions of the Royal Historical Society,* 5th ser., 33 (1983): 169–92.

_____. *Modern Ireland, 1600–1972.* London: Allen Lane, The Penguin Press, 1988.

Froggatt, Peter. "The Demographic Work of Sir William Wilde." *Irish Journal of Medical Science* 6th ser., no. 473 (1965): 213–30.

Garvin, Tom. *The Evolution of Irish Nationalist Politics.* Dublin: Gill and MacMillan, 1981.

Gash, Norman. *Sir Robert Peel: the Life of Sir Robert Peel After 1830.* Totowa, N.J.: Rowman and Littlefield, 1972.

Green, E. R. R. *The Lagan Valley, 1800–50: A Local History of the Industrial Revolution.* London: Faber & Faber, 1949.

Gwynn, Denis. "Denny Lane and Thomas Davis." *Studies* 38 (1949): 16–27.

_____. "John E. Pigot and Thomas Davis." *Studies* 38 (1949): 144–57.

_____. *O'Connell, Davis, and the Colleges Bill.* Cork: Cork University Press; Oxford: B. H. Blackwell, 1948.

_____. "William Smith O'Brien." *Studies* 35 (1946): 448–58; 36 (1947): 29–39; 37 (1948), 7–17, 149–60.

_____. *Young Ireland and 1848.* Cork: Cork University Press, 1949.

Hachey, Thomas E., and L. J. McCaffrey, eds. *Perspectives on Irish Nationalism.* Lexington, Ky.: University Press of Kentucky, 1989.

Hayley, Barbara, and Enda McKay, eds. *Three Hundred Years of Irish Periodicals.* Mullingar, Co. Westmeath: Lilliput Press, 1987.

Hepburn, A. C. *The Conflict of Nationality in Modern Ireland.* London: Edward Arnold, 1980.

Hempton, David. "The Methodist Crusade in Ireland, 1795–1845." *Irish Historical Studies* 32, no. 85 (March 1980): 33–48.

Hickey, D. J., and J. E. Doherty, eds. *A Dictionary of Irish History Since 1800.* Dublin: Gill and MacMillan, 1980.

Hill, Jacqueline. "The Intelligentsia and Irish Nationalism in the 1840s." *Studia Hibernica* 20 (1980): 73–109.

_____. "The Meaning and Significance of Protestant Ascendancy, 1787–1840." In *Ireland After the Union: Proceedings of the Second Joint Meeting of the Royal Irish Academy and the British Academy, London, 1986,* 1–22. Oxford and New York: Oxford University Press, 1989.

_____. "Nationalism and the Catholic Church in the 1840s: Views of Dublin Repealers." *Irish Historical Studies* 19, no. 76 (September 1975): 371–95.

_____. "The Protestant Response to Repeal: The Case of the Dublin Working Class." In *Ireland Under the Union: Varieties of Tension: Essays in Honour of T. W. Moody,* edited by F. S. L. Lyons and R. A. J. Hawkins, 35–68. Oxford: Clarendon Press; New York: Oxford University Press, 1980.

Hogan, Daire. *The Legal Profession in Ireland 1789–1922.* Dublin: Incorporated Law Society of Ireland, 1986.

Holmes, Finlay. *Henry Cooke.* Belfast: Christian Journals, 1981.

Hone, J. M. *Thomas Davis.* London: Gerald Duckworth; Dublin: Talbot Press, 1934.

Hoppen, K. Theodore. *Elections, Politics, and Society in Ireland, 1832–1885.* Oxford: Clarendon Press; New York: Oxford University Press, 1984.

_____. *Ireland Since 1800: Conflict and Conformity.* London and New York: Longman, 1989.

Hughes, T. Jones. "Society and Settlement in Nineteenth-Century Ireland." *Irish Geography* 2 (1965): 79–96.

Hutchinson, John. *The Dynamics of Cultural Nationalism: The Gaelic Revival and the Creation of the Irish Nation State.* London and Boston: Allen & Unwin, 1987.

Inglis, Brian. *The Freedom of the Press in Ireland, 1784–1841.* London: Faber & Faber, 1954.

_____. "The Press." In *Social Life in Ireland, 1800–45,* edited by Robert B. McDowell, 98–111. Dublin: Colm O'Lochlain, at the Sign of the Three Candles, 1957.

Jamieson, John. *The History of the Royal Belfast Academical Institution, 1810–1960.* Belfast: W. Mullan, 1959.

Jupp, Peter J. *British and Irish Elections, 1784–1831.* Newton Abbot: David & Charles, 1973.

Kearney, Hugh. *The British Isles: A History of Four Nations.* Cambridge: Cambridge University Press, 1989.

Kee, Robert. *The Green Flag: a History of Irish Nationalism.* London: Weidenfeld and Nicolson, 1972.

Keenan, Desmond. *The Catholic Church in Nineteenth Century Ireland: a Sociological Study.* Dublin: Gill and MacMillan; Totowa, N.J.: Barnes & Noble, 1983.

Kelly, Charlotte. "The 82 Club." *Studies* 33 (1944): 257–262.

Kemp, Betty. "The General Election of 1841." *History* 37 (June 1952): 146–57.

Kennedy, B. A. "Sharman Crawford's Federal Scheme for Ireland." In *Essays in British and Irish History, in Honour of James Eadie Todd,* edited by H. A. Cronne, T. W. Moody, and D. B. Quinn, 235–54. London: F. Muller, 1949.

Kennedy, Liam, and David Johnson. "The Union of Ireland and Britain, 1801–1921." In *The Making of Modern Irish History,* edited by D. George Boyce and Alan O'Day. London: Routledge, 1996.

Kennedy, Liam, and Phillip Ollerenshaw. *An Economic History of Ulster, 1820–1940.* Manchester: Manchester University Press, 1985.

Kerr, Donal A. *Peel, Priests and Politics: Sir Robert Peel's Administration and the Roman Catholic Church in Ireland, 1841–1846.* Oxford: Clarendon Press, 1982.

Kerrigan, Colm. *Father Mathew and the Irish Temperance Movement: 1838–1849.* Cork: Cork University Press, 1992.

Langer, W. L. "Europe's Initial Population Explosion." *American Historical Review* 69, no. 1 (October 1963): 1–17.

_____. *Political and Social Upheaval, 1832–1852.* Rise of Modern Europe Series. New York: Harper, 1969.

Large, David. "The House of Lords and Ireland in the Age of Peel, 1832–1850." *Irish Historical Studies* 9, no. 36 (September 1955): 367–99.

_____. "The Wealth of the Greater Irish Landowners, 1750–1815." *Irish Historical Studies* 15, no. 57 (March 1966): 21–47.

Larkin, Emmet. "The Devotional Revolution in Ireland, 1850–75." *American Historical Review* 77 (June 1972): 625–52.

———. "The Quarrel Among the Roman Catholic Hierarchy Over the National System of Education in Ireland, 1838–41." In *The Celtic Cross: Studies in Irish Culture and Literature*, edited by Ray B. Browne, William Roscelli, and Richard Loftus, 121–51. West Lafayette, Ind.: Purdue University Studies, 1964.

Lecky, W. E. H. *Leaders of Public Opinion in Ireland*. London: Saunders Otley, 1861. Revised edition, 2 vols. London: Longmans, 1903.

Logan, John. "How Many Pupils Went to School in the Nineteenth Century?" *Irish Educational Studies* 8 (1989): 23–36.

Lyons, F. S. L. *Culture and Anarchy in Ireland, 1890–1939*. Oxford: Clarendon Press; New York: Oxford University Press, 1979.

Lyons, F. S. L., and R. A. J. Hawkins, eds. *Ireland Under the Union: Essays in Honour of T. W. Moody*. Oxford: Clarendon Press, 1980.

Lysaght, Moira. "Daniel Murray, Archbishop of Dublin, 1823–52." *Dublin Historical Record* 27, no. 3 (June 1974): 101–8.

McCaffrey, L. J. *Daniel O'Connell and the Repeal Year*. Lexington, Ky.: University of Kentucky Press, 1966.

McCartney, Donal. *The Dawning of Democracy, Ireland 1800–1870*. Dublin: Helicon, 1987.

———. *Democracy and Its Nineteenth Century Irish Critics*. O'Donnell Lecture. Dublin: National University of Ireland, 1979.

———. *W. E. H. Lecky: Historian and Politician, 1838–1903*. Dublin: Lilliput Press, 1994.

———. "The Writing of History in Ireland, 1800–1830." *Irish Historical Studies* 10 (September 1957): 347–62.

———, ed. *The World of Daniel O'Connell*. Dublin: Mercier Press, 1980.

McCormack, W. J. *Ascendancy and Tradition in Anglo-Irish Literary History from 1789 to 1939*. Oxford: Clarendon Press, 1985.

Macdonagh, Oliver. "The Contribution of O'Connell." In *The Irish Parliamentary Tradition*, edited by Brian Farrell, 160–69. Dublin: Gill and MacMillan; New York: Barnes and Noble, 1973.

———. *The Emancipist: Daniel O'Connell, 1830–47*. London: Weidenfeld and Nicolson; New York: St. Martin's Press, 1989.

———. *The Hereditary Bondsman: Daniel O'Connell, 1775–1829*. London: Weidenfeld and Nicolson; New York: St. Martin's Press, 1988.

———. *Ireland: the Union and Its Aftermath*. London: G. Allen & Unwin, 1977.

———. *The Nineteenth Century Novel and Irish Social History: Some Aspects*. O'Donnell Lecture. Dublin: National University of Ireland, 1971.

_____. *A Pattern of Government Growth, 1800 to 1860: The Passenger Acts and Their Enforcement.* London: MacGibbon & Kee, 1961.

_____. "The Politicization of the Irish Catholic Bishops, 1800–1850." *Historical Journal* 18, no. 1 (1975): 37–53.

_____. *States of Mind: A Study of Anglo-Irish Conflict, 1780–1980.* London: Allen and Unwin, 1983.

McDowell, R. B. *The Irish Administration, 1801–1914.* London: Routledge and Kegan Paul; Toronto: University of Toronto Press, 1964.

_____, ed. *Public Opinion and Government Policy in Ireland, 1801–1846.* London: Faber & Faber, 1952; 2nd edition, Westport, Conn.: Greenwood Press, 1975.

_____, ed. *Social Life in Ireland, 1800–1845.* Dublin: Published for the Cultural Relations Committee of Ireland, in association with Radio Éireann, by Colm O Lochlainn, Sign of the Three Candles, 1957; reprinted 1963.

McDowell, R. B., and D. A. Webb. *Trinity College Dublin, 1592–1952: An Academic History.* Cambridge: Cambridge University Press, 1982.

McGrath, Fergal. *Newman's University: Idea and Reality.* Dublin: Browne & Nolan, 1951.

MacIntyre, Angus D. *The Liberator: Daniel O'Connell and the Irish Party, 1830–1847.* London: H. Hamilton, 1965.

MacManus, M. J., ed. *Thomas Davis and Young Ireland.* Dublin: Stationery Office, 1945.

Malcolm, Elizabeth. *Ireland Sober, Ireland Free: Drink and Temperance in Nineteenth Century Ireland.* Dublin: Gill and MacMillan, 1986.

Mansergh, Nicholas. *The Irish Question, 1840–1921.* 3rd ed. London: Allen and Unwin, 1975. First edition published as *Ireland in the Age of Reform and Revolution.* London: 1940.

Meenan, F. O. C. "The Georgian Squares of Dublin and the Professions." *Studies* 58 (winter 1969): 405–14.

_____. "The Victorian Doctors of Dublin: a Social and Political Portrait." *Irish Journal of Medical Science* 7th Ser., 1, no. 7 (July 1968): 311–20.

Meenan, James, and Desmond Clarke, eds. *RDS: The Royal Dublin Society 1731–1981.* Dublin: Gill and MacMillan, 1981.

Miller, David W. *Queen's Rebels: Ulster Loyalism in Historical Perspective.* Dublin: Gill and MacMillan; New York: Barnes & Noble, 1978.

Mokyr, Joel. *Why Ireland Starved: A Quantitative and Analytical History of the Irish Economy, 1800–1850.* London and Boston: Allen & Unwin, 1983. Paperback edition with corrections, 1985.

Moley, Raymond. *Nationalism Without Violence.* New York: Fordham University Press, 1974.

Molony, John N. *A Soul Came Into Ireland: Thomas Davis, 1814–1845.* Dublin: Geography Publications, 1995.

Moody, T. W., ed. *The Fenian Movement.* Cork: Mercier Press, 1968.

_____. "The Irish University Question of the Nineteenth Century." *History* 43 (1958): 90–109.

_____. *Thomas Davis, 1814–45.* Dublin: Hodges Figgis, 1945.

_____. "Thomas Davis and the Irish Nation." *Hermathena, A Dublin University Review* 103 (1966): 5–31.

Moody, T. W., and J. C. Beckett. *Queen's, Belfast, 1845–1949: The History of a University.* 2 Vols. London: Faber & Faber, 1959.

Mulvey, Helen F. "The Historian Lecky: Opponent of Irish Home Rule." *Victorian Studies* 1, no. 4 (June 1958): 337–51.

_____. "Nineteenth-Century Ireland, 1801–1914." In *Irish Historiography, 1936–70,* edited by T. W. Moody, 71–136. Dublin: Irish Committee of Historical Sciences, 1971.

_____. "Sir Charles Gavan Duffy: Young Irelander and Imperial Statesman." *Canadian Historical Review* 33 (1952): 369–86."

Murphy, Maura. "The Ballad Singer and the Role of the Seditious Ballad in Nineteenth-Century Ireland: Dublin Castle's View." *Ulster Folklife* 25 (1979): 79–102.

Ni Chinnéide, Síle. "The Gaelic Contribution to Irish Nationalism." *University Review* 2, no. 9 (1960): 67–76.

Ni Chinnéide, Veronica. "The Sources of Moore's Melodies." *Royal Society of the Antiquarians of Ireland Journal* 88 (1958): 109–34.

Noonan, John D. "The Library of Thomas Davis." *Irish Book Lover* 5 (October 1913).

Norman, Edward. *A History of Modern Ireland.* London: Allen Lane, Penguin Press, 1971.

Nowlan, Kevin B. "The Catholic Clergy and Irish Politics in the Eighteen Thirties and Forties." *Historical Studies* 9 (1974): 119–35.

_____. *Charles Gavan Duffy and the Repeal Movement.* O'Donnell Lecture. Dublin: National University of Ireland, 1963.

_____. "The Meaning of Repeal in Irish History." *Historical Studies* 4 (1963): 1–17.

_____. *The Politics of Repeal: A Study in the Relations Between Great Britain and Ireland, 1841–50.* London: Routledge and Kegan Paul, 1965.

_____. "Writings in Connection with the Thomas Davis and Young Ireland Centenary, 1945." *Irish Historical Studies* 5 (March 1947): 265–72.

Nowlan, Kevin B., and Maurice R. O'Connell, eds. *Daniel O'Connell: Portrait of a Radical.* Belfast: Appletree Press, 1984.

O'Brien, Conor Cruise. "Revolution and the Shaping of Modern Ireland." In *The Celtic Consciousness*, edited by Robert O'Driscoll, 427–35. Portlaoise: Dolmen Press, 1982.

O'Brien, Eoin. *Conscience and Conflict: a Biography of Sir Dominic Corrigan, 1802–1880*. Dublin: Glendale Press, 1983.

Ó Broin, León. *Charles Gavan Duffy: Patriot and Statesman*. Dublin: James Duffy, 1966.

O'Cathaoir, Brendan. *John Blake Dillon: Young Irelander*. Dublin: Irish Academic Press, 1990.

O'Connell, Maurice R. *Daniel O'Connell: the Man and His Politics*. Foreword by Conor Cruise O'Brien. Dublin: Irish Academic Press, 1990.

Ó Cuív, Brian, ed. *A View of the Irish Language*. Dublin: Stationery Office, 1969.

O'Day, Alan, ed. *Reactions to Irish Nationalism*. Dublin: Gill and MacMillan; London: Hambledon, 1987.

O'Driscoll, Robert. *An Ascendancy of the Heart: Ferguson and the Beginnings of Modern Irish Literature in English*. Introduction by Maire Cruise O'Brien. Dublin: Dolmen Press, 1976.

_____, ed. *The Celtic Consciousness*. New York: Braziller, 1982.

O'Farrell, Patrick. *England and Ireland Since 1800*. London: Oxford University Press, 1975.

O'Ferrall, Fergus. *Catholic Emancipation: Daniel O'Connell and the Birth of Irish Democracy, 1820–30*. Dublin: Gill and MacMillan; Atlantic Highlands, N.J.: Humanities Press International, 1985.

_____. *Daniel O'Connell*. Dublin: Gill and MacMillan, 1981.

Ó Gráda, Cormac. *Ireland Before and After the Famine: Explorations in Economic History, 1800–1925*. Manchester: Manchester University Press, 1988.

O'Hegarty, P. S. *A History of Ireland Under the Union*. London: Methuen, 1952.

O'Malley, Eoin. "The Decline of Irish Industry in the Nineteenth Century." *Economic and Social Review* 13, no. 1 (October 1981): 21–42.

Ó Raifeartaigh, Tarlach O. "Mixed Education and the Synod of Ulster, 1831–40." *Irish Historical Studies* 9, no. 35 (March 1955): 281–99.

_____, ed. *The Royal Irish Academy: a Bicentennial History, 1785–1985*. Foreword by W. A. Watts. Dublin: The Academy, 1985.

Ó Tuathaigh, M .A. G. *Ireland Before the Famine, 1798–1848*. Dublin: Gill and MacMillan, 1972.

_____. *Thomas Drummond and the Government of Ireland, 1835–41*. O'Donnell Lecture. Dublin: National University of Ireland, 1978.

Owens, Gary. "Hedge Schools of Politics: O'Connell's Monster Meetings." *History Ireland* 2, no. 1 (spring 1994): 35–41.

Philpin, G. H. E., ed. *Nationalism and Popular Protest in Ireland*. Cambridge: Cambridge University Press, 1987.

Porter, Roy, and Mikulas Teich, eds. *Romanticism in National Context*. Cambridge: Cambridge University Press, 1988.

Reynolds, James A. *The Catholic Emancipation Crisis in Ireland, 1823–1829*. New Haven: Yale University Press, 1954.

Riach, Douglas. "Daniel O'Connell and American Anti-Slavery." *Irish Historical Studies* 20, no. 77 (March 1976): 3–25.

Sadleir, Michael. *Dublin University Magazine: Its History, Contents and Bibliography*. Paper read before the Bibliographical Society of Ireland, 26 April 1937. Dublin: Juverna Press, 1938.

Schenk, Hans G. H. V. *The Mind of the European Romantics*. London: Constable, 1966.

Senior, Hereward. *Orangeism in Ireland and Britain, 1795–1836*. London: Routledge and Kegan Paul; Toronto: Ryerson Press, 1966.

Shaw, Francis. "The Canon of Irish History: a Challenge." *Studies* 61 (1972): 113–53.

Sheehy, Jeanne. *The Rediscovery of Ireland's Past: The Celtic Revival, 1830–1930*. Photographs by George Mott. London: Thames and Hudson, 1980.

Sismondi, Jean Charles Leonard Simonde de. *Economie Politique: Sur la Balance des Consommations avec les Productions*. Paris: n.p., 1824.

Sloan, Robert. "O'Connell's Liberal Rivals in 1843." *Irish Historical Studies* 30 (May 1996): 47–65.

Tessier, Thérèse. *The Bard of Erin: a Study of Thomas Moore's Irish Melodies (1808–1834)*. Translated from the French by George P. Mutch. Salzburg, Austria: Institut für Anglistik und Amerikanistik, Universität Salzburg, 1981.

Thornley, David. *Isaac Butt and Home Rule*. London: MacGibbon & Kee, 1964.

Thuente, M. H. "Violence in Pre-Famine Ireland: the Testimony of Irish Folklore and Fiction." *Irish University Review* 15 (autumn 1985): 129–47.

Tierney, Michael. "Thomas Davis, 1814–45." *Studies* 34 (1945): 300–310.

Touhill, Blanche M. *William Smith O'Brien and His Irish Revolutionary Companions in Penal Exile*. Columbia, Mo.: University of Missouri Press, 1981.

Turpin, John. *John Hogan, Irish Neoclassical Sculptor in Rome, 1800–1858: a Biography and Catalogue Raisoné*. Blackrock, Co. Dublin: Irish Academic Press, 1982.

Vale, Mary. "The Origins of the Catholic University of Ireland, 1845–1854." *Irish Ecclesiastical Record* 5th Ser., 82 (1954): 1–16, 152–64, 226–41.

Vance, Norman. *Irish Literature: A Social History*. Oxford: Basil Blackwell, 1990.

Vaughan, W. E. *Landlords and Tenants in Mid-Victorian Ireland*. Oxford: Clarendon Press, 1994.

_____, ed. *A New History of Ireland: Ireland Under the Union, 1801–1870*. Vol. 5. Oxford: Clarendon Press, 1989.

Wall, Maureen. "The Decline of the Irish Language." In *A View of the Irish Language,* edited by Brian Ó Cuív, 81–90. Dublin: Stationery Office, 1969.

_____. *The Penal Laws 1691–1760*. Dundalk: The Dundalgan Press, 1961.

Ward, Alan J. *The Irish Constitutional Tradition: Responsible Government and Modern Ireland, 1782–1992*. Washington, D.C.: The Catholic University of America Press, 1994.

Wheeler, T. S. "Sir Robert Kane: Life and Work." *Studies* 33 (1944), 158–68, 316–30.

Wheeler, T. S., M. A. Hogan, D. W. Bishopp, J. A. O'Riordan, A. E. J. Went, and T. Clear. *The Natural Resources of Ireland: A Series of Discourses Delivered Before the Royal Dublin Society of April 12th, 13th and 14th, 1944, in Commemoration of the Centenary of the Publication by the Society of Sir Robert Kane's the Industrial Resources of Ireland*. Dublin: Royal Dublin Society, 1944.

White, Terence De Vere. *The Road of Excess*. Dublin: Browne and Nolan, 1946. (Isaac Butt)

_____. *The Story of the Royal Dublin Society*. Tralee: Kerryman, 1955.

Whyte, John H. "Daniel O'Connell and the Repeal Party." *Irish Historical Studies* 11, no. 44 (September 1959): 297–316.

_____. *The Independent Irish Party, 1850–59*. London: Oxford University Press, 1958.

_____. "The Influence of the Catholic Clergy on Elections in Nineteenth Century Ireland." *English Historical Review* 75, no. 295 (April 1960): 239–59.

Williams, T. Desmond, ed. *Secret Societies in Ireland*. Dublin: Gill and MacMillan, 1973.

Index

茶芸茶

A Year's Work by Thomas Davis, 102
agriculture, 45–47, 90, 103, 150, 165, 187
Anglicans and Anglicanism, 8, 59, 95, 175–76, 233–34, 239; *see also* Church of Ireland
Anster, John, 68, 231
Antisell, Thomas, 112
Archer, Charles Palmer, 30
aristocracy, 34, 77, 104
Army Ordnance Survey, 229
Australia, 3, 6, 9, 23, 58, 189–90n, 239–40

Barrett, Richard, 139
Barry, Michael Joseph, 2, 109–10, 157, 159, 179, 189, 237
Beaumont, Gustave de, 88
Belfast, 52, 54–55, 58, 61, 111, 162, 166, 169, 173, 175
Board of Works, 94–95
British army, 21, 150–51
Burton, Frederick, 157, 194, 232–33
Butt, Isaac, 26–27, 68, 124–25, 231

Campbell, Lord, 45, 138
Canada, 2–3, 104, 110, 125–28, 148, 189
Cane, Robert, 158–59, 170, 184
Carleton, William, 60–61, 69, 231
Catholics and Catholicism, 1–2, 9n, 25, 33, 38, 53–54, 56, 77, 108–9, 118–20, 123, 127, 131n, 148n, 163, 176–86, 200–201, 203, 226, 233, 237–40; emancipation, 60–61, 80–82, 84–86, 90–91, 101, 103, 114, 120, 129, 138, 143, 153, 172–73, 177, 182, 205, 210; and Irish nationality, 63–64; magazines, 67–69; monarchies, 209–14; political appointments, 91–92, 95–98; priesthood, 167–71

Catholic Association, 84–85
Caulfield, Henry, 162
Cavour, Camillo, 76–79, 97, 127, 166, 239
Celtic ethnicity, 13, 56, 64, 105, 190, 200, 202, 231, 243
Christian Examiner, 67
Church of Ireland, 22n, 112, 114, 210; *see also* Anglicans and Anglicanism
Citizen, 35, 43, 49–51, 57–58, 60, 70, 104, 117, 125–26, 150, 164, 214; *see also Dublin Monthly Magazine*
Church of Ireland Gazette, 67
Cloncurry, Lord, 130
Clontarf meeting, 106, 137–38, 142–44, 161, 163
Colby, Thomas, 229–30
Colleges Bill, 115, 173, 176–86, 225–26, 237
Comerford, Vincent, 202
Commercial History of Ireland, 236
Congress of Vienna, 40, 72
Convention Act (1793), 130–31
Conway, Michael, 179–80, 183
Cork Southern Reporter, 110
Corn Laws, 27, 31, 35, 138, 175
Council of 300, 122, 130–34, 136
Crawford, William Sharman, 161–63
Crolly, George, 55, 69, 177
Curran, John Philpot, 16, 34, 199, 207, 222

Daunt, Alice O'Neill, 5, 151
Davis, Anna Maria, sister of Thomas, 21
Davis, Charlotte, sister of Thomas, 21, 114, 154, 194, 196–97, 200
Davis, James, brother of Thomas, 21, 22n, 200
Davis, James Thomas, father of Thomas, 21–22

Davis, John, brother of Thomas, 21–22, 114

Davis, Mary, sister of Thomas, 21

Davis, Mary Atkins, mother of Thomas, 21–23, 114, 139

democracy, 6, 29, 32, 34–35, 77, 81, 96

Denmark and Danes, 74–76, 118, 122, 243–45

Derrynane, 160, 162, 185

Dillon, John Blake, 1, 16, 30, 33, 42, 48–49, 51–52, 56–58, 84, 89, 99, 104, 107, 111, 138–39, 157, 184–85, 239

Dissenters, 28, 63, 127, 174–75, 233

Doheny, Michael, 2, 30, 107, 112–13

Drummond, Thomas, 92, 95, 167, 229

Dublin, 16, 35, 40, 42, 64–65, 92–93, 97, 112–14, 131, 134–37, 144, 185, 211, 222; Charles Gavan Duffy in, 52–53, 55–56; Daniel O'Connell in, 82, 99, 160–62; Thomas Davis in, 2, 12n, 21n, 22–27, 45–46, 58, 100, 109–10, 138–39, 157–58, 181, 187, 193–94, 200–202, 204, 207, 228–33

Dublin Castle, 92, 97, 124–25, 195

Dublin Corporation, 97, 122, 125, 200

Dublin Historical Society, 27

Dublin Literary Gazette, 67

Dublin Monthly Magazine, 49, 65, 207, 210, 214; *see also Citizen*

Dublin Penny Journal, 69, 230

Dublin Review, 69, 168

Dublin University Magazine, 68–70, 111, 203–4, 231

Dublin Weekly Register, 169

Duffy, Charles Gavan, 13, 17–19, 58, 61, 64, 84, 112, 131, 137, 139–40, 158–60, 166, 171, 179, 185, 88, 195–96, 198–200, 238; as an author, 2, 9–11, 23–24, 28, 39, 43, 57, 65, 109, 111, 115, 116, 122, 134–35, 145, 148n, 149n, 155, 163–64, 191, 210, 214, 240; life history of, 52–56, 104–5, 137, 179; and the *Nation,* 1, 16, 49, 66, 70–71, 99, 102, 107, 142, 157, 87, 193, 206

education, 6, 12, 26–27, 32–34, 45, 78, 80, 83–84, 93–94, 167, 173–82, 185, 187, 189, 191, 212, 228, 232, 234–36, 39; mixed, 31,

177, 180, 183; National Board of Education, 46, 152

Education Commission Report (1838), 173

Edwards, Dudley, 18–19

Eighty Two Club, 200

Eliot, Lord, 172

emancipation, Catholic, *see* Catholics and Catholicism

emigration, 6, 27, 89, 96

England, 4–5, 8, 11–15, 17, 21, 26, 30, 35–38, 40, 60, 68, 72, 74–99, 103–7, 121, 128, 130, 138, 143–44, 147, 148n, 153, 163–64, 172, 174–75, 187–90, 209, 211, 213–14, 222, 226–27, 232, 236n, 237–39, 244, 246, 249; Davis in, 39, 70; *see also* Normans, Conquest of England; Great Britain

English East India Company, 207, 215–18

Europe, 3, 6, 13, 15, 37–40, 44, 50, 68, 70, 72–81, 89, 93, 97, 104, 117–18, 120, 122–23, 127–28, 144, 150, 167, 203, 206, 209, 214–15, 217–20, 222, 234, 240, 249

Examiner, 54

famine, 2–3, 6, 14, 90, 199, 228, 229n, 238

Federalism, 161–67

Fenians and Fenianism, 2, 8, 12, 113, 202

Ferguson, Samuel, 12, 68, 203

Finland, 75

First Principles by Thomas Davis, 190

France and the French, 3, 6, 34–35, 37–38, 47, 51, 77, 79–80, 83, 87, 103–4, 117–18, 144, 211, 214, 219–20, 222, 224, 237, 244; French Revolution, 60, 73, 80–82, 123, 190

Freeman, 65, 101

Freeman's Journal, 112, 155

Gaelic, *see* Irish language

Germany and Germans, 34, 37–40, 73–74, 103, 113, 121

Gladstone, William, 4, 201

Graham, James, 172–73, 176

Grattan, Jr., Henry, 9, 49, 125, 130, 143, 153, 180, 212

Gray, John, 112, 114, 139, 154–55

Great Britain, 69, 78, 81, 86n, 87, 103, 124, 126, 147, 149, 162, 173, 175; *see also* England
Grey, Lord de, 130, 172
Griffin, Gerald and William, 136, 183
Griffith, Arthur, 14–17

Havlicek, Charles, 73–74
Herder, Johann Gottfried von, 38, 40, 74–75
Hermathena, A Dublin University Review, 18
Hogan, John, sculptor, 100, 135–36, 140, 202, 232
Home Rule, 10–11, 17, 240
House of Commons, 3, 27–28, 42, 79, 86, 92, 96n, 144, 153
House of Lords, 28–29, 86, 89, 96–97, 139, 143, 158n, 163
Hudson, William Eliot, 70, 117, 156, 164
Hungary, 74, 78–79, 122
Hutton, Annie, and family, 162, 193–204

India, 5, 31, 49, 103, 207, 214–18, 240
Ingram, John Kells, 99
Institute for Historical Study, 207
Irish Archeological Society, 190, 232
Irish Arms Bill, 146
Irish Catholic Magazine, 67
Irish cooperative movement, 14
Irish Historical Studies, 19, 205
Irish history, 4–5, 12, 14, 19, 27, 35–36, 41, 66, 69, 76, 88–89, 93, 102, 118, 121, 125, 134, 142, 153, 161, 189, 204, 205–27 (Chapter 6: Davis and the Writing of History), 234, 243
Irish Land Court, 3, 239
Irish language, 40, 69, 72–73, 94, 111, 114, 117, 120–22, 127, 187, 190–92, 217, 220, 230, 233–35
Irish Literary Society, 11–13, 210
Irish Local Government Act (1898), 96, 239
Irish Penny Journal, 230
Irish Penny Magazine, 69
Irish Protestant and Faithful Examiner, 66–67

Irish question, the, 3–4, 14, 73
Irish Tribune, 112
Italians and Italy, 10, 34, 37, 73, 76, 78–79, 127, 128n, 195, 200, 209, 219

Kearney, Francis, 25, 30
Kickham, Charles, 202

Laing, Samuel, 50
Land Act (1881), 3, 239
Landor, Walter Savage, 36–37, 48
Lane, Denny, 2, 109–10, 114, 134, 182–86, 228–29
Larcom, Thomas, 229–30
Le Fanu, Joseph Sheridan, 26, 30
Lecky, W. E. H., 4, 9–10, 50, 70–71, 211
Leinster, 129, 158; Duke of, 163; Leinster House, 46
Lessing, 38, 40, 156
Letters of a Protestant on Repeal, 117–21
Lever, Charles, 67–68, 231
London, 2, 4, 13, 15, 22n, 24, 26–27, 29, 41–42, 54n, 57, 59, 69, 80, 82, 84, 91–92, 108, 125, 131, 135–36, 145–47, 149, 154, 156, 186, 189, 200, 222, 229, 232–33
London Times, 106
Loyal National Repeal Association, *see* Repeal Association
Lyceum System, 34

Macaulay, 79, 153, 206
MacHale, Archbishop, 177
Maclise, Daniel, 232
MacManus, Henry, 53, 69–70
MacManus, Terence Bellew, 53
MacNevin, Thomas, 2, 26, 107, 109–11, 114, 120, 137, 170–71
Maddyn, Daniel Owen, 24–25, 29–31, 41–43, 58, 64–65, 108, 110, 125, 131–34, 136–37, 167–68, 171–72, 181, 188, 193–94, 225–27, 229n
Magee, William Conor, 30
Mallow, 21, 24, 29, 156; Mallow Defiance, 122
Mangan, Clarence, 55, 56, 231
Martin, John, 193

Mathew, Theobald, 14, 37, 55, 65, 99, 129, 159

Maynooth, 12, 53, 55–56, 69, 135, 168, 173–74

Maynooth Bill, 173–76, 237

Mazzini, Giuseppe, 76–79, 127

McCarthy, Denis Florence, 2, 109, 111, 158

McCullagh, Torrens, 25, 70, 199

McGee, Thomas Darcy, 2–3

McSkimmin, Samuel, 222–23

Meagher, Thomas Francis, 2, 7

Melbourne ministry, 78, 91, 93, 95, 97–98, 239

Mitchel, John, 2, 7, 16–17, 193

Moody, T. W., 18–19, 38n

Moore, Christopher, 192, 201

Moore, Thomas, 8, 55, 111–12, 117, 159, 220

Morning Register, 47–48, 104, 169

Morpeth, Lord, 28, 92

Mulready, William, 232

Municipal Reform Bill (Ireland), 146

Munster, 23–24, 129, 136n, 158

Murphy, John, 134–35

Murray, Daniel, 46–48, 177–78

Murray, Patrick, 69, 168–71

My Life in Two Hemispheres by Charles Gavan Duffy, 4, 52

Napoleonic wars, 72–73

Nation, 1–3, 7–8, 11–12, 14, 16–17, 38–39, 42–45, 49, 51–52, 54–58, 60–61, 65–71, 75, 78–79, 84, 89, 91, 99, 101–8, 110–19, 121–22, 128, 135–37, 139–41, 142–43, 151–52, 157–61, 166–70, 176–78, 180, 185–87, 190–91, 193, 198, 202, 204, 206–7, 217–24, 226, 228, 230–31, 233, 236–37, 240

National Library of Ireland, 4, 22, 46, 144, 155, 207

National Museum, 46, 230

National Repeal Association, *see* Repeal Association

nationalism, 6–7, 18–20, 31, 33, 38, 40–41, 43, 64, 76, 79, 97–99, 101, 114, 127, 129, 148n, 167, 203, 206, 209, 218, 232, 235, 240, 243

Newry Examiner, 109

Nicholls, George, 96

Normans, 44, 118, 209, 243–45, 248; Conquest of England, 31, 51, 117, 219, 224

Norway and Norwegians, 50, 75–76, 123, 229, 236n

O'Brien, Lucius, 143

O'Brien, William Smith, 5, 130, 136–37, 142–50, 158, 163, 166, 169, 172–73, 178–83, 186, 189, 237–40

O'Connell, Daniel, 5, 9, 12–13, 23, 36, 55, 70, 73–74, 76–80, 93, 95, 98–99, 106–8, 111, 113, 122–25, 127–40, 142–43, 146–50, 152–72, 177–86, 196, 225, 237, 241; life history, 82–86; repeal activism, 1, 6, 36, 77, 97, 228; and the Repeal Association, 8, 33, 101, 149; writings, 19, 24, 48–49, 90–91, 202–3

O'Connell, John, 139, 189, 237

O'Curry, Eugene, 191, 229–30

O'Donoghue, D. J., 14, 16, 120

O'Donovan, John, 69, 190–91, 229–31

O'Gorman, Richard, 2, 201

O'Hagan, John, 2–4, 10–11, 13, 17, 25, 107, 108n, 109, 112, 114, 136, 158, 159, 160, 162, 181, 193–94, 199, 201, 239

O'Hagan, Thomas, 39

O'Leary, John, 8, 12

O'Loghlen, Colman, 97–98, 181

O'Loghlen, Michael, 97, 167

O'Neill, Eoghan Ruadh, 252–53

Ordnance Memoir, 146

Otway, Caesar, 26, 67–69, 230

Parliament, 1, 3, 9, 31, 35, 46–50, 76–78, 80–81, 84–87, 89, 91, 93, 107, 112–14, 119, 122–25, 130–31, 137–38, 143–46, 148–49, 158, 161–66, 174–75, 187–89, 207, 210–14, 218, 222, 236–39

Parnell, Charles Stewart, 3, 12, 188, 239

Patriot Parliament of 1689 by Thomas Davis, 210–14

patriotism, 11, 15, 25–26, 32–33, 36, 49, 66, 74, 114, 132, 143–45, 148, 152, 165, 174, 178, 184, 208, 221, 240

Pearse, Patrick, 16–17

Peel, Sir Robert, 17, 19, 59, 65, 73, 86, 95, 96n, 98–99, 101, 115, 130, 133, 137–38, 165, 172–79, 182, 186, 237

Petrie, George, 12, 67, 69, 229–31, 232
Pigot, David, 97, 108, 158n
Pigot, John Edward, 2, 42, 75, 98, 107, 108, 112, 117, 135–36, 149–50, 154–58, 160, 194, 199–200, 202n, 229n, 230, 233, 239, 240
Pilot, 101, 182
Plunkett, Horace, 14, 45, 167, 235
poetry and poets, 55–56, 73, 75, 99n, 104–6, 111, 159, 202–4, 220, 228, 230–31; as influence on Davis, 25–26, 36, 66–67, 117; of Thomas Davis, 9–12, 15, 17, 24, 43–44, 55, 66, 105, 127, 139–40, 146, 194, 202, 204, 207, 211, 226–27, 232, 241, 243–54 (the Appendix)
Poles and Poland, 37, 73, 78–79, 122
Poor Law, 27, 35, 95–96, 165
Porter, Grey, 163
Precursor Society, 98
Presbyterians, 53, 176–77
Prospectus for the *Nation*, 61–64, 79, 102, 108
Protestant Letters by Thomas Davis, 7, 117–21
Protestants, 2, 7, 25, 33–34, 38, 48, 53–57, 60–61, 63–64, 68, 77, 80–81, 86, 95–96, 106, 112, 114–15, 118–21, 123, 127, 148n, 163, 168–71, 173–74, 178–79, 182, 185, 203, 209–14, 226–27, 232–33, 237, 239–40

Ray, Thomas Matthew, 139, 149, 151–52, 203
Reform Bill (1832), 28, 86, 146
Relief Act (1793), 81
Repeal and Repealers, 6, 13, 36, 49, 60, 77, 86, 91, 97–98, 101, 103, 106, 116–19, 122, 125, 127–31, 134, 142–48, 153, 156, 160–64, 167–68, 170, 172, 177, 180, 185–89, 200, 207, 211, 223, 226–28, 234, 236, 237; Act of Repeal, 50n; Repeal Association, 1–2, 8, 33, 44, 48, 84, 110, 113, 136–39, 150–51, 183, 200, 203, 223–24, 232, 236n
Repeal Association, *see* Repeal and Repealers, Repeal Association

Repeal Reading Rooms, 149, 151–52, 156, 161, 234
Repeal Registries, 188
Ross, David, 162
Rowan, Archibald Hamilton, 195
Royal Dublin Society, 46–48, 67, 202, 235, 236n
Royal Irish Academy, 67, 116, 126, 174, 200, 228n, 230, 235, 237
Russell, George, 14, 59, 69, 235
Russell, Lord John, 138, 172
Russell, Matthew, editor of the *Irish Monthly*, 154

Saxons, 105, 118, 209, 243–44
Scots and Scotland, 12, 28, 38, 92, 118, 128, 148n, 222, 229
Scott, Sir Walter, 159, 220
Slavs, 73–74
Smiles, Samuel, 4, 56
Society of United Irishman, 81
Songs of Ireland by Michael Joseph Barry, 110
Spirit of the Nation, 16, 105, 159, 233
St. Patrick's College, 69
Staunton, Michael, 48, 52, 54, 104, 125, 169
Steele, Thomas, 139
Stokes, William, 12, 156, 198–99, 229n, 230
Sugden, Edward, 130
Sweden and Swedes, 75–76, 123, 236n
Swift, Jonathan, 9, 14, 34, 212
Sympathy by Thomas Davis, 78–79

taxes and taxation, 27, 93, 150, 153, 165
tenures, 51, 102, 125, 165, 175, 250
The Reform of the Lords by Thomas Davis, 27–29
Thomas Davis: The Memoirs of an Irish Patriot by Charles Gavan Duffy, 4, 21n
Tocqueville, Alexis de, 32, 88n, 144
Tone, Theobald Wolfe, 13, 17, 20, 44, 81, 83, 153–55, 198, 221
Tories, 27, 59–60, 68, 165, 176, 247
Treaty of 1921, 15–17
Treaty of Limerick, 205

Trinity College, 2, 8, 16, 18, 23, 25, 29, 38, 40, 46, 53, 68, 81, 107, 114, 177, 207
Trinity College Historical Society, 16, 26, 27, 29, 34, 36, 38, 41, 45, 49, 56, 61, 104, 107, 110, 207
Trumble, Matt, 53

Udalism and Feudalism by Thomas Davis, 50, 150, 235–36
Ulster, 4, 53–54, 58, 64, 87, 118, 129, 164, 237; Ulster Tenant Right, 150
Union, Act of, 1, 66, 77, 84, 122, 138, 143, 164–65, 205
Union, the, 5, 13, 66, 77, 82, 84, 86–87, 92, 101, 113–14, 123, 127–28, 130, 138, 143, 145, 147, 183, 204–6, 222, 241; see also Repeal
Unionists, 27, 29, 40, 61, 134, 162, 196, 203–4, 231, 233, 237
United States of America, 1–2, 4, 6, 26–28, 30, 35, 38, 60, 79–80, 86, 88n, 103–4, 112–13, 144–45, 154, 239
Utilitarianism, 59–60

Vienna Congress, see Congress of Vienna
Vindicator, 52, 55–58, 62, 104–5, 111, 170
Voice of the Nation, anthology of articles from the Nation (1842–1843), 102; see also Sympathy by Thomas

Davis; Udalism and Feudalism by Thomas Davis
Volunteers of 1782, 111, 137, 212

Wales and the Welsh, 21, 28, 39, 118
Wallis, Thomas, 7, 15, 25, 41–46, 57, 70, 116, 227
Warder, 106
Webb, Robert, 48–49, 58, 136, 200
Wellington, Duke of, 86, 101, 152, 164–65
Whately, Archbishop, 95–96
Whigs, 28, 45, 59–61, 68, 70, 91, 96–98, 113, 133, 137–38, 146, 158, 176, 229, 247
White, Terence De Vere, 12, 47
Wicklow, Earl of, 146–47
Wilde, William, 201
Williams, Richard D'Alton, 112
Wordsworth, William, 25, 36, 72, 159
Wyse, Thomas, 85, 156, 173, 189

Yeats, William Butler, 8, 11–12, 210–11
Young Ireland by Charles Gavan Duffy, 4, 7, 9, 64, 107, 115
Young Ireland, 1–7, 9–10, 14, 16, 18–19, 26, 42, 58, 64, 70, 73, 76–78, 79n, 82, 84, 86n, 98–99, 102, 106–7, 109–11, 113–15, 128, 144–45, 158–60, 167, 170–71, 179–82, 185, 197, 227, 229, 235n, 239–40

Thomas Davis and Ireland: A Biographical Study was designed and composed in Minion by Kachergis Book Design of Pittsboro, North Carolina. It was printed on 60-pound Writers Offset Natural and bound by Thomson-Shore, Inc. of Dexter, Michigan.